INSIGHT GUIDES

Series created by Hans Höfer

HUNGARY

General Editing and Updating by Marton Radkai
Edited by Ulrike Segal and Heinz Vestner
Translated by Susan James and Barbara König

Editorial Director: Brian Bell

APA PUBLICATIONS
Part of the Langenscheidt Publishing Group

L

ABOUT THIS BOOK

Hungary is one of the exciting destinations of the 1990s. It entered the decade with a new lease of life, free of travelling restrictions, when its doors were thrown open for everyone to view its secrets and delights. Apa Publications had foreseen the changes and by the time the new Republic was declared in October 1989, the first edition of *Insight Guide: Hungary* was coming off the presses to join what is now nearly 200 titles in the award-winning series. Created by **Hans Höfer** in 1970 with a guide to Bali, Insight Guides pioneered the award-winning formula of excellent photojournalism and incisive writing, which combine to broaden travellers' horizons. This book, like its companions, starts with essays on the country's history and culture, followed by a Places section detailing everything there is to see. Finally, the Travel Tips section is a handy reference for the visitor's travel needs.

The demanding task of editing the first edition of the book went to **Marton Radkai**, an American then living on Lake Starnberg in Bavaria, with a Hungarian father, a Bavarian mother and a German wife. He was born in New York and had a turbulent youth. Before studying History, German and Communications in the USA, he lived in France, England and Switzerland. He had settled in Germany where he was working as a freelance writer, translator and radio reporter and announcer.

It was a considerable challenge for Radkai to go back to his roots on assignment for Apa and investigate modern Hungary. He was accompanied by his father, **P. László Radkai** who had not been back to his native land since 1934. Their journey through the entire country formed the basis of this travel guide to Hungary.

A multi-faceted country such as Hungary will demand an unusual team of authors. **Dr Wolfgang Libal**, a resident of Vienna and longtime reporter for DPA (German Press Agency) lent a poetic streak to the chapters on Hungary's northeastern region, Lake Balaton and the meandering Danube. He has also published works on the entire Balkan region and has written a guide to the Dalmatian Coast.

Dr Günter Treffer, another Viennese who originally hails from Innsbruck, Austria, is an expert on Hungary's western border. He also wrote the chapter on Hungary's magnificent castles.

As if by magic, the extremely rich natural and cultural life of the famous Hungarian Great Plain and southern Transdanubia fits perfectly within the narrow confines of the guide. The painstaking labour was undertaken by **Erika Bollweg**, a multi-talented personality who until her move to her native Cologne, lived in Tutzing near Munich. After 20 years on the concert and opera stages, she learned Hungarian and started a second career as a translator of literary works and as a writer.

The excruciating task of compressing the capital, Budapest, and its surroundings into a concise handful of pages fell to **Dr Cornelia Topf**, who studied economics in Giessen. She worked for many years as a commu-

M. Radkai

P.L. Radkai

Libal

Bollweg

Topf

Coston

Artru

Szász

nications manager and editor and is currently also using her skills as a business consultant. She brought her talent for brevity to bear on her work for the guide.

Grace Coston, who peeked with Virginian humour behind the scenes of Hungary's kitchens, had already been closely involved with *Insight Guides* to France and Paris. She lives in Paris where she is a playwright, novelist, editor, translator and teacher.

Philippe Artru, who lives in Brunoy, near Paris, was in his element when writing about thermal baths in Hungary. Although his academic trajectory began with economics and ended at art and archeology, passing by literature, he has made water one of his specialities, and has worked with such publications as *Piscine Spas*, *Espaces Aquatiques* and *Piscine Oggi*.

Writing about people and culture requires an encyclopaedic knowledge and a journalist's sense of observation. **Judit Szász** combined all the necessary elements to be able to write about such diverse matters as religion, Gypsies, the Hungarian people, literature and the university city of Pécs. She was born in a typically tri-cultural town in Transylvania, Rumania: Tirgu Mures/Marosvásárhely/Neumarkt. She studied English, German, Polish and Sociology in Bucharest, Warsaw, Munich and Great Britain. She has lived and worked in Hungary. When asked to contribute to this book, she was living in Munich, working as a free-lance journalist and translator.

To help with an overview of Hungarian music, Szász invited **István Balázs**, an *enfant terrible* of contemporary Hungarian musical scholarship, to contribute a piece. Balázs lives in Budapest and was at the time working on a book about *koiné*, the common languages of modern music.

Ferenc Bodor, whose *Tölgyfa* (oak tree) gallery in Budapest is devoted to collecting artifacts of Hungary's social culture, contributed the insider pieces on Hungary's folkloric life and coffee houses.

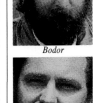
Bodor

Skupy

The main photographer for the guide was **Hans-Horst Skupy** who, assisted by his companion **Helene Hartl**, an indefatigable traveller who has visited four continents, shot well over 10,000 photos of Hungary. Skupy was born in Bratislava/Pressburg/Pozsony, capital of Hungary from 1563 to 1830, and has lived in Germany for 30 years. Equally proficient with prose, he has written travel books on Mexico and Hungary, compiled collections of aphorisms and has published extensively on topics ranging from the history of sun-dials to Mikhail Gorbachev. He and Hartl provided the Travel Tips section.

Other participant photographers were **Mark Read** and the young team **Jürgen Zilla** and **Heidi Malten**.

The Hungarian Institute in Munich was a tremendous help when it came to generously opening its library and archives. Finally, thanks go to Olga Zobel of Munich who provided much advice, encouragement and valuable criticism.

This book was produced from Apa Publications' editorial offices in London, where the text was copy-edited and proof-read by **Jane Hutchings**. This edition has been revised and updated by **Michael Ivory**.

CONTENTS

WELCOME TO HUNGARY

Hungary and the Hungarians as we know them today were at one time two quite different entities. The land, a large and fertile plain defended in the east and north by the Carpathians and in the west by natural obstacles – swamps, rivers and the foothills of the Alps – served as a haven to tribes before the Magyars took over in 896.

Hungary's history is relatively short but complex. Survival as an independent nation at the intersection of Western and Eastern Europe and the Balkans imposed the need for a cunning foreign policy not all Hungarian leaders could provide. Ever since it became a kingdom sanctioned by the Pope in 1001, Hungary has acted as a bastion for Western Europe, to be abandoned to its own devices when the going got rough. Internecine struggles between powerful magnates, nobles, the king and a galaxy of fine political leaders, tyrants and mountebanks also sundered the nation from within.

Hungary has waxed and waned with the tides of history. At times it exhibited boundless wealth which was then coveted by others. Under the Angevin King Lajos I, the realm stretched from the Adriatic to the Black Sea and almost to the Baltic in the north. After World War I three-fifths of Hungary was distributed to Romania, Czechoslovakia and Yugoslavia, and two-thirds of her population, including many ethnic Hungarians, went with the land.

The forces of circumstance have conspired to keep the Hungarians in a nomadic state. Today, 30 percent live and die outside Hungary. They survive well, judging merely from those who have become famous. They fill the ranks of the world's orchestras, of Hollywood, of the gossip columns, of Lawrence Livermore Laboratories, trade commissions, publishing houses. The roster of Nobel Prize winners is well garnished with Hungarian names.

Despite their turbulent and often painful history, Hungarians have by and large preserved a spirit of friendliness, tolerance and resignation. When history blusters with an evil breath they wait for the zephyrs. Their patriotism has been less a blind love for a piece of land than an intangible and perhaps unachievable ideal of freedom. They were (and remain) incurable romantics well before the 19th century, confronting their enemies at hopeless odds and earning acclaim for their many gallant defeats.

Preceding pages: Painted doorway; Fertô Palace; hang-gliding in the country's colours; grille of a bank building in Pécs; thoroughbred Nonius horses in the puszta; Hungarian-German folk dance group from the south; Busó carnival mask in Mohács. Left, the Parliament Building in Pest.

THE MAKING OF A STATE

Before the Hungarians established their presence in Hungary, the area was inhabited by a number of different peoples. Archaeologists using everything from shovels to the more sophisticated C-14 tests have provided evidence that human life has existed in Hungary since about 500,000 BC. When the Romans arrived in Transdanubia (the area west of the Danube) around 35 BC, it was inhabited by the Illyrians and the Eravisks, who were descendants of the Celts. In 14 BC this region, which went under the name of Pannonia, was officially incorporated into the Roman Empire.

A continuous onslaught: In AD 6, irritated by Rome's excessive recruitment policies and by heavy taxation, the Pannonians joined the Dalmatians in a rebellion that took three years to crush. After that fright, Emperor Tiberius set up various strongholds and *municipae* (independent cities): Scarbantia (Sopron), Soponiae (Pécs), Aquincum (Budapest) and Arrabona (Györ), to name just a few.

Stretched beyond its own human and financial reserves, and pummelled by the continuous onslaught of various tribes of barbarians, the Roman Empire withered away. When the Huns arrived in the Carpathian Basin in the second half of the 4th century, the Romans, daunted by the wide River Danube and the hostile Carpathian Range, still had not progressed eastwards.

After history had swallowed the Huns, Transdanubia and the Nagyalföld (Hungarian for the Great Plain, the region east of the Danube) were occupied by a hotchpotch of peoples – Avars, Ostrogoths, Slavs, Bulgars and various Eastern Franks. The Magyars were on their way.

The exact origin of the Hungarian people is still the subject of long lectures and heated debates in certain halls of *mons academiae*. The chronicles, written centuries after the facts, tend to be unreliable.

Some refer to Avars, others to Turkish tribes. The widespread derivatives of the term "Hungarian" recall the days when, it is speculated, the Hungarians were associated with a larger Turkish community known as the Onogurs ("10 arrows" in Turkish – in other words, 10 tribes). The name "Magyar" was first noted at the beginning of the 9th century.

In the 19th century the distinguished Hungarian linguist Antal Reguly (1819–58) investigated the languages used by the tribes living near the Ural mountains in central Russia. More linguists followed up the investigation and on their heels came a motley crew of archaeologists, ethnographers, ethnobiologists and anthropologists. Their united efforts over the past 140 years suggest that the Hungarians were once part of a Finno-Ugric speaking people living near the Urals.

Some time during the third millennium BC the community dispersed, with one group of tribes migrating westwards. By 600 AD the group consisted of seven tribes living between the Danube, the Don and the Black Sea as part of the mighty Khazar Kaganate. They led a semi-nomadic existence, moving to rivers in winter and back onto the plains in summer. The Magyars repesented the single most powerful tribe, and thus their name became the eponym for the whole group.

A dual monarchy: The Magyars rendered important military services to the Khazars and, in return for these, they enjoyed a special status. The Kagan either chose or sanctioned a figurehead leader (*kende*), while the tribes elected an executive leader (*gyula*) of their own.

The relationship became strained, however, when the Magyars not only declined to aid the Kagan in quashing a rebellion which had risen in the empire, but even granted asylum to the refugee rebels. Sensing that the Kagan would ultimately seek revenge, the Magyars began to look westwards for new homelands.

Riding as mercenaries for various European monarchs took them often into the Nagyalföld, which they soon coveted for its fertile ground and the defensible Carpathian Range.

Life on the open steppe was indeed hazardous. In the east a powerful Turkish tribe, the Pechenegs, had cut a swath through the dwindling Khazar empire and were threatening the weakly defended Magyar rear. The *gyula* Árpád had begun to move the tribes under his command westwards over the Carpathians. He crossed the Verecke pass in the spring of 895 and the rest of the tribes were huddling

the battle of Bresalauspurc (modern Bratislava).

The Magyars were not invincible. After staving them off for a time, the Emperor Henry the Fowler organised a division of heavily armed knights and defeated them in 933. A repeat performance by Emperor Otto I in 955 at the field of Lechfeld near Augsburg proved decisive. The Magyars ceased their visitations in the west and Otto I was rewarded for his efforts with the title "the Great".

National conversion: The Lechfeld collapse was no accident. Over-confidence and laxity within the ranks had eroded the

in the relative safety of the Nagyalföld by the following year.

The "adventure": The Magyars' new homeland was thinly settled by a mixture of Slavs, Avars and Franks. After establishing their presence, Magyar riders sought out their new country's borders west of the Danube. Hungarians call this period the "adventure". The chronicles are of a different opinion.

The Magyars plundered northern Italy and Bavaria, where a last-ditch attempt to rid the Western world of this new Eastern scourge failed miserably on 4 July 907 at

fighting will of the riders, and Western military organisation finally overcame their turbulent assaults. The Magyars were faced with the choice of either forming a cohesive state of their own or following the Huns into oblivion.

Árpád's grandson Géza, leader of the Magyars after 972, read the writing on the wall: integrate or disintegrate. Both Eastern and Western churches were wooing this potentially influential and important ally. Géza opted for Rome. In 975 Géza had his family converted. In 996 his son István, who would later become emperor, married Gisela of Bavaria, the daughter of Henry II.

Western religious medicine had proved more powerful than the Magyar scourge. Thus Géza, with a little force, could bring Christianity to many of his subjects. His son, a true believer as well as being a pragmatist, continued the policy of conversion. Named Vajk at first, he was baptised István (Stephen) after the Bishop of Passau, and his teacher and mentor was the great Bishop Adalbert of Prague.

István manoeuvred to propel Hungary towards the Western world. In AD 1000 he sent envoys to Rome to negotiate official

Bavarian knights, István defeated his rival's army near Veszprém in 997. Koppány's corpse was cut in four, and the head sent to his refractory uncle Gyula, who got the message. Later, just to make sure the fate of his victims was sealed, István confiscated his lands and imprisoned members of his family.

Prince Ajtony also proved to be a resilient enemy, but István's general Csanád (according to legend) was advised by St George when and where to attack, thus saving the Hungarian nation.

Besides consolidating his own power, István also gave Hungary its first set of

recognition, and in early AD 1001 he was anointed king. He later made Gran (Esztergom) his royal seat.

Paganism, however, still ruled in many parts of the country, but the Árpáds, a large family, stood behind István.

Koppány, Prince of Somogy (south of the Balaton), challenged the prospective king. With the help of his father-in-law's

Left, decorative Roman fountain in Gorsium, Tác, near Székesfehérvár. **Above**, an ivory horn in the local history museum, Jászberény, said to belong to the Magyar commander Lehel (d. 955).

laws, established a network of bishoprics and ratified the social order. The magnates, descendants of the first Magyar tribal chiefs, were considered a privileged class, probably because they owned large estates and did not owe the king anything other than loyalty and military obligation.

The magnates gathered in a parliament which possessed advisory rather than executive powers. Whatever land not belonging to this group of aristocrats would be placed under the control and ownership of the king. A second noble class existed, privileged, serving in the military, and legally free, but basically without land.

István divided Hungary into administrative units (counties), each led by a royal agent from a fortress (*vár*). These territorial divisions have since remained intact. The royal agents collected taxes from the "unfree" population, the majority of whom were poor peasants, and generally maintained small armies of freemen.

Apart from an attempt by Conrad II in 1030 to turn Hungary into a vassal of the Empire, István's rule was peaceful. His only son Imre, groomed for succession, was killed in a hunting accident in 1031. Suspecting his cousin Vasoly of closet

heathenism, István opted for his nephew Péter to succeed him. Vasoly was understandably miffed and may have been the author of an attempt on István's life. To seal the fate of Vasoly, the king had his eyes gouged, poured molten lead in his ears and even banished his three sons from the kingdom.

Troubled times: Fifty tumultuous years followed the death of István in 1038. Péter proved a misfit and was soon overthrown by Samuel Aba, István's brother-in-law. Henry II, the German emperor, was only too willing to help Péter resume power in

exchange for a little vassalage. King followed after king, army followed after army. Vasoly's sons re-emerged to claim their fair share of power and only last-ditch efforts prevented powerful tribes from the east – Pechenegs, Kumans and Uzes – from taking over the frail kingdom.

László I and Kálmán: The task of reconstruction fell to László I (1077–1095). The struggle raging between the popes and the Holy Roman Empire allowed him to pull strings on both sides. The popes, afraid of new enemies, were willing to overlook the Eastern taint of the Hungarian church and its total subservience to the king. They endowed Hungary with its first saints, including István. László I pursued a vigorous foreign policy, pushing into Transylvania and Croatia, and thrashing the aggressive Kumans.

Having promised the throne to his younger nephew, the dashing Almos, László changed his mind and ultimately opted for Kálmán, a hunchback who was supposedly bound for priesthood. The aristocracy was displeased at the last minute switch, and civil war almost engulfed the nation. But Kálmán proved an able if at first rather ruthless leader. He had Almos and his son Béla imprisoned and their eyes gouged.

Kálmán, nicknamed "könyves" (literally, "beset with books") because of his extensive education, ran a rational ship. Overall, his laws were fair and humanitarian for the times, and included such weighty statements as: "There will be no talk of witches, for they, we repeat, do not exist." He married the daughter of Roger of Sicily, and had his cousin (the daughter of László I) married to the Byzantine heir, thus ensuring allies on both sides of the country. Kálmán also made sure that the wild knights of Godfrey of Bouillon behaved themselves as they moved south on their crusade. He also furthered the expansion of Hungary into Dalmatia and Bosnia.

Left, the legendary Turul bird which led the Hungarians to their promised land. **Right**, the battle of Lechfeld, 955 AD, when the Magyars were decisively defeated.`

Noch nun auff die zeitt Otto des kayſers vmb ko
men ſo wil ich von den dingen ſagen die zu ſei
nen zeytten zu auffſpurg geſchehen ſend Do ſich d
kayſer otto beraittet wider berengarium den kunig bo
lomparden als wider ain vnietrich vnd geitigen vn
der alle gerechtikait vmb gelt gab Doch ſo forcht
in der ſelb vnietrich wan er die machtikait des kay
ſers wol wiſſet vnd durch ratt des hertzogen bo Luth
ringen kam er zu dem kayſer vnd begeret ſrid Do

Udita vo morte regis magni: puenit vniuersa multitudo nobiliu hungarie ad fratre eius Ladislaum Et eu comuni cosensu parili voto z cosona voluta te ad suscipiedu regni gubernacula cocorditer elegerut: imo fere magis affectuosissimis pcib copulerut. Oés eni nouerat ipsum esse vestitu psumarioe

By the Middle Ages, Hungary was a fairly large country with a cosmopolitan population. Besides the resident Slavs, Magyars and Székelys (another Magyar tribe that lived in the Carpathian basin prior to 896), throngs of Western Europeans had left their crowded homelands to settle and work in the fertile plains of Hungary. Many Germans, broadly and erroneously called Saxons, favoured Transylvania in particular, where they applied their skills in developing cities. They were considered freemen, and had the protection of a royal charter.

The generosity exhibited by Hungarian kings at the time may seem rather remarkable to the modern onlooker, used to hearing governments perpetually complaining about the influx of immigrants. The policy of inviting foreigners to settle in Hungary had two vital bases. First of all, King (and Saint) István had made an explicit point of it in his *Exhortations* to his son, a small book outlining his views on how to conduct the affairs of the state.

"Strangers and foreigners are most useful," he wrote. "They bring different values and customs, weaponry and sciences with them. These are all ornaments to a royal court to make it splendid, to the dismay of arrogant foreigners. For a land with one single language and uniform customs is weak and easily shattered." (The nationalists of the 19th century should perhaps have been wise to follow this "exhortation" to the letter.)

The ulterior motive for inviting people to settle on royal lands, however, was that, under the ancient tribal laws, power rested with the man who had the most people working on his land, which meant that it was in the king's interests to maintain the largest estates and the largest number of workers.

Left, a strong medieval ruler, László I. **Right**, a statue of the founder of Church and State, István I, at Székesfehérvár.

The tug-of-war: As long as the Hungarian king steered a successful course in his foreign policy and demonstrated his strength to the magnates and the nobles, Hungary was secured. Given the opportunity of a weak ruler, the magnates in particular, often venal and corrupt, vied for greater hold and power. Unfortunately much royal time and energy was expended in dealing with uncles, nephews and brothers, all of them squabbling over who should claim the throne.

A golden period in Hungarian history was the rule of Béla III (1172–96) who had been raised in Constantinople. He was firm without being tyrannical. He ran a well organised state apparatus, put the finances in order, kept the magnates and the nobles in check and conducted a sound foreign policy. The Byzantine cross was added to the Hungarian emblem, but Béla also relaxed his control of the Catholic church.

In matrimonial diplomacy, he first married Anne de Chatillon, who was related to the imperial family. His second wife was Margaret Capet, the widow of the English heir.

In a few years, Béla III's successors brought the country to the brink of ruin. András II (1205–35) spent most of his incumbency leading the leisurely, dissipated, bellicose life of the typical *roi fainéant*. He gave away royal real estates to his knights and lords, raised taxes and rented out lands and privileges to the highest bidder. Favouritism flourished and those who did not profit from it – disgruntled magnates, dispossessed nobles, the freemen who served in the army and the church

evolution of the nation. For the immediate future, however, the Bull, apart from making a few changes, could not restore the orderly kingdom left by Béla III.

The Mongols: News of the Mongol invasions of the Russian steppes began seeping through to the West in the 1220s, brought by Russian and Kuman fugitives from the scourge. Béla IV (1235–70) knew what awaited him but stood his ground. The Kumans provided him with 40,000 riders, and he hoped that the Western powers and the Pope would be able to provide more manpower before the arrival of the Golden Horde.

– rebelled. In 1222 András was forced to promulgate the "Golden Bull", a charter laying down the rights of the nobility and fixing the relationship between aristocracy and king. The Bull also permitted resistance to royal actions deemed illegal or harmful to the nation and freed the magnates from obligatory participation in foreign ventures.

The Golden Bull had an effect on posterity. All Hungarian kings would have to swear to it, and it created a consolidated social class of freemen and nobles who were to play a major role in the political

Instead of forming a united front, however, Europe fell apart. Emperor Frederick II's lackadaisical attempts to form a coalition of armies was stymied by the Pope, the fossilised Gregory IX, who was convinced that the Emperor, not the Mongol general Batu Khan, was the Antichrist. The Kumans meanwhile were involved in a civil war.

In 1241 the five-pronged Mongol invasion began in earnest. On 9 April Henry II, Duke of Lower Silesia, thrust himself and 10,000 knights suicidally at one of the prongs near Liegnitz. Two days later, a Hungarian army disintegrated at Muhi, at the confluence of the Hernad and Sajo rivers. The king escaped west over the Danube, which the Mongols did not cross until February 1242, when it was frozen solid. They then proceeded with their ravaging joyride, sparing only such virtually inaccessible forts as Pannonhalma and Székesfehérvár which was surrounded by swamps. Less fortunate areas were virtually depopulated. The Mongols' principal aim was to capture the king, for according to their rules of warfare (rules interestingly shared by the Hungarians, which is perhaps suggestive of the eastern origins of the Magyars), only when the king had been

IV set about building a series of fortresses for future defences. Pest, ravaged in 1241, was relocated to the mountainous west bank of the Danube where Buda stands today. At the same time Frederick of Austria, assuming Hungary to be prostrate, tried without much success to swipe at a small territory. Hungary later returned the favour. But, of course, it was Béla's urgent need of support that forced him into making several concessions to the magnates and the nobles.

The last of the Árpáds: Hungary recovered relatively quickly, but a deep bitterness remained from the justified feeling that the

taken prisoner could the country they had invaded be considered conquered. Béla IV, was escorted to the safety of an island off the Dalmatian coast.

In 1242 the Mongols disappeared as quickly as they had arrived. The supreme Khan Ogödei had died and Batu Khan had to return to the Far East to handle the succession. The Mongols had gone forever, but no-one was taking chances. Béla

Left, the chronicler *Anonymous* in the City Park of Pest. Above, the royal insignia attributed to St Stephen (István I).

Hungarians had been left on their own to fight off the Mongols. It was with reluctance that Béla IV married two daughters to Ruthenian princes and one to a Pole, for the sake of alliances and sources of information in the East. In a letter to Pope Vincent IV, written in 1253, he poured out his heart without any success. He particularly regretted the growing influence of the heathen Kumans. "Further, in the interests of protecting Christianity," he wrote, "We married our first born son to a Kuman girl... in order to secure the possibility of converting these people to Christianity..."

That first born, István, died soon after succeeding his father. His son László, finally crowned after a troubled period of regency, turned out to be one of the strangest royal figures in the dwindling line of Árpád rulers.

He married Isabella of Naples, but soon developed a strong attraction for the culture of his mother's people. He threatened to behead the Hungarian bishop, he locked up his wife, he dressed up as a Kuman, took in a string of young Kuman girls as mistresses, adopted various Mongol and Kuman customs, earned himself the nickname "the Kuman" and was finally mur-

government. This electoral system was unique in Europe at the time. The criteria included a trace of Árpád blood, a noble title and a certain amount of competence.

Potential candidates could for their part influence the magnates by virtue of their friends, their wealth or their willingness to bow to the magnates' demands.

Seven years went by while the magnates tried out a number of potential candidates for the succession. Wenceslas of Bohemia spent four years on the throne, Otto of Bavaria three. Finally, with help from the Pope, Charles Robert of Anjou secured the Hungarian crown for his dynasty. He

dered by a Kuman, probably in connivance with the exasperated magnates.

As luck would have it, the Árpáds were thinning out. For all intents and purposes, László IV had died childless. His sister, the Queen of Naples, placed her son András III on the throne. He, too, died after a brief reign, leaving a daughter, and thus ending the male line of the Árpád dynasty.

The elective monarchy: With the absence of a central authority, power in Hungary reverted to the magnates, who had to seek, investigate and then elect someone they considered fit to take over the reins of

reigned as Charles I, and both he and his son Louis I ruled wisely for many years.

In the absence of royal supervision, the magnates had become accustomed to certain freedoms. In 1312, aided by irate nobles, Charles I demonstrated who was boss. From then on, he centralised power. A new upper class developed, drawn from the ranks of his ministers, all of whom were hand-picked and therefore loyal. No parliament was convened after 1323 and the nobles were thus left to their own governing schemes, serving in the administration of the counties, which was a welcome move as it increased their independence.

Liberal mining rights and the introduction of a gold and silver currency increased the country's trading ability. The Northern Hungarian and Transylvanian mines produced an average of 3,000 pounds of gold annually, making Hungary Europe's biggest producer of gold, and therefore one of its richest nations.

Prosperity, in turn, attracted artists, scholars and new settlers, and resulted in a significant population growth in spite of the effects of the Black Death. Most of the pioneers came from the southeast region –

Strong resistance immediately came from the Papal States, backed by Venice; the merchant city frowned upon Hungarian ventures on the Dalmatian coast of the Adriatic.

In the north, Poland, too, became a Hungarian dominion for a while when Louis I, on the basis of an earlier treaty, acceded to the throne in 1370. But he had little control over the Poles, and even less time to devote to the dominion. His attention was, in fact, drawn to the Balkans, where major changes had been taking place.

Bosnia belonged by marriage to Hungary, but Serbia had experienced a politi-

Ruthenians, Romanians and Wallachians.

Foreign policy: Not all the kingdom's money went into supporting such ventures as the short-lived University of Pécs (1367). The complex diplomatic ventures of Charles I and later his son Louis I relied on a standing army. The Angevins wanted to establish their headquarters in Naples. The Hungarian army tried on three occasions to occupy the city but failed each time.

Left, arrival of the Mongols, 1241 AD. **Above**, the castle of Diósgyör near Miskolc was built as a reaction to the Mongol invasion.

cal renaissance under Stépan Dusan (1331–35) and was testing its strength. Rumblings from various nationalities now threatened regional Hungarian overlordship. But even more dangerous was the growing Turkish empire. By the 1350s it had reached European soil and started its military and diplomatic involvement with the Balkan states which lie along the lower Danube.

In 1377 Louis I defeated the Sultan Murad. At the same time, on Hungary's western flank, the Habsburg dynasty was looking for new territories of Europe to include in its domains.

The death of Lajos I in 1382 precipitated a crisis in the palace grounds. The Hungarian king had arranged for the elder of his two daughters, Maria, to succeed him in ruling the two kingdoms of Hungary and Poland, but the Poles would recognise only the younger Hedwig as their queen. Moreover, Lajos I had promised his daughter and the crown to Sigismond of Luxembourg, who had been educated at the Hungarian court. The noble estates preferred the Neapolitan Angevins. The Queen Mother, supported by the court paladin Miklós Garai, had her eye on Louis of Orléans.

Sigismond ultimately won the three-way contest. His reign, until his death in 1437, was controversial but by no means poor. His brutality in crushing the Bohemian-bred Hussite rebellion which overflowed into Hungary repulsed many. In spite of a rather productive economy, the lives of the indentured peasants were hardly improving, providing the Hussites fertile soil in which to spread their ideas. Only a coalition of Saxons, Szekels and Hungarian gentry could end the resulting peasant uprising in 1437.

A European power: Sigismond was active in European affairs, becoming titular king of Bohemia and even Holy Roman Emperor. During his long and often resented periods of absence, he neglected Hungary's domestic problems and left the duties of the state in the hands of faithful deputies. Amid growing discontentment, parliament took on greater responsibilities in governing the country, and the nobles and magnates were now required to provide armies of mercenaries.

In 1396, Sigismond led an ill-fated crusade against the Islamic "infidel", suffering a crushing defeat at the battle of

Nicopolis. In 1417 the Turks reached Wallachia and by the end of Sigismond's reign 20 years later, they carried out successive raids into Hungarian territory.

During his brief reign, Albrecht of Habsburg (1437–39) began work on fortifications for the nation, but he died leaving a pregnant wife. The estates, in search of some strong ally, selected the Polish king Wladislaw III Jagiello, who gallantly charged off to battle with the Turks at

Varna in 1444, and laid down his 19 years on the field. Albrecht's wife had in the meantime given birth to László, who was duly elected king, while the regency was entrusted to János Hunyadi, an inspired magnate and soldier. Despite two major defeats, Varna and Amselfeld in 1448, he was able to stave off the overall advance of the Turks.

Other magnates seethed with envy behind his back. Young László's uncle, Ulrich von Cilli, Count of Styria, intrigued, fearing for his nephew's crown. The Habsburgs also had to be warded off. By the time

Left, dominating the Buda hills is the Church of Our Lady, also known as the Matthias Church, after King Mátyás, or Matthias (**right**), had it extended and decorated during his reign.

Hunyadi died, of an illness contracted during the brilliant freeing of Nándorfehérvár (Belgrade) in 1456, Hungary was torn apart by internal strife. Cilli was murdered, but his clique had one of Hunyádi's sons killed and the other, Mátyás, imprisoned in Prague. In 1457 László died – possibly poisoned – without having achieved notoriety. As a result, the magnates had little choice but to recover the young Mátyás Hunyadi from Prague.

The last hurrah: Perhaps the magnates thought a 16-year-old boy could be easily pushed around. Certainly Frederick III of Habsburg, leering from the west, thought

1490 – another case of poisoning? – Hungary had acquired Lower Austria, Moravia and Silesia. Mátyás also led a successful campaign against the Turks in 1476.

The might of Mátyás Corvinus: Mátyás Corvinus' foreign ventures did not prevent him from keeping a lid on dissent at home. He operated through hand-picked delegates and he courted the free towns, the large peasant communities and the nobles, setting them against the magnates. Mátyás scraped together a standing army of mercenaries to be used when he thought necessary. He had a chain of fortresses built along Hungary's vulnerable borders, and

so, as he declared himself king with the support of a few Hungarian nobles. All of them were mistaken. Mátyás Corvinus (Latin *corvinus*=crow, from the crow on his emblem) proved tough and autocratic, yet remained fair in his dealings. By 1463 he had recovered the crown from Frederick III and hammered out a tenuous peace treaty with him.

In 1446 the two warred against the Bohemian King George Podiebrad who was apparently tainted with Hussitism. A few years later, Mátyás was again battling Frederick III. By the end of his reign in

also let the magnates' armies stand and fight, intervening when necessary.

Like Francis I of France in the following century, Mátyás had something of the Renaissance man with an eye for Italy. He raised vast sums to promote the arts and to beautify castles and churches. The court at Buda was considered to be the most important centre of Renaissance culture north of the Alps. Artists and scholars met here frequently; Italians and Germans contributed to the glories of the city and its Castle. Although the first book was printed in Buda in 1473, King Mátyás had a definite preference for the old handwritten codices, which ultimately made up the famous volume, *Bibliotheca Corviniana*. Thriftier Hungarians felt a little uncomfortable at the lavish disbursements, but the Hungarian court shone throughout Europe and the country's literary heritage of the period was indeed impressive. When Corvinus died, it all fell apart.

The estates, this time bent on a malleable king, chose Wladislaw Jagiello of Bohemia to succeed Corvinus. Affairs of the state, including defence, were left to this indecisive, mild and incompetent fellow, while the magnates and the lower

without ever being ratified by parliament.

By the time of Verböczy's Tripartium, however, most of Mátyás' territorial gains had been lost and the fortifications were ramshackled. Friendly relations between the kingdom and the sorely exploited serfs of the Corvinian days had atrophied. The Reformation, which made headway among the exploited as well as the nobles – as in Western Europe – gave impetus to a violent rebellion among the oppressed peasants in Transylvania, led by the soldier, György Dózsa. The voivode of Transylvania, an influential landowner by the name of János Zapolya, distinguished himself

nobility battled for greater power.

In 1514 the court judge, a noble named István Verböczy, prepared the Tripartium, which reiterated the privileges of the nobility while taking care to reaffirm their rights over serfs. The set of laws, which replaced the 1222 Golden Bull, remained in force until feudalism vanished in 1848,

Far left, memorial plaque for the Transylvanian leader and diplomat Bethlen, in Nyíregháza. **Left**, marble statues in Buda commemorating the peasant leader Dózsa. **Above**, the religious reformers Zwingli and Calvin in Debrecen.

through his ferocious suppression of the revolt. The Diet voted to condemn the peasants to "real and perpetual servitude" for their pains.

Disaster at Mohács: The Reformation sundered every facet of Europe's political and social life. It coincided with the high tide of Turkish power under Suleiman II "the Magnificent". Desperately in need of reinforcements, Lajos II of Hungary, married to a Habsburg, tried to convince a divided parliament of the need to re-establish the national army of Corvinus. He sought aid from every "Christian" monarch, including Francis I of France, who was secretly in cahoots with the Turks, in an attempt to surround the Habsburgs. A plea to the magnates of Transylvania and Croatia came too late. Plucking up courage, Lajos II placed himself at the head of a small army of less than 20,000 and quickly rallied together to stall the Turkish summer offensive of 1526. On 29 August that year, the armies clashed at Mohács.

It turned out to be a catastrophe for the Hungarian army. King Louis II died, drowned while crossing a swollen stream, those men who survived the battle were afflicted with serious injuries.

tively divided Hungary in two. Royal Hungary subsisted as a small strip of land in the west with Pozsony (today Bratislava) as its capital.

In the southeast of Hungary, the nobles elected Zapolya, who proved only too willing to make deals with the Turks in return for relative peace in his region of Transylvania. One glowing and relatively selfless figure to shine through the dark age was György Martinuzzi, also known as Friar George, a Dominican monk and cardinal who had the ears of both Zapolya and Frederick I. In 1538 he concluded a secret agreement between the two rulers,

A double monarchy: The Turks moved on to capture Pécs and Buda. They would have penetrated further had they not feared that the Europeans were maintaining a secret force more substantial than the pitiful Mohács division in reserve.

In fact the Hungarians had nothing up their sleeve besides Mohács. They quickly elected Frederick I of Habsburg in the vain hope that the Austrians would scheme assault strategies against the Turks, but apart from a few successful skirmishes, nothing else happened. By 1541 the Turks occupied a large chunk of land that effec-

that when and if the heirless Zapolya died first, the other would be crowned king of Transylvania. Two years later Zapolya died, leaving an infant son, János Zsigmond to claim the throne. Friar George became regent.

In 1551, during the lull in between wars, a small Habsburg army occupied Transylvania, and promised to compensate Zapolya's heir. Friar George prepared to counter the Turkish wrath at this blatant upset of the balance of power with a number of diplomatic and financial panaceas. But the Austrian general Castaldo became suspicious and had Friar George executed, whereupon the Turkish army moved in and helped János Zsigmond to the throne.

Transylvania's glory: Royal Hungary meanwhile puttered along, a mere latifundium of the Austrian Empire. Its magnates and nobles grew disgruntled, and Protestantism, synonymous at the time with political rebellion, immediately made headway. Transylvania on the other hand enjoyed a turbulent period of glory. Turbulent, because of its many nationalities, and its panoply of religious faiths living together in harmony – unique in Europe at the time. The Saxons opted for Lutheranism, the Székely uprising which he managed to suppress in such exemplary fashion that the Székelys no longer remained a source of trouble for centuries to come.

The glory stemmed from the independence Transylvania gained from paying tribute to the Sultan and allowing him the honour of sanctioning every newly chosen voivode. Now and then, war broke out; villages were plundered and lives were lost. On the other hand, the Transylvanian nobles officially recognised the Habsburgs through the Treaty of Speyer in 1570, only a timetable for reunification had not yet been set.

Székelys remained Catholic, the Hungarian nobles found Calvinism to their liking and the Romanians remained steadfastly Greek Orthodox. Turbulent also because these nationalities, notably the Székelys whose star had been gradually fading through the centuries, were not always happy with the status quo. In 1569 János Zsigmond was confronted by a dangerous

Left, the signature of Suleiman the Magnificent, engraved on a window of the Town Hall in Mohács. **Above**, the forlorn memorial of Sátorhely near Mohács.

Transylvania also produced a string of brilliant leaders. In 1571 István Báthory seized power, and not long after, was crowned King of Poland while his brother Christoph acted as Prince at home. Báthory's son Zsigmond distinguished himself by gaining several victories against the Turks. In 1595, after sealing an alliance with Rudolf I of Habsburg, his army under István Bocskay won a major victory at Giurgiu. The following year, the Turks won a minor victory at Mezőkeresztes.

The Haiduks: The war flickered on with skirmishes and brutal retaliatory expeditions that devastated the outlying areas of Transylvania. After a promising beginning, Zsigmond suddenly lost his senses and capriciously delivered the principality into the hands of Rudolf I of Habsburg, who sent an army headed by the brutal General George Basta into Transylvania. The local magnates and nobles suddenly owed total allegiance to the emperor, while General Basta began spreading a small fire and brimstone Catholicism on the tolerant Transylvanians.

Pressure soon passed the point of endurance. Putting himself at the head of a colourful gang of peasants – among them

He gambled for allies in Royal Hungary by extending official protection to all Hungarian Protestants, and kept the Habsburgs busy with a series of small wars. The Treaty of Nicolsburg, one of several treaties to be signed in the course of the Thirty Years' War, gave Bethlen the title Prince of Hungary and a chunk of Silesia. His successor György Rákóczi II pursued policies of expansion, even securing the Treaty of Westphalia in 1648 to recognise Transylvania as an independent state.

Transylvanian strength rested partially on the weakness of the Habsburgs and the Turks, whose leadership since the death of

the famous Haiduks – nobles, city-dwellers and discharged soldiers, István Bocskay, the valiant commander of Giurgiu, trounced the Habsburgs led by Basta and installed himself on the Transylvanian throne in 1606. He quickly restored religious freedom and diplomatic relations with Turkey. When he died, it was the Turkish Sultan who proposed his successor Gábor Bethlen (1613–29), the most famous prince of Transylvania. An ardent supporter of the arts, Bethlen like his contemporaries, invested huge sums on beautifying the palace courts.

Suleiman II left much to be desired. Bethlen's wooing of the nobles in Royal Hungary was facilitated by the poor treatment received from the Habsburgs, and by the atrocious behaviour of the Austrian soldiers while on campaign. Yet his efforts were countered by the brilliant Cardinal Péter Pázmány (1570–1637), who re-Catholicised most of the magnates and nobles, and by the plain fact that Transylvania had dealt with the "infidel".

Tatar invasion: The second half of the 17th century was full of highly dramatic events. In 1657 György Rákóczi II made common cause with the Protestant King Karl Gustav of Sweden and attacked Poland without permission from the Turks. The Sultan dispatched an army of Tatars who quickly ended the expedition and invaded Transylvania, effectively putting an end to 150 years of Transylvanian greatness.

Leopold I, the Habsburg Emperor, seized the chance to take the initiative away from Transylvania. From then on, the war against the Turks and for the liberation of Hungary rested in the hands of the Austrians. The ensuing war lingered until 1663, when the Austrian general Montecuccoli defeated the Turks at Szentgotthórd. Leopold I could

hardly wait for the eastern front to be closed to resume his war against the French king Louis XIV, so the treaty signed in nearby Vasvár not only failed to get territorial concessions from the Turks, but it promised them a small sweetener of 30,000 gulden to leave Europe alone.

The Hungarian magnates were incensed. An anti-Habsburg conspiracy of nobles

Left, statue of Prince Ferenc II Rákóczi in the palace park of Sarospatak. **Above**, site plan of the siege of Temesvár (today Timi oara, Rumania) in Translyvania.

received kind blessings from Louis XIV of France, but it was soon uncovered and fiercely repressed. Apart from executions and dispossessions, the Hungarians in the army were also expelled, and the governing of Royal Hungary was placed directly under Leopold I. Prince Imre Thököly of Transylvania, a young enthusiastic leader with little political wisdom, forged an army of discharged soldiers and disgruntled nobles, the so-called Kuruzes, and successfully forced Leopold back to the bargaining table.

The final thrust: Pope Innocent XI, finally putting some money where the Vatican's mouth had been for decades, decided it was time to finance a major operation against the Turks. While hoping for support from the Kuruzes, the Sultan also began an offensive in 1683. The alliance collapsed when the Turks were defeated at the gates of Vienna. Thököly was crowned king, but his army deserted him to join the Austrians.

By 1686 Buda had been repossessed. Within a few years, most parts of the country including Transylvania were cleared. The Peace of Karlovic in 1699 ended the war, temporarily, leaving only a small section between the Maros and the Tisza in Turkish hands. It was later ceded to Hungary in 1718.

Redistributing the land to its rightful owners and settling various other claims after 150 years of occupation would have been a difficult task even in the best of times and under the best possible administration. Now it seemed impossible. Corruption, extortion, unusually high taxes, the sale of land and property to foreign speculators and a violent spate of Counter-Reformation measures quickly brought the Hungarians to the boil. In 1703 Ferenc Rákóczi II initiated a rebellion that was to last until 1711.

Fortunately for Rákóczi, the Hungarian military leader of the Austrians, Count Pálffy, offered to negotiate some sort of settlement. The Peace of Szatmár restored the status quo of 1686. The treaty was hardly ideal but it did finally bring peace to Hungary.

When the Hungarian tribes streamed into the Carpathian basin during the 9th century, they found a land that was anything but empty or pagan. Christianity had already obtained a foothold in Pannonia by the 4th century. However, several of the churches, together with their congregations, were swept off by the whirlwind of the Great Migration. Quieter times had barely returned when both the eastern and the western churches sent their missionaries to the Great Pannonian Plain.

In the course of their raids and conquests the Magyars acquired new lands and also became familiar with Christianity. Some of them even submitted themselves for conversion and baptism. The spread of Christianity began under Prince Géza (c. 971–997) and was followed up by his son King István I (997–1038) with the influence of Bavarian and also Italian, French, Polish, Czech and Flemish emissaries of the faith. About 500 years later, the inspiring words of Lutheran and Calvinist preachers also landed on fertile soil.

The Babel of the religions: However, the largest denomination was and still is the Catholic Church, closely followed by the Reformed Protestant Church. The third largest denomination is the Lutheran Protestant Church. Most of the members of the Orthodox Church are either ethnic Romanians or Serbs, but the small Unitarian community, based in Transylvania, is almost entirely composed of Hungarians. The Council of Hungarian Free Churches is an umbrella organisation for various small Protestant communities such as the Adventists, Baptists, Anglicans, and Methodists. However, the Jehovah's Witnesses and the Church of the Latter-Day Saints are two denominations officially prohibited.

The Jewish community has some 80,000 members. In the early summer of 1944, about 500,000 Jews were deported to German concentration camps, most of them from provincial areas. The Jewish Ghetto in Budapest was the only one to survive the war fairly intact. It contains a rabbinical school, the only seminary for rabbis in Eastern Europe.

The People's Republic: After World War II, all the churches suffered great losses, both in terms of property and of social status. In 1949, the separation of Church and State was declared, and religious instruction was no longer permitted in schools – "The [ertswhile] People's Republic of

Hungary guarantees its citizens freedom of conscience and the right to practise their religion freely." However, this right was placed under the following constraints: in 1948 the leaders of all the churches were forced to resign, and the Catholic primate Cardinal József Mindszenty was even arrested and sentenced to life imprisonment for defying orders.

Property belonging to the churches was confiscated, the monastic orders were promptly dissolved and their members persecuted, interned and deported. Only one female order (the teaching order of Our

Lady) and three male orders (Benedictines, Piarists, Franciscans) were eventually spared.

Since 1951, religious affairs have been the concern of the State Ecclesiastical Office (*Allami Egyházügyi Hivatal*), which also has a right to be consulted when religious leaders are appointed within the churches. For instance, no priest can be ordained or bishop consecrated without the agreement of this office. The state gives financial support to the churches; the annual amount is decided every five years. The relationship between the Catholic Church and the state is regulated by a

partial agreement with the Vatican dating from 1964.

In the two large religious communities of the Protestant Church, a basic theological thesis which goes beyond the guidelines laid down by the state has been worked out. It has developed from the ideas of the theologian Karl Barth, and is based on a view of the Bible which claims that Jesus fitted in with the political and social systems of his day and did not try to exceed

Left, Serbian Orthodox bishop in Ráckeve. Above, synagogue railings in Eger.

their limits. Despite this thesis (which is often disputed even among theologians) it is the Protestant Church which provides political opposition more often than the conformist Catholic Church. A kind of quiet opposition is taking shape within the Catholic Church, in the form of grassroots groups, mostly led by lay preachers who hold prayer and Bible study meetings. The activities of these cells are viewed with distrust by both the authorities and the upper echelons of the church, as they are suspected of political dissent.

In recent years, the assistance that has been offered by the Reformed Church to Hungarian refugees from Romania has not only been tolerated, it has been supported by the media.

Variety of journals: All the churches have their own public information systems, with publishing houses and regular journals. "Quality" journals are the Catholic monthly, *Vigilia*, and its Protestant counterpart, *Confessio*, both of which include contributions from well-known Hungarian writers and intellectuals. The Jewish religious community publishes the weekly *Uj élet* (New Life), and since the autumn of 1987 an underground magazine, *Magyar Zsidó* (Hungarian Jew), has been appearing on the newstands. It deals less with religious issues and more with the general problems of being a Jew, as well as matters on Jewish history in this country.

The Catholic Church has five seminaries and eight high schools, the Reformed Church two theological academies and a high school in Debrecen. During the last few years, the Lutheran Church has been trying to obtain official permission for a high school in addition to the existing theological academy.

Religious freedom was restored after 1989 and in its wake came a revival of religious movements, with more denominational schools and the appearance of other sects and religions, Mormons, Baptists, Buddhists, Jehovah's Witnesses. The new freedom of expression has also, on the negative side, revealed that anti-Semitism is still latent in certain circles, even politically influential ones.

In 1723 the Hungarian parliament, still seated in Pozsony, ratified the Pragmatic Sanction establishing the legality of female succession and the indivisibility of Habsburg territories. As a result, the military and the government became more attached than ever. Vienna attracted Hungarians who wanted the better things in life; the nobles continued to enjoy their privilges. The issue of freeing the serfs, raised by Rákóczi, was toned down.

Maria Theresa (1740–80) ascended the throne to become Hungary's favourite ruler. She was both gentle and firm. In 1741, after Austria's squabble with Prussia suddenly developed into a major conflict following the secession of several provinces, she turned to parliament in Pozsony as a last resort and, dressed in mourning, appealed for help. The chivalrous Hungarian nobles could not resist and in return Maria Theresa did not forget to be grateful. More importantly, she restored peace to a war-torn Hungary and with her persuasive diplomatic style, easily gained the confidence of both magnates and the peasants.

The empress also proved to be a tough and autocratic woman. There were instances when she refused to succumb to parliament after it challenged her policies. A fervent Catholic, Maria Theresa "discouraged" Protestants from working in government service.

Transylvania was granted independent status and a fortified line placed between it and Hungary. The Székelys, who felt more attached to Hungary, rebelled. After their crushing defeat at Madefalva in 1764, many chose to migrate to Hungary, tipping the population scales in Transylvania in favour of the Romanians. Two decades later, the Romanians in turn rebelled when a series of land reforms in Hungary were not implemented in Transylvania.

Left, Empress Maria Theresa, Hungary's favourite ruler, who was crowned in Pozsony (modern Bratislava). Right, detail of a gateway in Hajós.

Liberalisation under Joseph II: The lull and peace of Theresan days ended abruptly with the coronation of Joseph II. Reared in the Age of Enlightenment, he rejected the hocus-pocus of symbolic power surrounding the Crown of St Stephen and, instead of wearing it, had it mothballed in Vienna. Being practical and believing in central government, he made German the empire's official language. He tolerated religions in an agnostic fashion which fright-

ened Catholic authorities. He turned cloisters into hospitals, regulated church building and practices, conducted a national census, replaced local administration with royal delegates and imposed a standard tax acccording to the area of an estate. He also began the process of freeing the serfs from bondage. By the end of the 1780s the conservative Hungarian nobles stood on the brink of rebellion. Joseph II retracted many of his reforms on his deathbed, while his successor, the short-lived Leopold II (1790–92), reversed others. Latin was reinstated as the official language, the nobles were given greater representation, and, most important, the crown was returned to Buda and the parliament again officially elected the king.

In 1789, the Enlightenment experiment blew up in the faces of Europe's enlightened monarchs. As the French Revolution turned from a mob screaming at the Bastille to a fire that spread across the continent, a pall of conservatism fell over the monarchies. After the death of Leopold II, the Diet ceased to be convened. A customs barrier was created between Hungary and Austria. The country was asked to pay its dues without question, and these were tween Hungary and Austria could only result in an explosion. Hungarian dissent consisted of equal parts reaction and republicanism. Count István Széchenyi footed the bill for unifying these two forces.

Széchenyi was a heartfelt patriot with a highly cosmopolitan background. His father had founded the National Museum in 1802, and he himself actively cultivated the Hungarian language, which had fallen into general disrepair during the dog days of the 18th century. His programme for a Hungarian revival involved social, political, cultural and industrial modernisation.

"Let us trust our own strength, and never

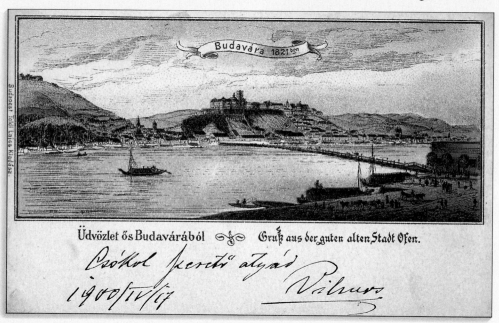

Üdvözlet ős Budavárából ⟶ Gruß aus der guten alten Stadt Ofen.

heavy as the Napoleonic wars absorbed increasingly large sums of money. Hungary also suffered a series of major currency devaluations.

The new consciousness: Though basically a kind-hearted fellow, the Habsburg, Francis I, looked suspiciously upon the Hungarians. He misunderstood the fundamentally conservative nature of the nobles' historic rebelliousness. Jacobinism had blossomed in Hungary in the mid-1790s, but when Napoleon called on the Hungarians to throw off their chains in 1809, he received no answer. Growing tension be-

do battle unprepared and administer our forces better; for in the rebirth of a nation... the modest bee and hardworking ant achieve a great deal more than golden rhetoric and the din of enthusiasm" Széchenyi stated in 1842.

Metternich, Austria's *éminence grise* until 1848, considered Széchenyi and his apostles dreamers (Metternich for his pains was nicknamed *Prinz Mitternacht*, or Midnight). Széchenyi, practising what he preached, busied himself building railways, shipyards and regulating the Tisza. His most famous work is the Chain Bridge which crosses the Danube in Budapest.

Revolutionary year: Széchenyi gathered support not only among his own class but among other nobles. Among the many to rise to prominence in his wake was the dispossessed landed gentleman and lawyer Lajos Kossuth, a brilliant orator and cunning statesman.

Vienna's attitude to the troubles brewing in Hungary changed from one of affable tolerance to that of police oppression. Kossuth, among others, had to cool his heels in prison for three years. In February 1848 the Parisians overthrew their monarchy. The revolution swept across Europe

drawn up reiterating Kossuth's demands and including freedom of the press, jury trials and reunification with Transylvania. Two days later, the far-sighted magnate, Count Lajos Batthyány, headed an autonomous cabinet which included some of Hungary's finest brains: Széchenyi, communications and transportation; Ferenc Deák, justice; Jozsef Eötvös, education; and Kossuth, finance.

Emperor Ferdinand, an exceptionally gentle Habsburg, kindly ratified all these changes while reactionary circles seethed with frustration. They had no choice; the whole empire was embroiled in revolution.

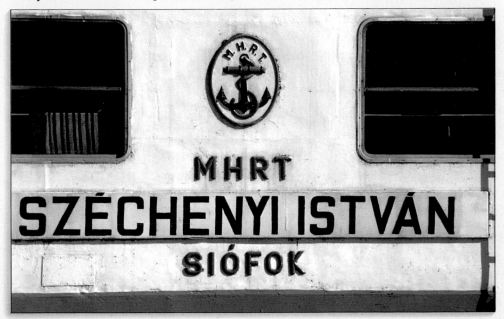

like wildfire. On 3 March, Kossuth addressed the Hungarian parliament, demanding in incomparable rhetoric, the revocation of tax privileges, extension of the franchise to non-nobles, freedom for the peasants – in short, an end to feudalism.

On 13 March, another major revolution shook Vienna. Two days later, 15 March, it reached Pest. At a stormy session in the Café Pilvax a 12-point programme was

Left, the castle of Buda before the construction of the Chain Bridge. **Above**, a ferry on Lake Balaton honors Count Széchenyi.

Resistance to the Hungarian revolution came from another quarter as well, and Vienna knew how to take advantage of it. Swept along by the events, Hungary's ethnic group – Romanians, Ruthenes, Croats and Slovaks – swamped an unwilling parliament with demands of their own. In June Serbia rebelled. The following month, Kossuth submitted a requested 42 million gulden to beef up the defence.

Batthyány tried hard to steer a non-violent course but was cornered. Vienna accused the Hungarians of breaking the Pragmatic Sanction and revoked the laws sanctioned in April. Széchenyi suffered a nervous breakdown. Batthyány and his cabinet members finally resigned and left Kossuth in power. The Hungarian revolution pulled itself together with the outbreak of hostilities in September. It coincided with a revolt by Romanian peasants under the command of Avram Iancu, but the newly formed army succeeded in fending off the various threats before it was stopped in its tracks near Vienna on 30 October.

After Ferdinand gave the throne to his 18-year-old nephew Franz Joseph, the war resumed. Kossuth moved parliament to

hopeless cavalcade. His declamations had given wings to the revolution, and with him went a glorious, tragic period of Hungarian history.

Görgey, who had surrendered to Field Marshal Paskevic at Vilagos on 13 August, 1849, slithered through the courts and lived to the ripe old age of 98. Kossuth reached exile through Turkey. Others were less fortunate. A wave of imprisonment, exile and execution followed. Batthyány and 13 other leaders of the revolution were summarily shot in Arad (today Oradea, Romania).

the relative safety of Debrecen, from where it proclaimed Hungary a republic on 14 April 1849. The Hungarian general Arthur Görgey, his ranks swelled by divisions of Italian, Polish, Slovak and even German patriots from Europe's failed revolutions, checkmated the royal troops. Then, the Russian Tsar led his army across the Carpathian basin and joined in the fray on the side of the Austrians. The Hungarians, outnumbered in every respect, were forced to surrender. Among the dead was Sándor Petöfi, his bones allegedly pounded into some forlorn field during a heroic but

Absolute rule and repression: The truculent General Haynau administered Hungary with an iron hand. All reforms were summarily revoked. Transylvania, Croatia and Slovenia were cut off from Hungary. Austrian and Czech bureaucrats rushed in to fill the shoes of the the Hungarian civil servants.

The heavy weight of absolutist rule reached its climax under the interior minister, Bach. The desired effect – pacifying the Hungarians – did not materialise. Instead repression created a pantheon of martyrs and further justified the need for reform. A few concessions to 1848 such as limited land reform and abolition of trade barriers failed to wash away the blood that had flowed between Hungary and Austria. They were counterbalanced by drastic increases in taxes and the shame of having to speak the official language German.

While Kossuth hovered over Hungary from exile, a new opposition formed in the country in the 1850s, made up mostly of conservatives and moderates left over from 1848. Their central figure was Ferenc Deák, an unglamorous, avuncular but very sharp little man. The Hungarians frequently gave

voice to their political sentiments, especially on historic anniversaries.

The Hungarians had a powerful ally in Vienna: the Empress Elizabeth who, perhaps roused by the romantic aspects of the Magyar resistance, often interceded in their favour. Moreover, times were changing. Austria's unsuccessful foreign policy ventures, such as the defeat by the Italians and the French in 1859, made the need for a

Monarchy versus republic. At the time of the coronation of Franz Joseph in 1867 (left), the republican Lajos Kossuth (right) was in exile.

safe domestic situation even more urgent.

In the October Diploma of 1860, Franz Joseph proposed a federal relationship between Hungary and Vienna, but the Hungarians refused to give up the idea of full restoration of the monarchy. They opted instead to wait until the emperor was ready for new negotiations. Deák wanted a return to the April Laws and more direct involvement in affairs of the state. He bided his time, steering himself into a position from which he would be able to bargain convincingly.

Compromise reached: The ice thawed in 1865 with the formation of a new cabinet in Vienna. There was talk of a compromise. Then, suddenly, in 1866 came the news of the disastrous Austrian rout in Sadowa at the hands of the Prussians. In February 1867 Franz Joseph convened a Hungarian ministry under Count Gyula Andrássy and gave his blessings to the April Laws. Further negotiations gradually restored the status of the crown lands. Transylvania had already voted independently to rejoin Hungary. The great Austro-Hungarian Compromise, sealed by the crowning of Franz Joseph as King of Hungary in the Mátyás Church in Budapest on 8 June 1867, signalled the beginning of a period known for its tawdry glitter.

Plans to unite the towns of Pest, Buda and Óbuda, which had been on the table since 1849, were finally realised and the newly formed municipality of Budapest was declared capital of Hungary. A city council was elected and Hungarian was nominated as the official language. An industrial boom, partly generated by the government, swept across the country, with greater emphasis on the processing of agricultural products. Budapest, one of the centres of this new economic activity, grew in Malthusian proportion, with slums springing up everywhere to absorb the influx of migrants from the countryside.

Between 1850 and 1914, the Hungarian population grew by nearly 60 percent to reach 19 million. A large community of aristocrats, spawned by both economic and social activities, became more socially aware as the decades wore on.

MAGYAR KIRÁLYI KONZULÁTUS

CONSULAT ROYAL DE HONGRIE

Under the conditions of the Austro-Hungarian Compromise of 1867, Hungary was allowed a sovereign government and its own defensive militia. The Ministries of Defence, Foreign Affairs and Finances were shared. The issue of the ethnic minorities was partially resolved by allowing the Croats proportional representation in the Hungarian Parliament. Within Hungary the old status quo remained, with the important land owners – including the church – oppressing a vast, disenfranchised, poverty-stricken class.

The "67ers" who supported *laissez-faire* liberal-minded economic and political programmes spent their first 10 years in power splitting hairs on policy and engaging in corrupt deals. A major bone of contention was the degree of compromise with Vienna. Nationalist fires fanned by the exiled Kossuth often singed the government associated with a partial cave-in to the Habsburgs. The Liberals were about to fall apart on this issue when the wily Kálmán Tisza succeeded in welding together a brand new Liberal coalition which held power until 1904.

Meanwhile, the strained social conditions in Hungary gave rise to a new political trend. Strikes broke out in 1871 which the government repressed with force. By 1880 Leo Frankel, who had cut his teeth as a minister of the Paris Commune in 1871, had organised the General Workers' Party. Its programme called for a 10-hour day, the abolition of child labour, equal pay for men and women and other human rights. Frankel was ultimately arrested, but the movement had developed a life of its own. In 1890 the Hungarian Social Democratic Party was called into being.

Magyarisation: Thanks to a concentrated effort, government and business were using Hungarian as a primary language by

the 1890s, and a substantial number of Hungarians used Hungarian as a mother tongue and viewed themselves as Hungarians first and foremost.

Magyarisation gently forced assimilation on the part of those who wanted to get ahead in life. Jews, for example, who had migrated in large numbers from neighbouring countries, adapted particularly quickly to Hungarian life. By 1910 they constituted 4½ percent of the population, and 75 percent used Hungarian as their mother tongue. They formed a major portion of the professional middle class. On the whole, Jews were tolerated and their contribution to Hungary's striving for nationalism acknowledged. Nevertheless, a parallel development was that of a rather sordid anti-Semitism which found expression in sporadic violent outbreaks and the creation of an Anti-Semitic Party under Gyözö Istóczy in 1883.

Ethnic rumblings: Magyarisation, on the other hand, did not please all of Hungary's ethnic minorities. Romanians, Slovaks, Serbians, Ruthenes and even the relatively well-assimilated Croats began claiming the right to statehood, fired by puissant orators and the spirit of the age. Even German nationalism was growing under the strident guidance of Vienna's mayor Dr Karl Lueger.

At the same time, the Hungarian nationalists, striving for independence from the Habsburgs, were gaining ground in government. By 1903 they were strong enough to block undesirable parliamentary measures. The parliament was dissolved. The new elections gave a coalition of Nationalists the majority, but Franz Joseph refused to sanction them until, secretly, they promised to abandon some of their demands. Faced with the threat of an extended suffrage, they agreed to rule in coalition with the Liberals.

By 1910 the "Party of Work", old Liberal wine in a new bottle, took power, but the nation was riddled with tensions, and

Left, memories of more blue-blooded days: this coat of arms is on the "royal" Hungarian consulate in Valetta, Malta.

in Europe the dogs of war were frothing at the mouth. The outbreak of hostilities in 1914, as in most participating nations, came as a welcome diversion from Hungary's internal strife. It was also the end of an uneasy, dynamic, silver-lined period, as the era's greatest poet Endre Ady expressed so beautifully in 1918:

An angel beat the alarm with power and
*   rage*
Down onto the sorrows of the earth.
A hundred youths he drove to madness,
A hundred stars fell down from heaven,
A hundred maidens fell, burning with
*   desire,*
What a night it was –
So strange, so curious, the summer night.

World War I: The initially unifying enthusiasm of August 1914 quickly faded as news of the first defeats and costly victories reached home. Heroic charges gave way to the muck and the mire. Discontent settled in with the strutting but ineffective military leadership and with the leadership in general. Peace negotiations began as early as July 1916. For Count Mihály Károlyi, head of the new Independence Party, separation from Austria, peace without annexation, major concessions to the ethnic minorities and land reforms were only some of the key proposals for Hungary's future.

The carefully balanced half-century of compromise began teetering with the death of Franz Joseph in November 1916. Charles I, his successor, made peace overtures with the Entente powers, but the war had gained its own momentum.

Throughout 1917 the country was in ferment. In May that year the unions in Hungary had already numbered over 200,000 smouldering members. Charles I's last-minute changes in the leadership did little good.

After years of calm the ethnic minorities issue re-emerged in the form of lacklustre performances in battle, mass desertions from the army and general bitterness in the face of the notion that this was someone else's war.

A wave of strikes and demonstrations swept through Austro-Hungary in January 1918, paralysing several domestic munitions factories. Some months later, a mutiny broke out in Pécs. By the time World War I ended, Hungary was divided along so many boundaries, social, political and ethnic, that only a miracle would have kept it together.

The long apocalypse: Károlyi formed a National Council on 25 October 1918. The war was lost, heavy casualties were incurred, and the great Danube monarchy was going to pieces. In better times, the 12-point programme hammered out mainly by the brilliant journalist and statesman Oszkár Jászi might have provided a solid

base upon which a modern state could have been forged out of a political Babylon such as Hungary.

Unfortunately the landowners seemed little inclined to follow the example of Károlyi himself and redistribute their huge holdings. The territorial integrity promised by Wilson's famous 14 points turned out to be inapplicable to Hungary. Moreover, the Hungarian ethnic minorities had quite a different understanding of the term "concessions" from that of the Hungarians. Jászi's direct efforts, especially with the Romanians, were in vain.

As no clear demarcation line existed at the close of the war, the Czech, Serb, and Romanian armies went about grabbing as much land as they could from the supine Hungarians, while the French army, bivouacked in Szeged, stood by and watched. With the entire economy at a standstill, and with virtually no army to speak of and no hint of an ally anywhere in the world, Károlyi and his cabinet were impotent.

Béla Kun: The newly established, very active Communist Party also put the Károlyi government under pressure. Its rank-and-file consisted partly of hordes of dissatisfied, disenfranchised workers and

east Hungary and let another allied division enter the country. Unable to control the nation's foreign policy, Károlyi decided to leave power to the Social Democrats, who in turn realised they could only rule together with the communists who might be able to find support and help in Soviet Russia.

On 22 March the Hungarian Soviet was declared. Béla Kun, commissar for foreign affairs, soon had the entire government solidly in hand. By 25 March Hungary had a Red Army which occupied the Ministry of Justice and also controlled the police force. Edict followed edict, nationalising

partly of demoralised soldiers returning from Russian POW camps where they had experienced the October Revolution at first hand. The leaders were imprisoned, but a chain reaction among their staunch supporters paved the way for their meteoric rise to power.

In February 1919, the Entente powers decided to create a neutral zone in south-

Left, Count Mihály Károlyi tried in vain to bring order to the post-war chaos. Above, the signs read: "Peace! Justice! Bread! Down with war, long live peace."

the banks and industries employing more than 20 people, reforming the education system, cutting back the power of the church and, of course, redistributing the land. Order was temporarily restored, but the price was fierce repression of real and perceived dissent.

Conservative reaction: The pendulum had started swinging to the left and was just heading back to the right. Conservative forces began forming conspiracies. The Western powers, who had already dispatched troops to fight the Bolsheviks in the Soviet Union, became more worried than ever about the possible emergence of another "Red" state.

Czechs and Romanians, saw an opportunity to gain more territory and played quite willingly into Entente hands. They attacked Hungary in mid-April. The Hungarians fought back – much to everyone's surprise, quite successfully.

Realising their strategy of using the Romanians as proxies against the communists had failed, the Allies took another course of action. The Hungarians were ordered to cease hostilities and the Romanians were told to return to their original positions east of the Tisza river. Kun ac-

and officers, students and wandering, homeless Magyars chased out of their native lands dished out summary justice to anyone accused or suspected of connections with the Kun regime. At the same time, a wave of anti-Semitism swept through the land.

Admiral without a ship: It took a few months for some form of political stability to return. The Romanians were finally persuaded to leave the capital in November after the interim Hungarian government (under Gyula Peidl) promised to set up a democratic system on a Western model with elections by secret ballot. Admiral

cepted, but the Romanians dragged their heels, agreed to the settlement, and waited for the Hungarians to disarm.

Kun decided to resume hostilities, but the attack which was launched on 20 July failed. On 3 August, Romanian troops reached Budapest and the Hungarian experiment with a communist government came to an end.

Chaos ruled for the remainder of 1919, with the Romanians and Entente delegations playing the role of spectators. The *Red Terror* gave way to a bloody *White Terror* as paramilitary bands of ex-soldiers

Miklós Horthy – admiral in a country without a fleet and one which no longer had access to the sea – had distinguished himself as a counter-revolutionary leader and now led an army of 25,000 into the capital, which the Romanians had thoroughly plundered. A new government was established under Károly Huszár to conduct the parliamentary elections.

Hungary's first free elections by secret ballot took place on 25 January 1920. Not all parties were represented; the Communists weren't, of course, and the Social Democrats boycotted the event in protest at the *White Terror* that still raged in the countryside. The two parties with the most votes were the colourless Smallholders Party with 40 percent and the Christian National Union with just over 35 percent.

The first issue that caused major dissension involved the status of the monarchy. Some believed Charles IV (Charles I of Habsburg) to be the legitimate heir. Others, however, insisted on the election of a new ruler. Finally, falling back on an ancient law, parliament chose Miklós Horthy as to be the regent of Hungary on 1 March.

Infamous Trianon: A sword of Damocles was hanging over the nation's destiny in much heated historic, geographic and legal argument. On 4 June, to the bitterness of the entire nation, they reluctantly signed the infamous Treaty of Trianon.

Overnight, Hungary's territory shrank from 125,641 sq. miles (about 325,411 sq. km) to 35,983 sq. miles (about 92,963 sq. km). The bulk of the land went to Romania, including the quintessentially Hungarian Transylvania. The loss of this region is resented even to this day, since the Hungarians still living in Romania represent an oppressed minority of over 2 million. A small territory around Sopron that had been granted to Austria earlier was re-

the form of a treaty. On 14 March 1920, Huszár relinquished the reins of government to a cabinet presided over by Sándor Simonyi-Semadam, whose first task was to send a delegation to Paris to see if anything could be salvaged from the wreck of World War I. Counts Apponyi, Bethlen and Pál Teleki achieved little with the Allies, in spite of having gone through

turned to Hungary after a plebiscite was convened. The overall population before the war was almost 21 million. Post-Trianon Hungary contained a mere 7½ million. Nearly 2 million Magyar speakers were in Romania, 1 million in what was then Czechoslovakia, and almost half a million in Yugoslavia.

To maintain internal order, the nation was allowed a militia of 35,000 men without heavy artillery. The economy was virtually non-existent after the war. The nation's capital had been hastily transferred out of the country during the Kun months

Left, national dishonour was sealed by the Treaty of Trianon in 1920. **Above,** a stricken family harbours poverty and misery-well-known companions during the period.

by frightened investors, and the Romanians had taken with them anything that could conceivably be removed. Trianon had cut off Hungary from its most important sources of raw materials. Still the Allies thought it necessary, on top of everything else, to exact reparations.

Hungarians between the wars had a single slogan to express their opinion of the treaty: *Nem, nem, soha!* (No, no, never!). As was the case in Germany, revising the blatantly unfair treaty became an *idée fixe* that helped to fuel the fiery furnace of right-wing nationalism.

and led to a new coalition between Anti-Legitimists and Smallholders, called the Party of Unity, under Count Bethlen. In October 1921, Charles IV gathered loyal army units and started a campaign against Budapest. The Allies looked on this sourly, and Horthy and Bethlen mobilised their forces, many from the ranks of the radical right paramilitary organisation of Gyula Gömbös, to expel the king. Their successful operation in Budaörs on 23 October 1921 finally ended Legitimist clamouring.

The Roaring Twenties: Count Bethlen, who led Hungary for a decade, combined saga-

Something had to be done about the economic and social situation. Soon after its assumption of power in July 1920, the cabinet of Pál Teleki introduced a string of modest land reform measures to break up some of the enormous holdings in the hands of the old magnate families. On paper and in discussions these measures satisfied the Smallholders Party, but in practice very little was achieved.

The complex issue of the monarchy flared up again in 1921 with the return of Charles IV to Hungary. It precipitated a crisis that split the Christian National Party,

ciousness with political cynicism and a hue of ruthlessness that gave Hungary, at least for the 10 years of his rule, apparent stability. His aim was to cultivate the international community, look for solid allies and then work hard on the economy. He struck deals with the Social Democrats to rein in worker and peasant rebelliousness, at the same time pacifying members of the radical right who still engaged in acts of *White Terror*. In September 1922, Hungary joined the League of Nations, and in the spring of 1924 it obtained from the League a loan of 250 million gulden which effectively put the brakes on escalating inflation and promptly restored investor confidence in the country. In 1927 a new currency, the *pengö*, was introduced.

As long as financial stability remained, Bethlen could maintain political stability. Many members of the far left had moved to Moscow, the Social Democrats were pacified. Labour unrest was put down with police force. Gömbös, however, was diligently rallying the forces of the right. His message had nationalist appeal, and was heavily peppered with racism and anti-Semitism. The fall in world wheat prices in

1929 and the financial crisis following the Wall Street Crash took their toll. Capital vanished and Hungary was once again insolvent. Discontent that was once dormant erupted. Bethlen chose to resign and, after the brief rule of Gyula Károlyi, Horthy appointed Gyula Gömbös in October 1932.

Social upheaval: Budapest at this time was expanding like a balloon. The rural population had shrunk dramatically nearly one-eighth of the population now lived in the capital, many in apalling conditions. Thousands were housed in box railway cars. City officials tried desperately to raise funds abroad for housing projects and so ease social tensions. From 1920 to 1941 there was a construction boom and the number of buildings in Budapest increased by 50 percent

The Nazi spectre: The excruciating weight of the Trianon Treaty might have made Hungary an ideal candidate for Nazism. Gömbös dreamt of a Berlin–Budapest–Rome axis – he even coined the famous term – but at the time Mussolini and Hitler were not on friendly terms. The ebbing of the world economic crisis also took some of the wind out of his sails. Moreover, Horthy did not trust Gömbös' constituents, and refused to allow elections until April 1935. Gömbös garnered over 43 percent of the vote, a comfortable majority. Later that year he visited Berlin, and returned convinced of the need to implement a system patterned on Nazi Germany. Gömbös' death in October 1936 prevented him from carrying out his schemes, but by then Hungary had already moved to the right and by extension towards Nazi Germany. Hitler courted the Hungarians by investing heavily in their industry and by providing a dumping ground for their agricultural products in the late 1930s. Hungary's re-armament programme depended on German products.

Successive Hungarian governments responded equivocally. There were Hungarians who sympathised with Germany and yet feared her. Others, such as the members of the overtly Nazi Nyílas or Arrow Cross Movement under Ferenc Szálasi, strove to implement Nazi rule in Hungary, including massacring Jews and any other groups of undesirables. And there were many, ranging from Conservatives to Social Democrats, who had no love lost for Germany, but found demonstrations of economic friendship rather attractive. Thus the Hungarian governments after Gömbös tried hard to lie in Hitler's bed without catching his fleas.

Left, the unfortunate alliance between Hungary and Germany, represented here by Göring and Regent Horthy. **Above**, Ferenc Szálasi, leader of the Nazi-style *Arrow Cross Movement*.

СПИТЕ СПО
ЗОЛОТЫМИ БУ
В ИСТОРИЮ

The funambulism so typical of Hungary's history grew ever more dangerous. Under Béla Imrédy a set of Jewish laws curbing the number of Jews in professions were passed, aimed at demonstrating how well the country was adapting to fascism. Simultaneous attempts to link up with Western democratic powers met with little success. The First Vienna Award (2 November 1938) gave Hungary a piece of its old Slovakian territory. A new set of Jewish laws then came into being. Hungary joined the Anti-Komintern Pact and passed a further set of Jewish laws, which were for the most part not enforced.

When Hitler attacked Poland on 1 September 1939, not only was the Wehrmacht banned from using Hungarian territory, but entire Polish regiments sought refuge in Hungary. The prime minister, Pál Teleki, tried to keep Hungary out of the war, as peace still allowed for possible negotiations with the West. But involvement was inevitable. A second Vienna Award in 1940 gave Transylvania back to Hungary, then the German army crossed Hungarian territory to occupy Romania. The pattern repeated itself with the invasion of Yugoslavia, only this time Hungary occupied Croatia and Great Britain threatened to declare war. Teleki, seeing his carefully planned compromise collapsing, committed suicide in early April 1941.

His successor, Bardossy, convinced that Germany could defeat the USSR and that a little commie-bashing would by no means offend the Western powers, sent a force into Russia to fight alongside the German armies. Great Britain finally declared war on Hungary in December 1941. In January 1942, Hitler called in old debts and demanded total mobilisation from Hungary. Meanwhile, Horthy was still hoping to reach some agreement with the Western

powers. The prime minister, Miklós Kállay, who had to preside over the virtual eradication of the Hungarian army near Stalingrad in January 1943, promised unconditional surrender to the Western powers if and when they reached Hungary. The Red Army moved faster.

Swedish saviour: In March 1944 the Nazis were given free rein in Hungary by the government of Döme Sztójay, appointed by Horthy to avoid a real German occupation. Political parties were suppressed by the Gestapo (the communists had been banned decades earlier), and Jews were removed to concentration camps. In Budapest countless Jews were temporarily saved by becoming citizens of neutral Sweden, thanks to the intervention of the 32-year-old Swedish attaché Raoul Wallenberg. This remarkable man was famous in an age known for despicable characters for his courageous, sometimes directly physical, intervention. He disappeared shortly after the fall of Budapest. His disappearance behind Soviet lines in January 1945 has never been conclusively proven, but he lives on in the hearts of the thousands he saved from the gas chambers. Recently a monument was erected to him not far from Moszkva tér in Buda.

In August 1944, Romania fell to the advancing Soviet army. Horthy decided that the time was ripe to make overtures to the USSR. In October he made a speech calling for an armistice and was promptly kidnapped by the Germans and taken back to their country. On 15 October, Ferenc Szálasi took power together with his brutal *Nyílas*. Efforts to deport Jews and other undesirables started in earnest.

For the Hungarian right wing the moment of glory came too late. On 6 October, the Red Army had begun its offensive to take Hungary. By 29 October, the vestiges of the Third Army surrendered at Kecskemét. Gradually the Russians encircled Budapest. On 28 December, a provisional government, made up mostly of

Preceding pages: the taking of Budapest by the Red Army in February 1945. <u>Left</u>, one of the many Soviet war memorials recalling the liberation.

exiled communists, was set up in Debrecen. On 11 February 1945, 16,000 Germans attempted a desperate sortie from the beleaguered capital. Only a handful managed to ward off the invaders. On 4 April, the last stragglers of the SS and Wehrmacht left Hungarian territory for Austria.

The Soviet military government ensured that all important positions in the supine nation were occupied by loyal communists, mainly those who had escaped to Moscow in the 1930s. Due perhaps to the enforcement of a popular land reform programme, the Smallholders, comprising a motley collection of political wanderers

hatred generated by the war was Czechoslovakia's requested expulsion of its 600,000-strong Hungarian minority. About 85,000 obeyed. The major communist flop at the polls was deceptive. Their real strength relied on three major factors: first, they had the backing of the Red Army and the occupation infrastructure; secondly, László Rajk, an active communist since the early 1930s, was put in charge of the vital Interior Ministry, which allowed him, with the help of the newly-founded police force AVO (later AVH), to gnaw away at the opposition using everything from calumny to murder. Finally, a strong centralised

without any "home base", gained an astounding victory in the November elections with 57 percent of the votes. The Social Democrats garnered 17.4 percent while the Communist Party came a close third with just 17 percent.

Republic proclaimed: The monarchy was abolished and a republic was proclaimed on 1 February 1946. Absolute power was in the hands of Mátyás Rákosi, leader of the Workers' Party. The Paris Peace Treaty, signed on 10 February 1947, reconfirmed the Trianon borders with a little more land removed in the west. A brutal result of the

government was needed to restore the country's economic balance. The pengö set a nonplussed world record for devaluation, reaching 1.4 quadrillion of its pre-war value by mid-1946. Unlike World War I, World War II had steamrollered over Hungary and left a holocaust. Over 500,000 Hungarians were killed in battle, and the retreating German army had confiscated all movables of value and destroyed any bridge it could along the way.

In November 1946 the great Ganz iron works and Weiss steel mills were nationalised, followed in February 1948 by the bauxite mines and the aluminium industry. In May the banks passed to the state. By then the Communists had cut themselves a large hunk of support from the Smallholders, and the Social Democrats had joined them in a newly founded Workers' Party. The coalition made headway in the face of a divided opposition, enacting in August 1947 a Three-Year Plan to put the country on its feet quickly. A plan to collectivise the land was introduced in 1948.

Church purged: By the middle of 1949 the Communists held power. A few Christian communities reluctantly accepted the provisions made for them. Generally, the op-

consolidating the power of his so-called Moscow wing of the party. The first sensational trial of the national communists – among them László Rajk – began with trumped-up charges of high treason and unlawful representation of the imperialist powers. (Rajk, whose dedication to his party led him to confess to these absurd allegations, was executed and buried in secret, but in 1956 his coffin was dug up and his bones were carried to the famous Kerepesi cemetery to be laid alongside his colleagues, friend and foe alike, who had died natural and mysterious deaths. About 250,000 people attended the funeral pro-

position had been chiselled down to manageable size. Even the powerful churches, notably the Catholics, had been reduced, or so it seemed. Cardinal József Mindszenty put up a vigorous resistance against the nationalisation of education, and was immediately thrown in jail on patently concocted charges.

Mátyás Rákosi, who had spent a good deal of the Horthy years in Moscow, began

Left, Hungary, a people's republic, declared in 1949. Above, seven years later, the uprising took place; the old coat of arms resurfaced.

cession on 6 October, 17 days before the revolution.) The domestic purges continued well into the 1950s, removing those party members who before the war had either been stationed in the West, in hiding in Hungary or even fighting Franco in Spain.

The AVO was reorganised by Gábor Péter in 1950 and became the AVH. Its scope of action was increased. A network of informants kept the state in touch with dissenters. The breath of Moscow stank of Stalinist paranoia, the prison doors yawned wide. Under the Stakhenovian posters, behind the banners proclaiming the workers' paradise, in such socialist Edens as the model city of Sztalinváros (Dunaújváros since 1956), discontent festered. Peasants were tired of being forced into collective farms; ideological schooling and AVH brutality were defeating the purpose of government. Conformism had made for sterility. After many years of belt-tightening Hungarians were looking for some basic comforts. Consumer goods, nylons and watches became hot black market items.

The avuncular Imre Nagy, who took over from Rákosi after Stalin's death in 1953, showed a certain willingness to re-

demonstration consisting largely of students marched to Parliament demanding reforms. At first the government dragged its feet, then Gerö (not in the country at the time) ordered repression by force.

Two days later, the entire country broke into revolution. All symbols of Communist rule during the upheaval were violently exorcised from the capital. The red stars were cut out of every Hungarian flag, the towering statue of Stalin in Budapest was blow-torched off its feet and dragged through the city. Even the soldiers found little cause to quell the revolution and switched sides. In the event, many mem-

dress the most obvious grievances. However, his rule did not last long after having failed to garner support from Russia. Rákosi returned to power untamed in 1955.

Stalin denounced: In July 1956, Khrushchev, who was wooing Yugoslavia, replaced the patently anti-Tito Rákosi with another unpleasant figure, Rákosi's second-in-command, Ernö Gerö. Earlier that year Khrushchev had denounced Stalinism in a long speech that shook communist parties around the world but apparently had little direct impact on the Hungarian leadership. On 23 October, a spontaneous

bers of the AVH were executed.

Political prisoners, among them Cardinal Mindszenty, were freed. Old and new political parties crawled out of the woodwork. Imre Nagy, who seemed to hold so much promise, was made titular head of Hungary and its improvised revolution.

In an interview with the German journalist Hans-Henning Paetzke, published in 1986, the Hungarian writer Béla Szász summed up the man and the politician, Imre Nagy, whom he knew personally: "He was a friendly man with a great sense of moral responsibility. He wavered between solidarity with the party and solidarity with the people… By the end of the revolution, however, he had come to a firm decision. He saw himself as the representative of the will of the people and put himself on their side, taking full responsibility for all the consequences."

Invasion excuse: The decision of General Pál Maléter to side with the rebellious nation and Imre Nagy gave the Soviet Union its much needed excuse to invade, claiming Hungary was illegally breaking away from the Warsaw Pact. The crushing of the revolution by Soviet tank divisions lasted only a few days. The cost in human

macious Magyars after 1956 was János Kádár, an adversary of Rákosi. Having been hand-picked by the Kremlin, his arrival amid the diesel fumes of the departing Soviet tanks had already made him a suspect from the start. Indeed, he appeased the USSR by faithfully conforming to every one of its foreign policy moves. In 1968, two Hungarian divisions were deployed, under his orders, into Czechoslovakia to help put an end to the Prague Spring.

There was another side to János Kádár. He pushed for better rapport with the Western powers. His close ties with the Austrians, then under Chancellor Bruno Kreisky,

lives was estimated at around 3,000. However, the exact number of executions still remains a mystery to this day. Nagy, holed up within the walls of the Yugoslavian embassy building, was persuaded by his victors to come out and when he stubbornly refused to recant, was executed. Thousands were sent to prison. Almost 200,000 Hungarians fled the country.

The yes-man chosen to lead the contu-

led Hungarians to joke of a new "dual monarchy". The boost achieved through trade, tourism and industrialisation helped to raise the standard of living.

In 1977, aiming to patch up differences with Hungary's strong Roman Catholic community, Kádár paid a visit to Pope Paul VI. This policy of rapprochement has spared Hungary the sharp conflicts between church and state that characterise countries such as Poland.

Economically Kádár at first stayed the old course, pushing through collectivisation and trying to increase industrial pro-

Left, Sculptor Imre Várga portrayed a relaxed Lenin in Jászberény. **Right**, one of the model socialist new towns, Leninváros.

duction. Poor harvests and an exodus from agricultural work drained Hungary's hard currency reserves. The 1960s were austere years, but Kádár did at least give hope in 1962 with his famous quote: "He who is not against us is with us." This effectively suggested that he was giving some credence to the claims of the revolutionaries.

The New Economic Mechanism (1968) allowed for some private sector work and gave various state-run operations a considerable degree of autonomy. Concrete results became the determining factor of success rather than the sheer volume of political kow-towing. Allowing farmers a

price was unemployment and growing poverty. Its heavy industry was also in dire need of retooling. With *glasnost* and *perestroika* loosening up regimes all over the Eastern Bloc, Hungary was able to push through reforms that would have been undreamt of several years before. At times it seemed that the government was just waiting to be ditched so as not to have to deal with the problems at hand.

Immigrant flood: In June 1988 a large demonstration in solidarity with the Transylvanian Hungarians received official sanction, an unusual provocation of Romania. A year later, Imre Nagy and his acolytes

certain leeway in the private sector partially relieved the problem of food distribution throughout the country. The soaring price of oil and other raw materials in the 1970s put the economy under pressure and fuelled inflation, but in comparison with many other Eastern Bloc nations, Hungary fared quite well.

The experiment with market socialism ultimately did not pay off. The country's foreign debt skyrocketed to 18 billion dollars, and while a few Hungarians were able to drive Western cars and buy computers and German washing machines, the final

were reburied in Parcel 301 of the Kozma Street cemetery where they had been hastily thrown after their executions. The ceremony was a media event attended by 300,000 people and organised mainly by the opposition MDF (Hungarian Democratic Forum). In September 1989 the Hungarians opened the Iron Curtain to let out a throng of East European refugees, precipitating the downfall of the East German Party Secretary Erich Honeker.

By the time of the elections of 24 March and 8 April 1990, several old and new parties had emerged. The winners in this tight contest were the MDF, with the Free Democrats (SZDSZ), the Smallholders and the Social Democrats as close contenders.

Under Prime Minister Antall (who died in February 1994), the MDF steered a course towards Europe and a market economy. No one expected an easy transition. Inflation soared to between 25 and 30 percent, unemployment increased sharply as old inefficient factories closed down for lack of subsidies.

Foreign investment: Switching from the penurious Russian market to the quality orientated West has also been difficult, although Hungary's toolmaking industry

mainly because of the political errors of the MDF. First, it drifted far to the right, adopting all sorts of old-fashioned chauvinistic stances to appease its more extreme fringe (István Csurka, an abominable anti-Semite feeding on the eternally disgruntled, was the most vocal of the far-right members; he finally left and founded his own party). If it were not for the fact that Hungary was at the centre of a tense region, and had a serious minorities problem of its own in neighbouring countries, this would have hardly mattered. Worse, privatisation was accompanied by large-scale corruption. Every minister has his

is extremely good. Foreign investors have shown interest in Hungary, with Audi and Opel opening plants in the country, for example, and Alitalia buying heavily into the national airline MALEV. In fact, the Czech Republic and Hungary have together received the lion's share of foreign investment in Central Europe.

The election results in May 1994 turned out in favour of the Social Democrats

Left, Imre Nagy's emotional reburial. **Above**, Hans-Dietrich Genscher, German foreign minister.

price. The MDF, somewhat wary of the democratic process, attempted to muzzle the press as best it could. None of this sat well with rank-and-file Hungarians.

If there is anything to learn from history, looking back over nearly 1100 years, it is that the Hungarians are a difficult bunch to govern. They are fickle, restless, creative when it comes to improvising solutions to a wide range of problems (using Mig fighters to blow out burning oil wells in Kuwait, for example), and naturally suspicious of the powers that be. Enough have tried to subdue them over the centuries, but failed.

What sort of people are the Hungarians? Extrovert Southern Europeans, mysterious people from the Far East, fighting nomadic tribes from the steppes of Northern Asia? Are they a people broken by the merciless blows of history, or a people who have proved themselves again and again?

The Hungarian philosopher Béla Hamvas believes that the Hungarian people comprise five archtypes corresponding to the five geographical regions: the eastern Great Plain, the northern provinces (including Slovakia), western Transdanubia, the south – the crossroads of many different civilizations – and finally the former principality of Transylvania, now part of Romania.

Landscape with people: The ancient Hungarian character is best preserved in the east. Here some people still live lives that are half nomadic and half settled. Their characters are determined by a desire for freedom, passion, a revolt against anything foreign, vanity, pride, indifference to religion and a concentration on the present.

A provincial lifestyle is dominant in the north, a culture that is close to nature but not markedly differentiated. Social ties tend to be loose, the people are not practically minded and their faces are clouded by an unfathomable melancholy, as if they are constantly amazed by the unreality of their own existence.

The west, however, is the home of practicality, civilization, reason and the everyday work ethic. A stable social order, loyalty, the desire for knowledge and an active life have left their marks on the lifestyle of the Transdanubian people, a lifestyle strongly influenced by Western European ideas of development. An easygoing, cheerful, peaceful and balanced attitude, together with restricted activity

and a harmonious enjoyment of life, are characteristic of the more contemplative people of the south of Hungary, who took no (or hardly any) part in the historic struggles but allowed them to pass by – and survived them.

The fifth archtype is only to be found in Hungary today among the refugees, the Transylvanian Magyars, forced to exchange their mountainous home for the Hungarian plains, forced to leave by the

political pressure of the late Ceausescu regime and abandon the region of ravines, of deeply-divided opposites and the (often grotesque) humour, the complexity and duplicity that bridged the divide. They offer the experience of a history rich in compromises and in rebirth, as well as a sound and practical change of mind, a high expectation of life, good taste and great cunning.

Language differences are never great enough to prevent to Hungarians from opposite corners of the country from understanding one another. Difficulties arise in making themselves understood to for-

Preceding pages: horse markets are firmly under Gypsy control; wine tasting festival in Balatonboglár; tuning up. **Left,** a smile found only in Kalocsa. **Right,** a young girl dressed up for the harvest festival in Köszeg.

eigners who don't speak Hungarian. But when language fails, the legendary hospitality springs into action. Like every cliché, this one is based on fact. Hungary has never been a country closed to foreigners. Ever since the Magyar conquest, foreign visitors – known in those times as *hospes* – have been welcome to settle in the country. Paragraph VI of the *Exhortations* of King István I to his son Imre shows what value hospitality to strangers had even in the Middle Ages: "Guests and immigrants are so useful that they well deserve their position as the sixth element of royal dig-

nority consists of the Slovenes (*Venden* in Hungarian). The conquering Magyars found an independent Slovenian kingdom in southwestern Transdanubia. Its capital was Mosapurc, probably in the region of modern Zalavár. The original population has not lost its individuality, despite the thousand-year rule of strangers. The Slovenes were Christians before the coming of the Magyars and spoke a Slavic language. They have kept their ancient language and culture to the present day, probably due to the isolated peasant society in which they have lived for centuries.

nity. For a country with only one language is weak and easily broken." Sound advice, which has not always been followed by Hungarian politicians in later centuries and particularly not in modern times.

Slovaks and southern Slavs: Hungary is not a simple nation state. Within its borders, apart from Hungarians, live small numbers of Germans, Croats, Romanians, Serbs, Slovaks and Slovenes. Most of them live on the borders of neighbouring states, but some are scattered in settlements throughout the country.

The smallest – and oldest – ethnic mi-

Within the borders of modern Hungary, between the rivers Mura and Rába, there are now nine Slovenian villages with an overall population of about 5,000. The Slovenian language is taught in the elementary schools of these villages.

When the subject of ethnic minorities is raised in Hungary, the topic of the Southern Slavs often comes up. This group, with a population of 100,000, comprises several ethnic groups. Apart from the Slovenes mentioned above, there are Croats, Serbs, Schokats and Bosnians. Ninety percent of the Southern Slavs are Croats. Most of them live in the south of the country on the borders of Slovenia, Croatia and Serbia, but you can find Serbian villages along the Danube, even north of Budapest. These settlements date from the time of Turkish expansion and were founded by refugees from the Turkish dominions who came to Hungary under the leadership of the Patriarch Arsenije Carnojevic in 1690.

The Serbs live in fairly scattered settlements, but the Croat population is mostly concentrated on the banks of the Dráva. The Schokats and Bosnians live mostly in county of Baranya. The Bosnians come

Industrialisation and the subsequent shift of the population away from the villages has brought about a high degree of assimilation into the Hungarian population, and yet the largest number of people who acknowledge their ethnic origins without embarrassment or neurosis, and are indeed proud of them, belong to this Southern Slav group. There are several reasons for the heritage. On the one hand there is the proximity and, in recent times, the almost unimpeded contact with other members of this ethnic group across the borders. On the other are the language classes in both

from the border areas between Bosnia and Dalmatia, hence their name. The Schokats acquired their name because, unlike the pravoslavic Serbs, they cross themselves using the whole palm of the hand (*saka*=palm of the hand). The Serbs and Croats are bilingual – as are almost all the members of the ethnic minorities – and are the most diligent in encouraging their mother tongue.

Left, spontaneity is most easy to find at unorganised festivals. **Above**, folk music and dance are undergoing a renaissance.

elementary and high schools and the Serbian and Croatian programmes of the local Hungarian radio stations. The Southern Slavs have always been loyal inhabitants of Hungary and have no real or imagined historical "guilt" weighing upon them.

The Germans: It's another matter when we come to the largest ethnic minority in Hungary – some 230,000 people – the Germans. Here you cannot help but notice a loss of language and of culture which, despite all the efforts of official departments, may well be too late to remedy. For a period of 1,000 years, the Germans entered Hungary at different times, from different places and in different numbers. For this reason they form a minority which has no economic, political or cultural unity. This is one reason for the high degree of assimilation. The first major wave of immigration came during the reign of King András II in the 13th century. Most of these immigrants settled in Transylvania.

Moving cultures: The Saxons of Transylvania received privileges from the king which allowed them to preserve their culture until well into the 20th century. But in the mid-1970s they were forced to move "home" to Germany by the rigorous

The rural German population came in large groups, but a German middle class had been slowly moving into townships almost since the time of the conquest. As a result, the bourgeoisie who lived in the cities of the Kingdom of Hungary during the middle of the 19th century comprised mainly Germans. They were subject to a continuous process of assimilation, but the village communities remained generally intact until the end of World War II.

The great split within the German population of Hungary came about in the years between the two world wars, influenced by racial ideas imported from Germany. De-

"Romanianisation" policy of the Ceausescu government. Germans also came to stay in Hungary after the Turks were driven out in the 18th century, arriving with the so-called "Swabian trains". The Habsburg emperors settled them in the areas of southeast Hungary that had been devastated by the Turks, in Batshka and Bánat, according to the proverb *ubi populus, ibi obulus* – where people live, there's money to be made. The counties of Tolna, Baranya and Somogy were popularly known as Swabian Turkey, and this is where most Germans live today.

velopments in Germany caused great confusion among the Hungarian Germans. In 1933, Jakob Bleyer, one of the leading political figures of the German minority, far-sightedly noted: "What is happening now to the German people is either our last chance of salvation or our final ruin."

In November 1938, the *Volksbund der Deutschen in Ungarn* (People's Federation of Germans in Hungary) split off from the *Ungarländischer Deutscher Volksbildungsverein* (Hungarian Society for German Culture). The former was a fifth column for the German national *Volksbund für das Deutschtum im Ausland* (People's Federation for German Culture Abroad). The Volksbund spread intensive Nazi propaganda among the rural populace and achieved notable success. In the autumn of 1942 about 40 percent of Germans were actually members of the Volksbund, while the number of fellow travellers could have been much higher. The German Reich had been secretly recruiting soldiers from among the Hungarian German minority since the beginning of the war. In February 1942, an agreement was reached with the government, which officially permitted the recruitment of volunteers to fight within

In 1946 forced emigration began, and it continued with interruptions until 1948. Final restoration of full civil rights did not take place until March 1950. However, complete rehabilitation could not be achieved by bureaucratic measures alone, and was even less likely as there were at that time neither schools nor the cultural and even political organisations of today, which could have helped the German group to affirm their deeply scarred ethnic identity. Many years of development were needed to heal, partially at least, the wounds of the war years.

Some 100,000 Slovaks in the northern

the ranks of the Waffen SS.

In May 1943, recruitment was sanctioned even among those liable for military service in the Hungarian army. After the Germans entered Hungary on 14 April 1944 all ethnic Germans between the ages of 17 and 62 were obliged to fulfill their military service in the German army. After the war, the Germans in Hungary suffered the same fate as those in Poland and what was, Czechoslovakia and Yugoslavia.

Far left, Serbian Orthodox cleric. **Left**, winter reveller. **Above**, the good life in Hungary.

counties live mostly in villages of mixed ethnic population. Like the Slovenes, they are in a manner of speaking the original inhabitants of these areas, since Slovakia was part of the Kingdom of Hungary up to World War I. The ethnic line between Hungarians and Slovaks cannot be clearly defined. Within modern Slovakia resides a minority of about half a million Hungarians. Today, the Romanian minority who dwell on the eastern borders of the country comprises about 25,000 people, most of them living in the town of Méhkerék and the villages surrounding it.

The Hungarian minorities: Since only about five percent of Hungary's population belong to an ethnic minority, it is hardly possible to talk about the country as a multi-cultural state. Nonetheless, since the mid-1970s, the Hungarian government has been trying, with the aid of some exemplary measures, to support the cultural independence of its minorities. Indeed, as far as policies for minorities are concerned, Hungary is an example to its neighbouring states, where many Hungarians live in minority groups. The largest group is found in Romania, 1.7 million according to the census of 1977, though the number is unofficially estimated at between 2 and 2.5 million. The anti-minority policies of Romania have over the last 20 years forced many Hungarians who lived there to return to their motherland.

The situation of the Hungarian minority in Slovakia is not all rosy, and the Hungarians of the Carpathian Ukraine, hope that the country's recent independence will allow their culture the freedom to develop freely. Many Hungarians still live in Serbia, in the Batshka. Of all the Hungarian minority groups, they have – relatively speaking – the most rights.

Since 1979, bilingual signs have been put up in those Hungarian villages in which at least one third of the population belongs to an ethnic minority, and the language of the minority can be used in all government departments. In practice, however, these measures can only be instituted with difficulty, partly because of the hostile attitude of some local officials, but partly also because the Serbs, the Germans and the Slovaks all converse in Hungarian and have been accustomed to speaking the national language for all official matters.

Ethnic groups: There are hardly any settlements in which members of a minority live without Hungarians among them. The various ethnic groups are scattered throughout 18 of the 19 counties, mostly in Baranya, Vas, Békés, Csongrád and Bács-Kiskun. The problems of deciding what makes up an ethnic group and what is defined as a mother tongue are shown by the results of a recent census. Some 70,500

viewed themselves as members of an ethnic minority, but twice the number described their mother tongue as non-Hungarian.

The figures quoted above are based on estimates made by the ethnic associations and probably could be much higher. Is a person who claims that his mother tongue is Romanian, but sees himself as Hungarian, a Romanian or a Hungarian? To which ethnic group does the German whose mother tongue is Hungarian belong? Is having Serb parents enough to make a person a Serb? To which group do the children of mixed marriages belong? In which particular group do they see themselves?

The children of the German minority have long grown up in families where German is mostly spoken only by the grandparents, but rarely by the parents, who did not learn it in their schooldays during the late 1940s, the 1950s and the 1960s. In general, they have found refuge in assimilation in a culture that was mainly suspicious of Germans and the German language, sometimes even hostile. Their children speak Hungarian in the street and in school, their feelings and thoughts are expressed in this language, even among those children who are lucky enough to attend a school with extra German classes. There are no German, Serbian, Slovakian or Romanian schools.

The efforts of the government to revitalise the culture of the minorities may retard the process of assimilation, but can hardly prevent it altogether. Even the various ethnic associations try to keep their culture alive through the mass media in the various languages. The minorities today may not harbour any more fears about their different languages, but they are not exactly confident either. Or, as a Serbian peasant woman once expressed in a double-edged manner, "Since democracy came, there's nothing left. We're not afraid of the devil, we're not afraid of death either; we're afraid of nothing." Proud words indeed.

Right, a puszta herdsman smokes a pipe at the end of a working day work in Hortobágy.

For nearly a century, the Hungarian intelligentsia and general public have been busily discussing folk art. The subject is brought up again and again, for a variety of reasons. It should be mentioned that folk traditionally referred only to the peasants, and that the idea of "folk" was never extended to cover other classes or social groups. Without doubt the Hungarian nation, which has always had a strong peasant economy, has produced a folk tradition with very rich, specific and individual traits, just as other European cultures have.

However, despite all its unmistakably Hungarian features, and because of its geographical position, the Magyar ethnic group with its folk traditions has always enjoyed a continual and lively exchange with the people around it, such as Romanians, Germans and the various Slavic groups. In the search for its identity and its roots, the Hungarian intelligentsia has always preferred to go back to the idea of a specific, unmistakably Hungarian culture – or to create such an idea.

This particular leitmotif, which has cropped up time and again for the last 100 years, has, to put it simply, guided the interests of the intellectuals towards "the art of simple, uneducated village people". The huge celebrations of the "Millennium", which were organised in 1896 to commemorate the 1,000-year anniversary of the Hungarian conquest, gave plenty of space to the exhibition of folk art. Masterpieces of craft and folk art, as well as examples of early craft traditions, were collected. A gigantic "folk" village was built, consisting of typical houses from the various regions. Institutes for the study of and research into folk art were founded.

By the 1880s, the value of collecting folk art had been recognised and many thousands of objects had been gathered from the villages. By the end of the last century, Béla Vikár was already recording folk

Left, traditions are revived in opulent costumes.

songs. Architects went out and measured farm houses and drew up plans of their layouts, artists drew the national costumes of regions rich in tradition, and the inseparable twins of Hungarian culture, Zoltán Kodály and Béla Bartók, set out on their famous travels in order to collect folk melodies.

The turn-of-the-century intellectuals were stuck with the idea that whatever was produced by the peasantry was not "refined" enough for polite society, but had to be altered and raised to the level of the "concert hall". Led by the deeply rooted paternalism of the city fathers, these intellectuals did not believe in the power of village art, but wanted to change it at all costs to fit "their own image", their own taste. These beliefs were not convincing, at least not when seen from today's viewpoint. The deeply moving lament of an old village woman for her son, fallen in the wars, often sobbed rather than sung, sounds quite wrong when performed in a taffeta gown in front of a grand piano.

In the years between the wars more and more people in Hungary became interested in rural culture, and their activities were more enlightened and better planned. Collecting continued, although at a slower speed. There were countless recordings of folk music, dances were filmed, and more and more photographs were taken.

Romantic tourists: The process also took another turn, inspired by visitors from abroad. Once the attraction of folk traditions had been discovered by tourists, the tourism industry concentrated all its energies on this topic and successfully promoted the image of Hungary as the land of "Csikós, Goulash and Fogas".

The beginnings of this romanticised image of Hungary, so attractive to foreigners, can be traced back to romantic nationalist ideals of the 19th century. It was only developed and promoted in such an abridged and aggressive form, however, during the 1930s. In some areas of Hungary, the tendency of the tourist industry to take over folk arts undoubtedly encouraged the survival of existing rich traditions, for instance, in the Matyó area (Matyóföld) east of the capital. The colourful costumes of this region, its surviving customs and the textile arts and crafts were used as enticing advertising material.

A similar fate befell the famous puszta in the east of the country, the Hortobágy. Here the cracking of whips can be heard virtually day and night, even if it means that the horses have to gallop tirelessly over the wide-open plain. Thanks to the

tained world of the Hungarian peasant farmer fell apart within a few years. The collectivisation of agriculture and industrialisation meant that a far smaller proportion of the population was living a traditional rural life. The popular storytellers and singers began to disappear; individual, handmade objects in daily use were replaced by faceless industrial mass-produced items with all their advantages and disadvantages and their uniform, sterile style. Taking all these points as a whole, the process was perhaps an unwelcome but inevitable one, dictated by the changing times. The old, traditional communities

radio Gypsy music, once discreetly fiddled in coffee-houses, spread in leaps and bounds adding to the cliché. And thus was created the ubiquitous stereotypes of the Hungarian in national costume being serenaded by a Gypsy in the *csárda*. Ever since, this symbolic trademark of Hungary, containing only half-truths, has been seen flashed across the puszta like a mirage as soon as any foreigner sets foot over the border. And yet it almost completely obscures the authentic rural culture that still lives on.

Following World War II, the self-con-

and their values were slowly, but surely, dying out, social and family ties slackened or came apart for good, the old village institutions lost their significance and their function. Only the rural singing and dancing groups survived the turbulence of the times.

After 1945, many amateur choirs, orchestras and dance groups were formed in the provinces as a result of individual initiatives. However, they too suffered from the competition of mass culture canned from abroad. It was much easier to sit in front of the television and take advantage of what the city had to offer than to spend time putting something together on your own. For some years, this passive consumerism virtually paralysed village life. It was only in the late 1960s that musical activities returned to the scene.

Revitalisation via TV: Oddly enough it was television, blamed above for all the damage, that played an important role in getting things started. A country-wide television competition for folk music uncovered unsuspected energies. Choirs and dance groups which up until then had existed more or less only on paper came out into public view. As the performance of Hungarian folk songs and music was a strict straightforward attractive music. At the same time, traditional handicrafts were also given greater attention. Potters, basket-makers, weavers, blacksmiths and indigo dyers set to work revitalising their age-old craft traditions.

Today, however, alongside the reborn rural culture and folk art, there exists a state-sponsored "folk" art aimed at the export and tourist markets. Foreigners unfamiliar with the country's language and domestic situation will have trouble sorting out those events that spring from this youthful folk art movement with its originality and genuine if sometimes hid-

requirement for participation, a number of previously unknown treasures and talents simultaneously came to light.

In the 1970s, a programme aimed at revitalising village life combined with a vigorous youth culture gave rise to a fascinating sub-cultural phenomenon: the dance hall. The dance house provides active entertainment, mixing elements of rock'n'roll jamborees of the 1950s and peasant festivals, including liberated youthfulness and

Left, musicians strike up at a country wedding and <u>above</u>,the dancers take to the floor.

den value, from the garish pastiches of touristic-folklore aimed at raking in hard currency. We don't want to deny well organised "state" folk traditions their right to exist or even the need for them, but for a visitor to Hungary it might be a positive experience to get to know authentic folk traditions as well.

The harmonious appearance once presented by the typical Hungarian village can today really only be admired in old photographs. We should also point out that the houses built in rural areas nowadays are functional but hideous. You can only find farmhouses in the traditional style in the various museum villages (*skansen*) and in the more isolated settlements. In some villages of southern Transdanubia (Adorjás, Kórós) and in the small communities of western Transdanubia (Öriszentpéter) and in the villages in the hills above the northern shore of the Lake Balaton, remnants of the traditional elongated Hungarian farmhouse with its typical pergola have survived. In these regions you will probably find the largest number of well-preserved houses, "thanks to the influence and the conservation work of intellectuals who have moved out into the

women who still dress in traditional garb. Some of the houses have been turned into bed-and-breakfast accommodation, and one serves as a museum featuring artifacts and utensils peculiar to the region still in daily use. An ethnic group known as the Palozzans live in this area.

Tourists mostly stray into the inner regions of the counties of Somogy and Tolna and their towns by accident. Here the elongated villages lying at the feet of the gentle lines of hills are often still inhabited by Germans. These villages have little or no tourist infrastructure and no hotels or restaurants. There is, however, usually a vil-

country". (From an architectural point of view, Szentbékkálla, Salföld, Kékkút, Kövágóörs and the surrounding villages in what is known as the Káli Basin constitute probably the most impressive region in terms of Hungarian building tradition).

There are also many beautiful farmhouses in the small villages of the region around Nógrád. Worth a visit, though somewhat museum-like, is Hollókö. Its old centre has been on the UNESCO list of world cultural monuments since 1988. It consists of 55 small houses (including the church) that are for the most part inhabited by elderly

lage inn or a simple bar which opens from morning or midday onwards.

If you want to have a particularly interesting tour, concentrating on the rural architecture, we recommend the following route: Budapest – Dunaföldvár (highway No. 6) – Cece – Kölesd – Gyönk – Högyész – Kalaznó – Bonyhád – Dunaföldvár – Budapest. This tour will not only familiarise the traveller with some exceptional examples of rural architecture, but also reveal some of the more typical small country noble residences (such as those in Gyönk, Kölesd, Högyész). Today they are mostly used as schools and cultural centres.

Open-air museums: If you can't make it to the more remote villages, which are often difficult to reach, you can instead visit several open-air museums. The largest is in Szentendre, where planners hope gradually to gather together the most characteristic buildings from nearly all the major regions of Hungary. For the moment Eastern Hungary is excellently represented (appropriately in the eastern part of the grounds) with a bell tower, crouching farmhouses, a small Reformed Church and a 17th-century wooden Orthodox Church. About three-quarters of a mile to the west

Landscapes, Periods and Museums. These brochure-like volumes are inexpensive and many of them are available in several languages. However odd it might sound, one of the most useful guides on this topic is the *Road Atlas of Hungary.* Any site that might be of special interest is marked by a red star next to the name on the maps and in the index. In the following section the names of these places appear in alphabetical order with a map and a brief explanatory text in Hungarian that can be deciphered using a small dictionary.

Religious architecture: In Hungary the Protestant churches (mainly Calvinist Re-

are houses from Western Hungary (known as Transdanubia). Here, too, folk music concerts are frequently held, as are craft courses for children. There are also fairly important museum villages in Szombathely, Nyíregyháza and Szenna. They can usually be visited from spring through to autumn. The visitor can obtain information about famous buildings that are difficult to locate and about places worth visiting from books in the series *Library of*

formed churches) are especially interesting sights because of their painted coffered ceilings. The decoration of the galleries, ceilings and pews of these churches combines the rich ornament of the Renaissance with naive floral decoration and other ornamental motifs of folk art. The artists were mainly travelling joiners whose names are unknown. We can only mention a few of the countless, absolutely unparalleled monuments here. Many lie in areas where transport poses a daily problem, out on the inaccessible fringes of the country. The Calvinist churches of the communities

<u>Left</u>, winter chill and fun time at the Mohács carnival. <u>Above,</u> a traditional riding display.

south of Pécs, Kórós, Adorjás, Drávaiványi and Kovácshida date from the early 19th century. To admire the coffered ceilings, those in the churches of Tákos, Vámosoroszi, Gacsály, Tivadar and Milota (in eastern Hungary) are highly recommended. The ceiling of the Reformed church in Csenger, completed in 1745, also deserves special attention. It features a central arrangement of leaves, flower ornaments (tulips, rosettes, wreaths) and some figural motifs.

A quintessential Hungarian speciality, though less well known outside the country, are the wooden bell towers. In them regional variations began to appear in the Hungarian national costume, which was still fairly uniform in its basic features. While the costume of the women changed more noticeably and reflected the "fashion" of the appropriate period, men's costume tended to be conservative. The most beautiful Hungarian costumes, with their perfect harmony of styles and colours, are now found outside Hungary, in the Magyar villages of Transylvania. Within the borders of the country, the prettiest costumes for festivals and holidays are still worn today by some in the communities of Transdanubian Sárköz.

"Hungarian folk art reaches the heights of great art", to quote the pertinent verdict of a learned dissertation. The superbly built wooden structures are evidence of the high level of Hungarian carpentry. In fact, the most beautiful wooden bell towers can be found in the region of the upper Tisza, and among them is the impressive Nyírbátor tower, standing tall and proud at 30 metres (85 ft). Another can be seen beside the Aras Reformed Church in Miskolc.

Regional costumes: The rural costumes of Hungary only became colourful in the middle of the last century. At that time If national costumes were at one time common place in Hungary, today they are only brought out of the wardrobe to be worn for special anniversaries and festivals. Village life leaves no room for fine dress. Yet the old garments are still kept and treasured.

The work of rural craftsmen can be seen in many places. Great masters of their craft, people with skill and formal training, allowing them to maintain their traditions, are members of the Council for Folk Arts and Crafts (*Népi Iparmüvészeti Tanács*). Committees of the council are responsible for quality control of the products, so that in principle only authentic quality work can leave the workshops of the masters. You can buy their products, which have a peacock as a trademark, in the shops run by the Co-operative of Folk Art and Crafts (*Népmüvészeti és Háziipari Szövetkezet*). The largest of these co-operative shops is located at the corner of Váci-/Régi Pósta utca in Budapest. In the exhibition rooms over at Corvin Square in district I of the Buda side, you can from time to time view informative collections of these products.

There are other places and opportunities for buying original pieces. You can obtain

flea market. It is known by the name Ecseri or Teleki, but its official designation is Second-Hand Market (*Használcikk-piac*). You can find the market, (Monday to Saturday, 8am–4pm) at Nagy-körösi út, at the beginning of motorway No. 5 in the direction of Kecskemét, on the left and facing the city outskirts. Here the odd piece of genuine folk art can turn up, whether it is traditional clothing, textiles or ceramics. The prices are high, and where at one time you could freely haggle (indeed it was expected that the customer should argue over the price), it is rarely the case today. Some of the private and state antique shops

useful information about master workshops from two main sources: the older representatives of their profession in the Council for Folks Art and Crafts, and the younger craftsmen from the Folk Art Association (*Népmüvészeti Egyesület*), both of which are centrally located at Corvin tér 6, Budapest I.

With a bit of luck, you can still find old items of craftsmanship in the Budapest

Left, flower festival at Debrecen. **Above**, a pasha flanked by women from his harem at the popular harvest festival in Köszeg.

have an extremely wide range of old samples of traditional crafts on sale (e.g. Folkart Centrum, Váci utca 14, Budapest V). The privately owned shops in the Buda castle district and in Szentendre also have a beautiful selection. Buyers should note that the prices are sometimes way above normal.

Street sellers: A few years ago, Hungarian farmers from Transylvania (mainly from the Székler region) started selling their woven and embroidered goods, such as cushions, tablecloths and skirts, in the pedestrian subways of the Pest inner city, not far from the Emke and Astoria hotels.

They sell original handicrafts at fairly reasonable prices. In more recent times, they have faced increasing competition from Gypsies, who build up their basketry wares like barricades.

Fairs and markets: A special feature are the regional markets. Once upon a time every part of the country had its traditional market-places. The more important market towns had developed along the trade routes. Even today, the larger markets still attract tens of thousands of people. The most famous markets are the "Bridge Market" in Debrecen (19–20 August) and the "Great Annual Market" in Pécs, which, despite its

generation are influenced by established folk art and follow its traditions and patterns. Besides flowery embroidery, Hungary is renowned for its leatherware, lace (from Kiskunhalás), and especially for its pottery using traditional floral motifs. A speciality inherited from the Turks is black pottery which has been fired in sooty coal. The designs are etched into the surface using a smooth pebble. Mohács is particularly famous for this type of work, but it is found in the Puszta as well. A good way to get a feel for the "right pattern" is to visit any of the ethnographically orientated regional houses *(tájház)*, or an ethnographic

name, takes place on the first Sunday in the month. The Pécs market is the one with the most traditional wares and is also the biggest. If the weather is good, huge crowds squeeze into the market square behind the railway station, where you can buy just about everything from young kittens to winter coats, used cars, and even *Playboy*. In the southern part of Hungary many villages keep their old traditions, and on market day rows of vendors sell their newly-woven linen, quaint cutlery, old-fashioned mats and bags among other items.

The products of the new arts and crafts

museum, where examples of old Hungarian pottery are frequently displayed. You can see these products in the markets all year round. Twice a year the young and not-so-young master craftsmen get together for a special occasion. The first date for such a meeting is on the last Sunday in March, when the dance-house dancers meet during the exhibition and market of traditional crafts in the Budapest Sports Centre (Budapest *Sportscarnok*, Hungária körút 44–52, Budapest XIV). This is a big event, and several hundred exhibitors come together – puppeteers, leather workers and saddlers, carvers of wood, bone and horn, to name just a few – to peddle their wares. The second major event is the "Crafts Fair" (*Mesterségek Ünnepe*) which takes place from 18–20 August in the old Castle District of Budapest.

Craft courses are held in several places during the summer months. In Velem in Western Hungary, young people staying in a specially built camp can learn wood carving, pottery and weaving. In Zalaegerszeg, you can learn wood carving, and in Magyarlukafa (Baranya district), besides working with wood, there are courses in basketry and weaving on handlooms.

also have the opportunity to learn about various crafts.

Of all the traditional arts available in Hungary today, folk dance and folk music perhaps offer the greatest variety and are the most accessible to the foreign visitor. However, it has recently become necessary to emphasise that Hungarian folk music is not the same as Gypsy music, although the former is also played by Gypsies. Apart from books on the subject, your own ear is not a bad guide here. The record store Rózsavölgyi in Martinelli tér 5 in District V of Budapest has a large selection of folk music and can start you off in the

Folk music: One of the most interesting courses is offered by the famous folk music group *Téka* and its friends and supporters. It is held in the second half of June in the eastern Hungarian town of Nagykálló, in a camp with the tents surrounding a mighty wooden barn that also serves as a dance-floor. Visitors not only take part in singing, dancing and music-making, but

<u>Far left</u>, painted eggs to symbolise the Easter festivities. <u>Left</u>, horse graveyard in Szilvasvárad in the Bükk Mountains. <u>Above</u>, garden of the Zsolnay museum, Pécs.

right direction. Here you will find recordings of the less "wild" popular Hungarian music, with colourful, decorative covers. One special type that should be mentioned is folk-rock or eszpresszó-rock, which is very popular in Hungary. Genuine bar musicians usually play in threes and fours on electric organ, saxophone and percussion, performing Hungarian songs in a rock style. Folk-rock first became popular in the Hungarian-settled regions of the former Yugoslavia, and then spread rapidly across Hungary. More educated mainstream audiences tend to dismiss it as somewhat lowbrow, and it is not played on radio, but in many places folk-rock is now popularised as a new type of folk music.

Where in Hungary today can you hear genuine folk music and see genuine folk dances? Usually, you have to rely on good luck, for instance if you should accidentally get caught up in a rural wedding. If you go to the bigger dances for young people, you will hear "canned" music or modern, electrically amplified sound. It can still happen that, in a small bar, you come across a traditional group. However, the minute the musicians notice a foreign tourist, they will strike up the tune to some

international hit or other. An appropriate gift will usually dissuade them from playing such music. The big Gypsy bands in the Budapest restaurants keep an eagle eye on the wealth of the guests and play tunes accordingly. If some tenor or other, or a female singer in red boots, should turn up, a critical point has been reached and it's high time to leave the restaurant as quickly as possible, without being too conspicuous, of course.

Festivals: Some of the festivals and folk music events are both entertaining and amusing, though they can seem quite lengthy to a visitor who does not understand everything that is going on. Information about the various events can be obtained from the House of Folk Dance (a branch of the Institute of Folk Culture), Szentlélek tér 8, Budapest I.

One celebration which you should not miss is the Kaláka Folklore Festival, which takes place every year at the beginning of July. The Kaláka Festival offers Hungarian folk – not folk music – of good quality and quantity. Information about this event can be obtained from from the Folk Culture Centre of the town of Miskolc (*Miskolci Városi Müvelödési Központ*), Árpád út 4, H-3534 Miskolc. A special event is the dance-house meeting, which takes place every year at the end of March. An endless procession of folk musicians and dance groups congregate for this Sunday festival, admired by the thousands who come to join in. Here the visitor can listen to the folk music of both Hungary itself and of the country's ethnic minorities. Some guest groups from abroad are also invited to perform.

This is the biggest folk music festival in Eastern Europe, and it is recommended for anyone who loves and appreciates live musical entertainment.

Dance-house culture: If you're only staying in Budapest for two or three days and feel that you can't survive without the strange and unfamiliar sounds of Hungarian folk music, or if you want to dance, a visit to a dance house (so-called) is highly recommended. The dance house is a large room where the old Transylvanian form of entertainment takes place; musicians play their hearts out for a modest fee while young people take to the floor. Some of the dance houses occasionally conduct dancing lessons. This is where you can learn Hungarian peasant dances, which can be rather complicated and require utmost concentration. The dance houses are popular good-time venues usually patronised by the young and the active.

Left, wine harvest in the "Valley of Beautiful Maidens" near Eger. **Right**, full folk dress hits the right note.

"Who has not seen in the dominions of our fatherland those wandering hordes, travelling from village to village in their covered wagons drawn by wretched nags? Who does not know of the dark strangers who live out their wretched lives in mud huts on the fringes of our villages? Whose heart has not been overcome by deep emotion on hearing these 'new Magyar' musicians strike up their wailing melodies? Surely each one of us has noticed how the dark olive, elongated faces of these guests from Hungary differ from those of all the other peoples of Europe, as do their dark, restlessly glittering eyes, their well-formed, lips, the wiry, dark curly hair, the slender supple forms, the delicate hands and feet, and their ever cheerful and jocular natures."

Archduke researcher: This portrait, sympathetically drawn in 1902, is the work of Archduke Joseph of Austria, one of the pioneers of research into Gypsy culture. It is a picture that is in many ways still applicable today. The external appearance and the cheerful, colourful clothing of the Gypsies hasn't changed. Even their way of life has remained true to their traditional nomadic culture. The difference is that they no longer travel the countryside in covered wagons, but use the "black train", the commuter train which at weekends brings the menfolk out of the capital back to their eastern Hungarian villages around Nyíregyháza and Debrecen.

After World War II, there were many changes in the Gypsy way of life, not all for the better. The traditional Gypsy occupations (begging, door-to-door selling, horse trading, small businesses) were either prohibited or redundant. Those Gypsies who had previously worked as labourers on the estates were also out of work, as the co-operatives only took in farmers who also owned land. All that remained was poorly paid unskilled work on construction sites and in factories. For this reason many Gypsies are casual labourers in Budapest and other industrial cities. They live in

workers' hostels and can only afford to visit their families once or twice a month. Theirs is an aimless way of life, comforted by drinking or gambling.

Only three percent of all Gypsies are professional musicians. A violin locked under the chin, they play in the bands that provide the local colour, so loved by tourists, in the hotels and restaurants of Budapest. Most of them live in the city, in contrast to the vast majority of the almost

half a million strong Gypsy population. Fewer Gypsies have to survive in mud huts, but mud brick houses and corrugated iron huts are by no means an unusual sight in Gyspy settlements. The Hungarian government is trying to ease the poverty, to remove the slums gradually and replace them with modern apartments. However, given the present general shortage of living accommodation these efforts only bring limited results. Even today there are still many areas without basic amenities. Streets are not paved; in an emergency no ambulance could drive down them. The dreary new housing developments are on the out-skirts. They form a clearly defined ghetto. The rules of the ghetto are not necessarily those of the rest of Hungarian society. Even nowadays, the Gypsies form the poor-est and weakest group in Hungary.

Social deprivation: Officially, their situation is described by the euphemism "potentially disadvantaged". Social deprivation affects 4 percent of the population, and Gypsies comprise the largest ethnic minority. Their birth rate is double or triple that of the Hungarians. Over the last few years, there has been a drop in the birth rate, but not enough to solve basic prob-

40 percent of Gypsy children successfully complete the eight grades of elementary school. About 70 percent of Gypsies speak Hungarian as their mother tongue, while 10 percent speak a Romany dialect, the rest Romanian. The Gypsies fall into several groups, divided along ethnic as well as cultural lines, and some are still organised in tribes. The latter applies to the Romany-speaking Gypsies, who consider themselves the "original". Assimilation is encouraged among Hungarian-speaking Gypsies, but cultural differences and racial prejudices still divide them from the rest.

The Hungarian government is trying to

lems in the foreseeable future.

Life expectancy for Gypsies is 15 or 20 years shorter than for the rest of the population. This means that there are increasingly more children than adults in the family – another reason for their poverty and poor educational qualifications. Children have to contribute towards the family income from a young age. Despite intense efforts by the Hungarian government, only

Left and above, Costumes and colouring mark out Romanies, who are still known as "Gypsies" in Hungary.

integrate the Gypsies, but with little success. In 1986 the dissolved Cultural Association of Hungarian Gypsies was reorganised. Whether this association succeeds in realising the ideals of Gypsy emancipation, with the help of Hungarian intellectuals, is doubtful. At present there are only two paths for Gypsies to follow: either they remain in a Gypsy environment with all its disadvantages, but within their own culture; or they make their labourious way up in Hungarian society, at the cost of giving up their own roots and sometimes even their language.

Within the mosaic of European languages, Hungarian is a stone with a colour and shape all of its own. Its only – and distant – relative is Finnish. Both belong to the group of Finno-Ugric languages, as do Estonian and the minority languages of the Lapps, Vogules, Ostiaks and Samoyedes. Like the language, Hungarian literature, too, is isolated within the European context. This situation has changed over the last few years, mainly as far as the German-speaking public is concerned, for new works are regularly translated into German. In this way, Hungarian literature is at least partially included in the circulation of European culture.

The Hungarians built up their European civilization rather late. Thanks to their conversion to Christianity the nomadic riders were able to take part in developments in Europe. Conforming to European medieval standards offered the Hungarians their only chance of establishing themselves on the Pannonian plain. This pressure to conform did not diminish over the ensuing centuries. Historical developments played an important role in this process. A frontier post between the East and West, the Hungarian Janus mask faced two directions at once. The eastern face was on the lookout for foreign invasions, the western one was trying to assimilate foreign influences.

Throughout its cultural development, Hungary was checked again and again by history. During the peaceful periods people tried desperately to fill in the cultural gaps, a process which repeatedly forced authors to use their craft for social and political ends. This development by leaps and bounds, caused by the continual need to catch up, explains the conflict of two basic attitudes of Hungarian literati – on the one hand, the complaints about their

fatal isolation and the treachery of the West (without its support, it is generally believed, Hungarian culture has very little chance of survival), and on the other, an arrogant self-sufficiency, a proud desire for isolation and a wholehearted trust in the nation's own strength.

Roman origins: Until the late 19th century, Latin was the language of the learned and the cultured. The influence of strict clerical literature is perhaps one reason why

texts in the Hungarian language do not appear until the 13th and 14th centuries. These are also clerical texts: a funeral oration, *Halotti beszéd*, and a lament for the sorrows of the Virgin Mary, *Ómagyar Mária siralom*. The chronicles, mostly a mixture of historical records and legends, were written in Latin, as were the poems of the first notable poet in Hungary, the humanist **Janus Pannonius** (1434–72). Around the time of the Reformation, the Hungarian language began to establish itself as a written form.

In 1590 **Gáspár Károli** finished the first complete translation of the Bible. Sermons became a popular literary form. They continued to be so until the time of the Counter-Reformation. Hungarian literature gained an accomplished stylist in **Péter Pázmány** (1570–1637), whose works had a decisive influence on the development of modern Hungarian prose. The translation of the psalms by the Calvinist **Albert Szenci Molnár** (1574–1634) encouraged the development of the lyrical form. He also devised a Latin-Hungarian dictionary and a Hungarian grammar, to make Hungarian accessible to the rest of Europe.

The more personal lyrical poetry of the troubadour and soldier **Bálint Balassi**

dependent. Here we draw attention to the writings of **Prince János Kemény** (1607–62), **Miklós Bethlen** (1642–1716), **Péter Apor** (1676–1752), the exiled **Prince Ferenc Rákóczi II** (1676–1735) and his loyal follower **Kelemen Mikes** (1690–1761), examples of philosophical and religious soul-searching of an exceptionally high literary standard.

The Romantic contributors: The poet **Mihály Csokonai Vitéz** (1773–1805) unfortunately died young. His work forms a bridge between the rococo style and national romanticism. However, the initiator of the decisive movement for renewal in literary

(1551–94), modelled after Ovid and indebted to the Renaissance, was the first example of poetry of European standard and written in Hungarian. Balassi was of the highest rank of the nobility, as was **Miklós Zrínyi** (1620–64), author of the famous baroque epic *Szigeti veszedelem* (The Siege of Sziget).

A hundred and fifty years of Turkish occupation limited literary creativity in the Kingdom of Hungary to a significant extent. By contrast, a rich literary tradition of memoirs developed in the Principality of Transylvania, which had remained in-

circles was the language reformer, publisher, translator and author **Ferenc Kazinczy** (1759–1831). Writers who previously had worked in isolation found common ground in his intellectual circle, which by the same token opened up channels between Hungary's noble houses and contemporary European influences, especially French and German classicism.

However, recent Hungarian literature was really born in the romantic period. The historical drama *Bánk Bán* by **József Katona** (1791–1830) was celebrated with wild enthusiasm as part of the national awakening. Human but also national suffering mingle in the poems of **Ferenc Kölcsey** (1790–1838), who wrote the Hungarian national anthem.

Discovery of the folk song: By contrast, the great master of Hungarian romanticism, **Sándor Petöfi** (1823–49) discovered the folk song – a simple and direct form for expressing the political and human ideals of freedom. In his poems, the liberal spirit of the French Revolution reached the Hungarian reader in familiar nationalist guise. It is hardly surprising that the reading of his *Talpra Magyar* (Rise up, Magyar) opened the 1848 revolution against

During the 19th century, the popularity of prose writing heightened. **Miklós Jósika** (1794–1865) and **Zsigmond Kemény** (1814–75) wrote historical novels. The entertaining romantic novels of **Mór Jókai** (1825–1904) are still read with enjoyment today. While the exotic world of this great storyteller is firmly rooted in the romantic tradition, the existential pessimism of the dramatic poem *Az ember Tragédiája* (The Tragedy of Man) by **Imre Madách** (1823–64) points the way to the modernism of the 20th century. The turning-point to realism came with the works of the novelist **Kálmán Mikszáth** (1847–1910). His

Habsburg domination. His friend **János Arany** (1817–82), who perfected and at the same time transcended the romantic style, was also inspired by folk song lyrics. He was an ingenious manipulator of language, who succeeded in convincingly conveying modern political and philosophical ideas in classic forms. His ballads and epics are masterpieces conforming to even the highest European standards.

Left, "Sweet homeland, sweet songs..." Above, statues of the poets Miklós Rádnoti (left) and Sándor Petöfi (right).

charming, anecdotal and critically ironic style was imitated by many, but only one raised it to the point of social criticism: **Zsigmond Móricz** (1879–1942). Zsigmond belonged to the generation of writers who established a circle around the journal *Nyugat* (The West), and who succeeded at integrating Hungarian and European, intellectual and literary values into a seamless whole.

With the entry of the lyric poet **Endre Ady** (1877–1919) onto the literary stage, a radical revision of the romantically idealised self-portrait of Hungarian culture began. It also signalled the beginning of modern Hungarian poetry. Ady's valuable contributions and his personality caused vigorous literary, political and moral debates and provided the decisive push that raised the standards and popularity of poetry in the years between the two world wars. We only need to look at the finely chiselled masterpieces by **Dezsö Kosztolányi** (1885–1936) – who was also an excellent prose writer – and at the explosive dynamism of the language of **Attila József** (1905–37).

Contemporary literature: By the 19th cen-

Gyula Illyés (1902–83) are among the most important representatives of the revolutionary trend. The poetry of Miklós Rádnoti, who was shot on a march towards the Mauthausen concentration camp in 1945, is filled with moving images in the romantic style. He paints in vivid colours the suffering of the Hungarian people during World War II.

Responsibility for the community is the marked characteristic of post-World War I Hungarian literature from Transylvania (part of Romania since 1920). The novelist **Aron Tamási** (1897–1966) has recorded

tury, literature had become an important factor in Hungarian politics, and writers often saw themselves pushed into a role of political responsibility for their people. This is a historical situation that repeats itself, and it is certainly still valid in modern times.

The struggle against social and cultural backwardness was the origin of the rich social literature of the years between the wars. The brilliant pamphleteer and novelist **Dezsö Szabó** (1879–1945), the author **Zoltán Szabó** (1912–84), who died in exile in England, the essayist and novelist **László Németh** (1901–75) and the poet

the language and attitudes of Transylvanian Szeklers in inimitable fashion. **András Sütö** (b.1927) is also influenced by the vocabulary of Transylvania, rich in archaic elements. He creates linguistic jewels out of the Hungarian language, which is so much at risk in Romania. The poets **Domokos Szilágyi** (1938–76) and **Géza Szöcs** (b.1955) convey the besieged situation of the Hungarian minority through a multi-layered, metaphorical language. Its poetic power breaches the bounds of nationalism to express existential and general human values.

The post-war years at first brought about

a complete reorganisation of the literary world. All publishing houses and journals were nationalised, and anything published had to undergo strict Party censorship. Most writers stopped writing or were forcibly silenced. Only after the 1956 rising did a gradual liberalisation come about. Authors who had begun their literary careers before or during the war began to be published once more. New on the literary scene were the poems of **Agnes Nemes Nagy** (b.1922) with their clear, refined language and thought, the frivolous elegance of **Sándor Weöres** (1913) and the

diamond clarity and hardness of the painful lyricism of **János Pilinszky** (1921–81). **László Nagy** (1925–78) and **Sándor Csoóri** (b.1930) were inspired by the language of folk songs and developed a system of metaphors based on images of nature. Since the 1960s they have become, together with Gyula Illyés, leaders of the intellectual movement which is slowly, but surely rediscovering national values.

The prose authors **Géza Ottlik** (b.1912) and **Miklós Mészöly** (b.1921) mingle European and Hungarian culture without conflict, and yet do not neglect the responsibility of intellectuals for their own people. As an essayist, **György Konrád** (b.1933) considers Central Europe to be the cultural and political home of thinking Hungarians. As a novelist he contributed to intellectual Central Europe with experimental, linguistically compact literary records of Hungarian history. Konrád, together with the poet **György Petri** (b.1943) – the author of formally audacious political poems – belonged to that group of dissident writers whose works were not published by the official houses in Hungary. They published in the *samizdat* press, in underground publishing houses and outside the country's boundaries.

The younger generation: Writing itself is a theme for many of the younger generation authors. Their personal style is by no means the result of a flight from reality, but rather a critical attempt to shed more light on time, space and history from an individual point of view.

Péter Esterházy (b.1950) is a brilliant experimenter of this kind. He dissects the present, with the help of extremely inventive and flexible language, from various different narrative viewpoints, which do not permit the amused reader any identification with the author, but rather force him or her to think. **Péter Nádas** (b.1942) is an author of more essay-like and philosophical novels of classic seriousness, which can be included in the great European tradition of novel writing.

Hungarian literature seems to have overcome the doctrinal mutilation of the 1950s and today is back on the same level as the rest of European writing. With censorship now very much a thing of the past, literary life in Hungary is more lively than ever as the scene has opened up. Coming to grips with the past 50 years still remains one of the main themes to write about. It is a process that is taking place mainly in the ever-increasing numbers of new periodicals and newspapers that crowd the newsstands.

The oldest Hungarian music goes back to the 12th century, to the songs of the Chermiss and other Ugric peoples living along the Volga and on the Ob. After the conversion of the Hungarian state established by István I at the turn of the millennium, the musical culture of Christendom played a formative role. For years, the hymns and chants existed alongside pagan ritual songs. The carriers of secular musical culture were the *ioculatores*, the professional "jesters", who transformed the legendary cycles of the Huns and Magyars into sweeping epics.

Under King Mátyás Corvinus, vocal polyphony influenced by the Flemish school appeared in Hungary. However, the conquest of Hungary by the Turks in 1526 brought courtly culture to a sudden end. In the divided country, the rhymed chronicle became the most common musical genre. The singing, travelling chroniclers, among them Sebestyén Tinódi (1505–56), were the sole keepers of the continuity of national consciousness. The most prominent musician was the lute virtuoso Bálint Bakfark Greff (c. 1507–69).

Cultural centres: The virginal became the most popular instrument in wealthy bourgeois houses. The best secular music was arranged for this instrument, although gospel music was also often included. Characteristic musical forms of the struggles against the Habsburgs are the Kuruz songs and the Hajduk dances. In those cities that were residences of the bishops, most importantly Györ and Eger, the music of the Counter-Reformation, the high baroque style, reached its peak.

In 1711 a collection of cantatas, *Harmonia Caelestis* by Prince Pál Esterházy, was published. From 1761 on, Josef Haydn served the Esterházy family for 30 years as court musical director. Bratislava and Sopron saw the first results of urban, bourgeois musical culture. Debrecen and Sárospatak, where the Reformed Church was strong, were the cradles of Hungarian choral music. The choir founded by György

Maróthi (1715–44), the *Cantus of Debrecen*, still exists today. The *verbunkos* soldiers' dance (music used as an aid to recruitment) gradually developed into a national dance form.

Thanks to the efforts of Ferenc Erkel (1810–93), the Hungarian National Opera was founded. In his earliest stage-works (the two most famous are *László Hunyadi*, 1844, and *Bánk Bán*, 1861), he was trying for a synthesis of Italian cavatina with the

sound of military music. Erkel also composed the Hungarian national anthem in 1844. Karl Goldmark (1830–1915) represented the German element. His opera The *Queen of Sheba* (1875) is an interesting example of the richly ornamental musical style corresponding to art nouveau. However, among 19th century Hungarian composers, only Franz Liszt (1811–86) achieved fame.

The anthropologist Béla Vikár (1859–1945) made sound recordings in Transylvania, and began research into previously unstudied peasant music. Following the initiative of Zoltán Kodály (1882–1967), his colleague Béla Bartók (1881–1945) decided to travel among the peasants in order to catalogue the rich treasure of folk songs. Peasant music also influenced their methods of composition. Bartók had the more philosophical view of the world, while Kodály's creative strength was most evident in his role as national musical educator. Composers such as Sándor Jemnitz (1890–1963), György Kósa (1897–1984) and Pál Kadosa (1903–83), who left a legacy in music and education, have been undeservedly forgotten.

Even in music, cultural monopoly was under attack. "People's Colleges" were founded, among them the music school of Békés-Tarhos (1946), to serve talented youngsters from peasant backgrounds. From 1948 onwards, contemporary Western music was branded as "bourgeois decadence", and Bartók was castigated as a "cosmopolitan". The Békés-Tarhos music school was closed in 1954. A conservative

Left, Béla Bartók gave modern Hungarian music its unmistakable sound. **Above,** court music for tourists at the Fishermen's Bastion.

folklore-style and an academic rigidity were the hallmarks of music. The most popular form at the time was the choral work in praise of Stalin and the party leader, Mátyás Rákosi.

New generation: Some consolidation took place, but freedom of musical expression was also promised. By 1959 the first works in the rediscovered new style were premiered – *Six Orchestral Pieces* by Endre Szervánszky (1911–77) and the *String Quartet* by György Kurtág (b.1926). By the early 1960s, the "New Wave" of Hungarian opera had arrived with works such as *Blood Wedding* by Sándor Szokolay (b.1931). A new generation of composers was starting to make itself known – András Szöllösy (b.1912), Zsolt Durkó (b.1934), Sándor Balassa (b.1935) and Attila Bozay (b.1939).

Jazz, too, began to free itself from ideological pressure and the first clubs were founded. Beat music was a new wave of unofficial music culture. New Hungarian compositions such as Szöllösy's *Third Concerto* (1970), *Balassa's Requiem* (1972) and Durkö's oratorio *Funeral Oration* (1975) won international awards. Reacting against the rigidity of the established New Hungarian Music, young composers searched for other possibilities. In 1971 the "Studio for New Music" was founded (Zoltán Jeney, László Vidovszky, László Sáry). In 1976 young musicians in the industrial city of Miskolc formed the "Workshop for New Music". Music centres were set up in universities and clubs. A forum, *Publicity for Free Music*, was held in 1987. In 1988, the Society for the Encouragement of Music, a pressure group, made a bid to promote the music industry.

Since the dawn of the 1990s, the raising of cultural restrictions on creativity and the reduction in government subsidies to the arts, Hungarian composers have had to face the same questions as their contemporaries in the West – questions such as should they increase accessibility or proceed further down the road of modernism for its own sake? And so the same dilemma remains for every artist: Do I have to conform in order to earn a living?

Hot springs are to Hungary what oil is to Texas. In Hungary the land is like a sponge, and hundreds of spas have been built on this ground with its springs of hot water, like derricks in the oilfields. You don't need to go through the country with a divining rod to find water – just stop somewhere and dig, and you'll soon discover a spring. In fact, a number of spas came into being when the government was drilling in search of oil. Zalakaros, southwest of Lake Balaton, is one such place.

Such abundance explains how the popular, traditional and typically Hungarian spa cult came about. The spas are almost always based on hot springs and are favourite meeting places. Of course, they are frequented by the sick, too, acting on doctor's orders, for the Hungarian spas are particularly effective in easing rheumatic ailments, stomach and intestinal conditions and gynaecological problems. But just as many healthy people regularly visit the spas, not only to give themselves a quick "general overhaul", but simply because it's a longstanding tradition.

Daily routine: For some, a visit to the spa is part of their daily routine. In the spas you meet familiar faces, and here you can bathe together with your family, your neighbours, or your friends, just as others might choose to meet at a popular local pub. The Hungarian people, more than any other, love anything to do with water, whether it's a matter of sport, fun or health. The water seems to "favour" the Hungarians, too, cleansing their bodies and at the right temperature.

A foreigner who really wants to become acquainted with the Hungarian way of life must visit a thermal spa at least once during his or her stay in the country, whether it's a traditional bath house in the Turkish

style or the more elaborate type of establishment in the style of Gellért in Budapest. However, it is wise to be aware that spa treatments are not always suitable for people with heart problems or high blood pressure, or for stroke victims. In such cases it is always advisable to consult your own doctor before partaking of any hot springs treatment.

Bathing traditions are as old as humanity

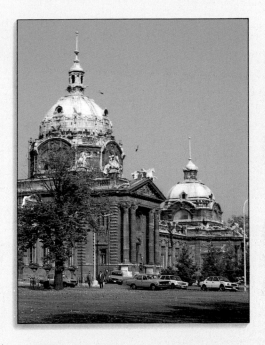

itself. Traces of *homo erectus* dating back 600,000 years have been found in the vicinity of some hot springs. This was not by chance; even in prehistoric times people were aware of the beneficial effects of the water, and since then the history of Hungary has always unfolded around springs.

The Romans were the first to make rational use of them. The ruins of their baths in Aquincum (Buda – Szentendrei u. No. 139) or in Gorsium are evidence of this. Many of the medieval chronicles tell of Saint Elisabeth, who would treat lepers at the foot of the Gellért Hill in Buda, in the

Preceding pages: the world-famous Gellért baths offer treatment in elegant surroundings. **Left**, Kiskunmajsa baths. **Right**, the Széchenyi baths in the Budapest City Park.

baths founded by the Knights of St John.

However, it is the Turks who have left the best-preserved evidence. They were keen bathers and created a genuine social rite out of the process of bathing and body hygiene. Between 1541 and 1686, they built a dozen bath houses in Hungary, all based on the same pattern, with copper domes and the Turkish crescent perched on top, almost similar to the ones of the Ottoman empire.

Budapest has five of these Turkish baths, also known as steam baths – **Király** (II Fö u. 8-10), **Császár** (II Frankel Leó u. 29–31), **Rudas** (I Döbrentei tér 9), **Rác** (I

they would not miss out on their daily bath when under siege. The dome was damaged by bombs in World War II and has been rebuilt. If you go to bathe, watch the time: the sexes bathe separately by the hour, as it is usual to take to the water almost naked. Don't take a camera – the steam will do it no good, and the other bathers are not likely to appreciate such an indiscretion. It is usual to wear a cloth to cover the genitals, but it is often laid aside when people actually go to bathe. You can choose the sequence of baths to suit yourself, but the usual cleansing procedure is to start with the warm rooms. One room (on the sauna

Hadnagy u. 8–10), and **Pesterzsébet** (XX Vízisport u. 2). They were not built with tourists in mind and are mainly visited by older people and the inhabitants of surrounding districts. That in itself is reason enough to leave the well-trodden track, if you really want to get to know Hungary and gain an impression of the traditional and Middle Eastern bathing rituals.

Király has the best preserved baths. They were built in 1556 under the rule of Pasha Arslan, and were at that time within the fortifications erected by the Turks around the quarter known as the "water city", so

principle) is heated to 113°F (45°C), in the steam rooms the temperature rises to (131°–149°F/55°–65°C). A leap into cool (79°F/26°C) water refreshes and revives. Then warm yourself in the hot pools, with temperatures of 82°, 97° and 104°F (28°, 36° and 40°C), until you are ready to submit to the hands of the masseur...

The favourite bath is the central pool under the dome, with its pleasant (body) temperature of 97°F (36°C). Here visitors often stay longest, and discuss various topics thoroughly, veiled in steam. On sunny days, you can see an unforgettable spectacle when the rays, broken by many panes of glass, enter through the dome in colourful bundles of light.

The pleasures of the table: Towards the end of the 19th century, under the rule of the Austro-Hungarian monarchy, the Magyar waters received international acclaim, which spread as far as America, where bathers also followed the call to visit the spas for the sake of their health. In 1907 a brochure introduced Budapest as "the greatest mineral water spa in the world". This was perhaps no exaggeration. Nowadays Budapest is the most important spa in Europe.

needed to round off the delights of bathing. Széchenyi, with its neo-baroque building, its domes and its equestrian statues, was at that time the biggest spa centre in Europe. A dozen baths, from mud to hammams, public baths to luxury baths, had something to offer every taste and every purse. The hottest springs in Budapest rise here, and for this reason you can bathe in the gigantic open air pool even in the coldest winter. The most difficult problem bathers experience when it snows is getting from the changing rooms to the water. But, of course, you soon forget the cold once you have dived in and your head has disap-

The **Lukács** baths (II Frankel Léo u. 25–29) are the most reputable even today for their mud baths which ease ailments of the joints. Spa treatments, just like ideas, follow fashionable trends. In 1913 the Széchenyi bath (XIV Allatkerti körút 11) was the favoured resort of the "spa tourists". The baths are in an exclusive little park, not far from the famous Gundel restaurant, for a good meal is just what's

Left, sculpture in splendour adorn the baths in Budapest. **Above**, cool dip in the popular Széchenyi baths.

peared in the warm steam. As in other baths, chess players can be seen in the water conducting their games with serious intent in the water. You should note, however, that the actual spa section of the Széchenyi, the men's section that is, is one of Budapest's well-known meeting places for homesexuals.

Fashionable Gellért: From 1981 on fashion drew the bathers to the newly opened Hotel Gellért and its baths (XI Kelenhegyi út 4). The list of VIPS who visited this temple of sophisticated treatment includes the Shah of Persia, Richard Nixon, Artur Rubinstein,

Raquel Welch and Luchino Visconti, and even Queen Juliana of the Netherlands, who spent her wedding night here in the hotel in 1937. This is a place of supreme elegance, and is today mostly visited by the upper classes of Budapest, tourists and foreign businessmen. The Gellért building is representative of Hungarian art nouveau, with unmistakable Middle Eastern–Moorish influences. If you do stay in this hotel, don't miss out on a visit to the baths. These are among the finest that any spa has to offer. If you have neither the time nor the inclination for the baths, let this at least be the one that you visit. Look at the Turkish

able history, but none of them apart from Gellért, has new medical equipment conforming to Western standards. However, the Thermal Hotel hotel on Margaret Island is a modern centre, with research laboratories, sports facilities and even a small open-air theatre for the patients. Unfortunately, the architecture of the 1980s is functional and by no means as impressive as that of the Gellért.

There are many baths and swimming pools in Budapest, particularly those called "beaches" by the Hungarians. These are mostly open-air pools in park-like surroundings. There are usually several pools

baths with their fascinating majolica decor, which covers all the walls and pools… or take the hall baths, where you can have your back massaged by the jets of water which contain carbon dioxide, as if you were in a Jacuzzi in elegant art nouveau surroundings. And finally, whatever you do, don't miss the wave pool in the open air. There are lawns, too, but try to avoid coming here on a Sunday – you would have to pay an additional entrance fee and probably spend hours queueing.

The "beaches" of Budapest: The spas and baths mentioned are places of consider-

of various types in one location, including a children's pool, a swimming pool and a therapy pool. You can even hire chalets for a holiday. The most popular is the **Szabadságpart** (XIII Dagály u.), the "Freedom Beach". A recent development at the Csillaghegy "beach" (II Puszta-kúti ut. 3) is a nudist zone.

Baths in the grotto: The spas elsewhere in Hungary have always been overshadowed by Budapest. They were simply forgotten; and hotel standards, medical treatment and hygiene did not meet the demands of an international clientele. The Hungarian government turned to the United Nations in 1971 to obtain technical assistance for a modernisation programme for the spas. The plans drawn up in 1977 called for new accommodation to be built (previously guests and patients had to lodge with local people), old spas to be modernised and for the equipping of new spas.

Several spas are now open to international visitors. **Gyula**, in the Great Plain in southeastern Hungary, specialises in the treatment of chronic rheumatic diseases. Its spa facilities are set in a protected environment, in a beautiful park just opposite the 16th century castle.

most popular spas in the country. This spa accommodates about one million patients every year and claims the dream results of a 90 percent cure rate. **Buk**, about 18 miles (29 km) east of Szombathely, is also very popular, even though the spa buildings are not the most attractive. The waters contain calcium, magnesium, fluoride and carbonates, and are used to help relieve a wide range of disorders from post-operative to gynaecological.

Hungary has some unusual physical features to offer the visitor, which make spa treatment even more interesting. In **Miskolctapolca**, a spa just a few miles away

Lying in the east of the country, **Hajdúszoboszló** is nowadays one of the most dynamic regions of Hungary. In 1925 they were looking for oil here, but drilling brought something else up from below – water at a temperature of 162°F (72°C). The water, it transpired, was particularly beneficial in treating open wounds, and after World War II, when thousands of veterans needed help, it became one of the

Left, **Miskolctapolca in the north is a popular spa. Above, three bathing beauties in the pedestrian zone of Nyíregyháza.**

from the industrial centre of Miskolc, you can bathe in slightly radioactive caves with a water temperature of 86°F (30°C), and can inhale wholesome steam if you suffer from asthma. This is truly spectacular bathing, in the half-light of tortuous caves, where in the gloom you may occasionally stumble across a courting couple by mistake.

Relief for rheumatism: The lake of **Hévíz** is one of the greatest hydro-therapy sites of Hungary. Close to Lake Balaton and only 40 miles (65 km) away from the Austrian border, Hévíz, the "Mecca of rheumatism sufferers", lies on the largest warm lake in Europe, with a surface area of 11 acres (4½ hectares). The water, at 104°F (40°C), sulphurous and slightly radioactive, bubbles up from a crater 125 feet (38 metres) deep and supplies 80 million litres of water a day! The thick layer of medicinal mud at the bottom of the lake is used for treating rheumatism and even exported abroad.

This lake was known to the Romans, but spa facilities were not developed until the end of the 19th century when bathing pavilions were built on piles in the centre. The village was rebuilt completely from 1977 to 1986. The old wooden platforms were

replaced by concrete, but the pavilions were reconstructed in the traditional style. Ladders lead down to the water, which is covered in lilies. The lake itself is an attraction, and bathing in it is extremely beneficial and relaxing. Holiday-makers swarm here in summer. They cluster in large groups on the wooden piers that stretch into the lake. Swimming is possible even in the winter as the temperature of the water never falls below 75°F (24°C).

The little spa resort on dry land, Hévíz, has gained an excellent international reputation in recent years. There are two new four-star hotels – the Hotel Thermal and the Hotel Aqua. Here the visitor can take to the waters and receive the best medical treatment to his or her heart's content, and at prices which are unrivalled for good value. These hotels have the most modern therapeutic facilities and are serviced by competent medical staff. They are evidence of the fact that spa provision is becoming an increasingly important factor in the country's tourist industry.

Heartfelt ease: Four other spas in the west of Hungary have made a name for themselves: **Balf**, where the water even splashes within the sacred buildings, and the ceiling of the baroque chapel is painted with a biblical bathing scene; **Zalakaros**, with its hot, almost boiling spring, which has proved successful in treating depression; **Harkány**, where the water and the mud baths are rich in sulphur and fluoride; and **Balatonfüred** on the north bank of Lake Balaton. This spa is not only a hydrotherapy centre, thanks to the medicinal waters of the lake, but also a spa because of the springs, which contain carbon dioxide. The spa is known around the world for its success in treating heart problems. In the ultra-modern hospital directly administered by the World Health Organisation and the United Nations, extensive research is being carried out in the study of heart diseases. Balatonfüred is also an elegant spa town, popular with summer visitors, and is one of the oldest spas in the lake district.

This chapter has highlighted the more popular spas. But wherever you go – to Pécs, Szeged, Györ, Kecskemét, Nyíregyháza – you will find a wealth of medicinal waters. Every town – or almost every town – nowadays has hot springs and baths. In fact, there are 1,100 springs in use, with a water temperature of 77°F (25°C), and 450 hot spring baths, of which a third were built in the last 30 years. Given these figures, it is perhaps not surprising that the hot springs are also used for central heating in homes and for agriculture and industry.

Left, a three-generation Hungarian family having some fun in the pool. **Right**, the Rudasfürdö baths – Turkish style.

If the Hungarian dishes you taste and savour during your visit bear little resemblance to the "Hungarian" cooking you sampled elsewhere, don't be surprised. Some of the ingredients are found fresh only in Hungary, and a number of philistine-operated restaurants abroad lack the delicate touch of devoted Hungarian cooks. It is interesting to note that the Hungarian food of today is quite different from that of a century ago, and that the turn-of-the-century influence of France has left its mark on many dishes. However, some traditions still hold sway in the preparation and enjoyment of food in Hungary.

Traces of "prehistoric" Hungarian cuisine are present in the hearty soups, rich in grains, and cabbage-based dishes. During the Great Migration, nomadic Magyars experimented with different ways of preserving food, including a recipe for kneading a paste and rolling it into balls which could later be cooked by dropping them into boiling water. *Tarhonya* is made with flour and eggs, and the small balls can be browned in lard, onions and paprika, and then served with meat.

Nomads since earlier times, Hungarians developed and refined their culinary wizardry by assimilating recipes and techniques from the lands they visited as friends or enemies. Their travels brought them into contact with Bulgarians and Turks on the Black Sea. Later, King Mátyás and his Italian wife Beatrix introduced Western habits into the royal kitchen. It was Mátyás who brought the turkey to Hungary, and history tells us that his royal feasts included up to 10 dishes per course.

Paprikás speciality: The best-known ingredient of Hungarian food today is paprika. *Paprikás* is a general name given to dishes seasoned with paprika and served with sour cream sauces, especially with fish, fowl and veal dishes. Red meat, pork

and fatty fowl such as goose or duck are not prepared as often with this spice. Hungarian goulash (*gulyás*), probably the most famous Hungarian creation (and the most abused in foreign kitchens), uses plenty of paprika in a meat soup or stew containing onions and small potatoes.

Onions are another mainstay ingredient, cooked to a glassy state, flavouring soup (but removed before serving), or raw and sliced in rings on top of salads or grilled

meat. Fresh spring onions are very popular in a sandwich filling made with sheep curd, butter and paprika. Parsley is a common seasoning ingredient in Hungary, though cooks elsewhere have to make do with turnips or parsnips in its place. Bay leaf, dill, caraway, marjoram and tarragon are used in many recipes. Some rarer spices such as saffron and ginger are found in special dishes. Finally, there is cream, cream and more cream. Cream in the soup, in the sauce, in the dessert – always delicious with a flavour that is never quite matched outside the country.

<u>Left</u>, ready-to-serve Hungarian delicacies. <u>Above right</u>, *lángos, fried dough.*

Catch of the day: Some of the most flavoursome and authentic dishes in Hungary are made with local fish, many varieties of which are only to be found here. The most famous – and some say the tastiest – is the silvery Lake Balaton pike-perch (*fogas* or *süllö*, the latter name referring to young fish). This lean, boneless fish, weighing eight to ten kilogrammes at maturity, has white meat full of flavour. It is best, of course, to enjoy the fish at its freshest, on the shores of the lake. Because the pike-perch is quite delicate, it cannot be transported alive, so if you eat it anywhere else it has probably been frozen. Another of the

with paprika and grilling until crisp. They are best enjoyed in this way in the open air, and go down well with a bottle of wine. If you head for the shores of Lake Balaton in fine weather, you'll find Hungarians with the same idea in mind.

Hungarian *fish paprikás*, or fish soup as it is sometimes called, has some loyal fans. Look for it on the menu as *az igazi halpaprikás* (the genuine). Traditionally, you can taste the dish at its best along the banks of the Tisza river at Szolnok or Szeged, in the middle of the puszta at Tiszafüred, by the Danube at Komárom or on the shores of Lake Balaton. Restaurants

savoury regional fishes is sturgeon (*tok*) from the Tisza, which is delicious and also boneless. Trout is found in Hungary, especially a common variety with red and black spots, and a gourmet's favourite.

In addition to these "star" fishes, there are other festive and lavish dishes such as *fish paprikás*. These include catfish, carp and pike. The many varieties of carp are popular and commonly served fried in breadcrumbs or "Serbian" style (*rácpaprikás*). Carp, bream and razor fish from Lake Balaton are also delicious when prepared by slicing them in two, sprinkling

serving this fisherman's delight have become rather popular, and some even prepare it in a giant cauldron over an open fire, and let the aroma lead you to your seat.

Halpaprikás should contain at least three kinds of fish, including catfish, carp and local fish (sturgeon or pike-perch), and is even better with small fry added. The fish is layered in a big pot, with the choicest morsel on top, then simmered in onions, paprika and water, unstirred. The smaller fish at the bottom of the pot often remain there, serving only to flavour the dish. The dish is usually supplemented with noodles, spaghetti or *túróscsusza* (cottage cheese noodles).

There are a small number of variations on this theme, including *halpörkölt* (fish stew flavoured with onions and lard), *halleves* (fish soup with vegetables), *ikerás* (fish soup with roe – highly recommended), *barátleves* (friends' soup), *halleves ikrafelfújttal* (fish soup with roe soufflé) and *halragu* (fish ragout flavoured with mushrooms, wine and sour cream).

Gulyás: Hungarian goulash (*gulyás*) is probably the most maligned and most loved meal to come out of Hungary. Maligned, because outside the country any dish made

lar, using small strips of meat, mushrooms, sour cream, peas and other vegetables. Paprika is sometimes replaced by pepper in this dish. A tasty regional speciality is *Székelygulyás*, Transylvanian goulash, which combines different types of meat with sour cream, paprika and cabbage.

Most of these stews are thickened with sour cream, though egg yolks are also used. In finer cuisine, flour is avoided as a thickener, but you may find this rather unpleasant flavour (and lumps) in thick sauces served in cheaper restaurants. Sometimes pasta is boiled into a dish at the end of cooking to give it more consistency. In

with paprika is mistakenly referred to as "goulash", as well as stews making good use of leftover meats, served in institutional cafeterias. The real thing has several forms – *gulyás, pörkölt, tokány*. Goulash *per se* is a meat soup prepared with onions and paprika, to which cubed potatoes and noodles are added. *Pörkölt* is a ragout made with meat and minced onion, the strong flavour of which predominates. The sauce is thick and smooth. *Tokány* is simi-

any event, goulash has earned its reputation as a filling meal, and one of the most traditionally popular dishes in Hungary. Even dieters will want to make an exception to taste the real thing.

The festive table: The end-of-the-year holidays in Hungary as in many other countries are times for good eating and the renewal of traditions. If you are in Hungary at Christmas or New Year's Eve you will delight in the seasonal customs and cuisine, especially if you are fortunate enough to be invited into a Hungarian home. There you may sample a walnut-

Left, kitchen in the museum of the Slovakian minority in Békécsaba. **Right**, fresh-baked bread.

fattened turkey, stuffed with chestnuts and prunes, poppy-seed rolls, Bishop's Bread...

Start with the celebrated *Krambambuli*, a spicy punch served flaming on New Year's Eve. The list of ingredients can include chopped fruit, stoned dates, raisins, candied orange peel, dried plums, walnuts, sugar, rum and brandy, all of which are flambéed before white wine, cinnamon, lemons and oranges are added. The aroma alone is enough to start the year off right.

A typical dish for this time of year is roast suckling pig, although a real suckling pig is a rare find and the usual fare is more

Pig-killing and sausage-making time is still an important winter tradition in rural Hungary. Some of the bigger farms welcome Hungarians and tourists, who arrive by the busload to witness the feast. This is the only way to taste *orja* soup, made on the spot with spicy spare-ribs. The soup is typically followed by boiled meat and horseradish, and by festive *stuffed cabbage*, making use of the different parts of the animal. The meat is also used to prepare the Hungarian sausages, of which many varieties exist. Hungary is considered a paradise for sausage-lovers.

Black sausage or blood pudding is made

like a young hog. Crisp and golden, an apple in its mouth, suckling pig is served with vinegary red cabbage, caraway seeds, sour gherkin pickles. Tradition has it that the suckling pig on New Year's Day brings good luck all the year round. If you are not game enough to enjoy a whole suckling pig, conjure good luck with a hearty *pörkölt* made of the same, served with *tarhonya* in red paprika gravy. *Carnival doughnuts*, which should really be served later in the year, are a popular winter dessert. Served piping hot and sugary, they are as festive and delicious as other treats.

by stuffing the large intestine with pig's blood diluted with milk and vegetable stock, pork and bacon, onions, black pepper and marjoram. *White puddings* are made with a liver base and may often use lemon, garlic, paprika and marjoram as flavouring.

If you should have the pleasure of partaking in one of these feasts, leave room for the supreme delicacy on the menu, *tenderloin roast in caul*. The *caul* is a fatty

Above, roast pig and fish soup are popular delicacies at public festivals all over Hungary.

PAPRIKA

"I owe a great deal to paprika, for this modest fruit has made the fulfilment of my scientific dream possible. Also, the good health of a not insignificant number of my people is based on this plant." —Albert Szent-Györgyi

Next to the salt and the toothpicks, the average Hungarian table carries either a shaker or a little dish with a deep red, sometimes orangey-red aromatic powder. This is, of course, the famous *paprika*, the spice that perhaps more than anything brings Hungary and the Hungarians to mind. The association is a little peculiar, as the use of paprika in official Hungarian cooking only dates back about a century. Moreover, the plant itself is not native to Hungary.

Paprika may have been imported either from Spain, or from India via the Turks, or even from America. The etymology of the name itself seems to be rooted in the Balkans. What the luminary of the paprika trade knows for sure is that first, paprika grows wild in Central and South America, and that second, Christopher Columbus brought it home with him in 1493.

Legend has it that a fair Magyar maid, haremed for the Sultan's pleasure during the long Turkish occupation of Hungary, succeeded in escaping, taking some paprika seeds with her. Post-doctorial gastronomists still puzzle over who gave the product to the Turks, though.

At first the "heathen pepper" served as a decorative shrub in genteel aristocratic gardens. Suspicions about its edibility are understandable as it belongs to the nightshade family, long considered exclusively poisonous. On the other hand, it provided poor people with a cheap and effective way of spicing up food, especially as its full flavour emerges best when cooked together with pork fat.

To this day, the southern Hungarian peasants keep a stash of home-grown and ground paprika. The simple "*tanyas*" under strands of drying peppers have become part of the romanticism of the Hungarian landscape.

Paprika's widespread usage in modern Hungarian cuisine is the result of a process of gentrification. The poor man's pepper was soon consumed by both kings and peasants. On top of savoury qualities the Nobel Prize winner, Albert Szent Györgyi, discovered in 1938 that paprika is extremely rich in vitamin C. What's more, the "hotter" brands have an invigorating effect on the body which can only be doused by

Right, "Heathen peppers", brought to Europe by Columbus and used by peasants and kings.

an immediate application of liquid or sour cream.

Ask along the way what homeopathic applications exist for paprika, and you may be surprised to learn that it cures everything from the common cold to premature hair loss. According to a 17th century manuscript, wreaths of paprika and paprika powder are supposed to keep off blood-thirsty vampires.

What makes Hungarian paprika so special is a complex issue. Attempts to transplant seeds into Israel produced a tasty fruit, very spicy, but not Hungarian. Under the continental climate, in the flatness of the Great Plain, Hungarian paprika – both sweet and hot varieties – develops a highly characteristic flavour.

Szeged, a beautiful city on the Tisza close to the border with Serbia, is the capital of paprika,

though many suggest that the true capital is Kalocsa on the Danube. The *Szegedi Paprika-feldolgozó Vállalat*, located on an industrial estate behind the station, has been growing, hybridising, grinding and packaging the red gold since 1951. Today, it employs 3,000 people and has extended its operations to the making of powdered soups and canned entrées. It also harbours the world's only research facility devoted entirely to paprika. In well-equipped laboratories, the "heathen pepper" is scrutinised for its flavour, its colour, and its chemical and molecular constituents. New grinding methods are tried and new strains tested. It is hardly any wonder that the casual, curious visitor is treated as if he or she had asked to visit a munitions plant. ■

membrane covering the large intestine, or "veil." It allows the tender pork to be stewed in its own aromatic juices. The feast continues with more courses of cottage cheese noodles, crackling, salads, plums pickled in spiced red wine, strudels, cakes and cream – all served with wine and topped off with fresh fruit and coffee.

Easter and the seasons: As elsewhere, one traditional Easter meal in Hungary is *Easter ham*, spiced, pickled or smoked, served in slices with fresh spring vegetables, spinach, onions, radishes, peas. The ham is left to cool in the water in which it has boiled (along with the Easter eggs) and should

for *breaded spring chicken*, a favourite dish in Hungary and one which, though quite simple, is delicious when prepared with care. Fresh *kohlrabi* and chilled cucumbers are also heralds of spring, along with tender young goose meat, sorrel sauce, fresh dill seasonings and May asparagus.

Strudels (*rétes*) are the pride of the Hungarian cuisine. It is the outstanding quality of Hungarian flour that makes them so delightful. The dough, made from fine flour, sour cream, lard and egg yolks, is rolled out as thin as tissue paper. The filling is spread over the pastry, which is rolled up and put into the oven. *Rétes* are

never be served re-heated. It is either eaten warm just out of the boiled juices or cold with horseradish and aspic.

Easter lamb is another seasonal favourite. Some of the forms it may take include *lamb's head soup, Transylvanian tarragon lamb, lamb paprika stew, paprika lamb with sour cream* and a variety of cutlets, chops, saddle, and leg of lamb preparations.

Horse-shoe cakes are festive pastries sprinkled with walnuts or poppy seeds that are associated with Easter celebrations. Easter Monday is traditionally reserved

delicious when served hot with cream and powdered with sugar.

Fruit soups (cherry, plum or gooseberry) are appetising on a hot day. Cold meats are garnished with salads of cool cucumber, cauliflower, tomatoes, mushrooms, beans, celery, lettuce and pepper.

At harvest time, you can enjoy ripe, delicious fruit. Chestnuts and walnuts are roasted and sold in paper bags in the parks and on street corners. *Csája*, a warming grog, is a favourite drink for this time of the year. It has taken the place of the traditional "must" made from the first pressings of newly harvested grapes. New wine made this way from *honigli*, the Buda white grapes, is especially delicious, and if you have the chance to sample some fresh chestnuts or almonds, jump at it.

A rich harvest: Autumn is the time for harvesting grapes, which brings us to the wines of Hungary. Though the selection is not as broad as in France or Italy, for example, the wines of Hungary are enjoyable and some are excellent. Wine is produced in many parts of the country. Some areas, such as the warm, fertile volcanic slopes of the northern coast of Lake Balaton (Badacsony and Bakony) are particularly

duction has resumed its normal course.

Among those wines which have obtained international recognition, two are particularly famous. The first, *Egri Bikavér* (Eger Bulls' Blood), owes its name to its beautiful deep red colour and undoubtedly also to its strength and aroma. It is made from various grape varieties, not always in the same proportions. The second famous wine comes from the area to the northeast of Eger, from the confluence of the Tisza and the Bodrog. Here lies **Tokay**, the capital of a small region famous for its extraordinary wines. The Tokay grape itself contains a lot of sugar, which affects the alco-

fertile. Grapes have been grown in the Buda region since ancient times. Under the Habsburgs, the drink became more common as vineyards spread further south and east. Its growth in popularity, as well as that of wine taverns (*borozó*) was hampered by phylloxera – a disease which destroyed vineyards all over Europe in the late 19th century. Thanks to new pest-resistant vines from America, wine production has resumed its normal course.

hol content of the wine. The range of wines is so great that the Hungarians have developed a special vocabulary to describe the various types. The top spot in the list is filled by Aszú. Its grapes are harvested at the end of October, when they have almost shrivelled up to raisins and become very sweet. The selection of grapes for pressing is very strict, and the number of baskets (*puttony*) it takes to make each barrel is carefully monitored. Naturally, the more baskets, the better the grade.

Miklós Pap, a Tokayan author on wine, is the curator of the local wine museum and owns one of the best cellars in Tokay. He claims that Tokay, taken in homeopathic doses, can ease an astonishingly varied number of ailments, including leukemia. At any rate, it is worthwhile keeping in mind the wine's alcoholic strength, and also the precaution that motorists should stick to mineral water or any of the tasty Hungarian fruit juices. The permitted limit of alcohol in the bloodstream of car drivers is zero, and checks are carried out on foreigners, too.

A place to eat: Hungary's culinary culture has spawned many a great restaurant, especially in the capital. The old coffee-

house (*kávéház*) has for the most part given way to rather pedestrian *eszpressós* with linoleum floors and stainless steel counters scratched to the colour of lead. However, finding a place to eat is never a problem.

Prices and menus vary. You pay more in a first-class restaurant, less in a second-class, and of course even less in a third-class establishment. Though the menu (*étlap*) expresses the difference quite clearly, most restaurateurs will prominently display a sign bearing either I, II or III *oszt* (*osztály*=class). *Caveat emptor!* The cost does not necessarily reflect the quality. In some inns of the I oszt, the food might be lukewarm, the waiter rude and the bill legalised highway robbery. On the other hand, a grubby, neon-lit hovel populated by beer-sodden Gypsies cursing in their own inimitable way might offer an unforgettable meal in unforgettable company. The majority of restaurants are privately run, in the wake of Hungary's attempts to enliven its economy and encourage entrepreneurship. The main difference between these places and the state-run operations is in the treatment of the customer. The privateers greet, offer help, bid farewell and invite the customer to come again.

Food for thought: The average menu usually has the following sections: *levesek* (soups), *köretek* (vegetables and side dishes), *saláták* (salads), *tésztak* (cakes), *készételek* (prepared meals), *frissensültek* (freshly fried), *különlegességek* (specialities). Salaták may mislead the diner to expect something green. The rubric applies mainly to the nation's wonderful pickled goods that help to cut through the pall of heavier foods but leave a constitution used to roughage stranded. Thus, life as a vegetarian here is difficult, unless that person is willing to believe that the Hungarians use butter and oil instead of *zsír*. (a lard mostly made from pork fat. It lubricates every cooking utensil and shortens every pastry dough.)

Music plays an integral role in restaurants. Where the old Gypsies have retired, they have been replaced by new-fangled electronic instruments played by either poor students or dropouts from the local music academy. In the more chic establishments, music is piped in from the ceiling. But let no romantic vision of sweltering, Byzantine, dancing Budapest vanish. Many Gypsies still maintain the old traditions and exercise their old profession. Their repertoire is international, from Strauss waltzes to German folk songs, and even Leonard Bernstein numbers, but all *alla zingara.*

<u>Left</u>, it keeps the head cool when you're dancing. <u>Right</u>, quality control at work in a salami factory in Szeged.

FACTS AND FIGURES

Official name: Magyar Köztársaság (Republic of Hungary)
Area: 35,910 sq. miles (93,030 sq. km)
Neighbouring countries: Austria, Slovakia, Ukraine, Romania, Slovenia, Croatia and Serbia.
Highest point above sea level: Kékes 3,330 feet (1,015 metres)
Major rivers: Danube (273 miles/ 439 km), Dráva, Tisza, Rába

Population: 10,296,000 (1980), circa 55 percent in rural areas
Capital: Budapest (pop. 2,016,000)
Major towns: Debrecen (pop. 215,000), Miskolc (197,000), Szeged (178,000), Pécs (170,000), Györ (130,000), Nyíregyháza (114,000), Székesfehérvár (109,000)
National flag: red, white and green (horizontal stripes)
Administration: 19 administrative counties, and Budapest

PLACES

Hungary is a relatively small nation covering 35,910 sq. miles (93,030 sq. km) and with slightly over 10 million inhabitants, a fifth of whom reside in the capital Budapest. It shares borders with Slovakia in the north, the Ukraine and Romania in the east, Slovenia, Croatia and Serbia in the south and Austria in the west. The Danube cuts Hungary into two unequal parts; the smaller Transdanubia in the west, and a wild eastern region defined by the almost painful flatness of the Great Plain and the rugged remoteness of the northern mountain ranges. The climate is determined by steppe, Mediterranean and even Atlantic influences, and guarantees plenty of sunshine and rain. The winters can be harsh, especially on the vast eastern plain.

A trip through Hungary – whether on foot, by car, bus, bicycle or on horseback – can be a memorable experience. Compared to the precision and servility of many other nations, catering for tourists in Hungary is at times surprisingly informal, not to say lackadaisical. Literature also testifies to the seductive qualities of the land and its people. Yet it is not easy to pinpoint the exact source of Hungary's beauty. There are few natural scenes on the Grand Canyon scale, few castles as overwhelming as some of the edifices of Louis II of Bavaria or Versailles. Hungary is a collection of subtle experiences: a purplish sun hanging over the baked plain, delicate stucco work on simple houses, horses pulling a coal load along a shimmering road, an organist struggling with his instrument in remote chapel.

Preceding pages: an early bird in the sulphurous springs near Eger; shepherd and his flock of sheep near Bonyhád surviving the cold; river bank along the Tisza against a golden backdrop.

Religion: Roman Catholics (56 percent), Reformed Church of Hungary (Presbyterian Calvinist) and Lutheran Church (22 percent), Greek Orthodox(5 percent)
Currency: 1 forint = 100 filler
Gross Domestic Product (per capita): US$3,755 (1993)
Universities: 10
Technical universities: 9
Roads: 65,507 miles(105,424 km)
Railways: 4,722 miles (7,600 km)

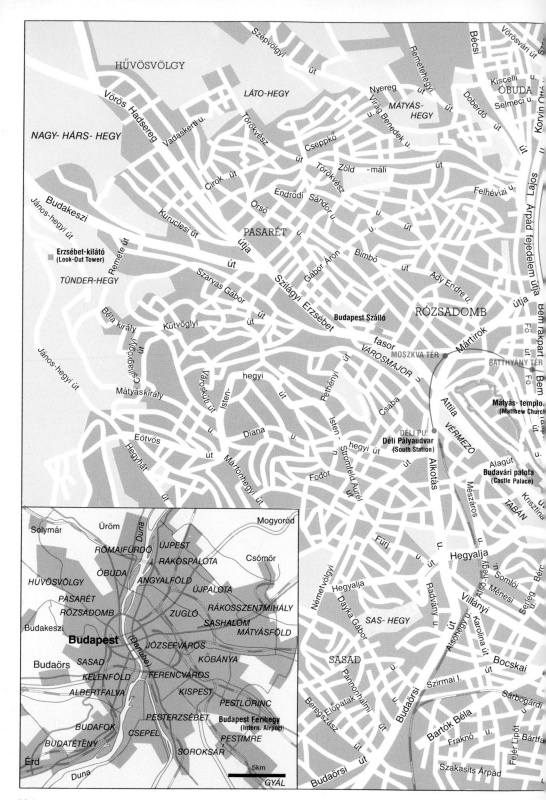

136

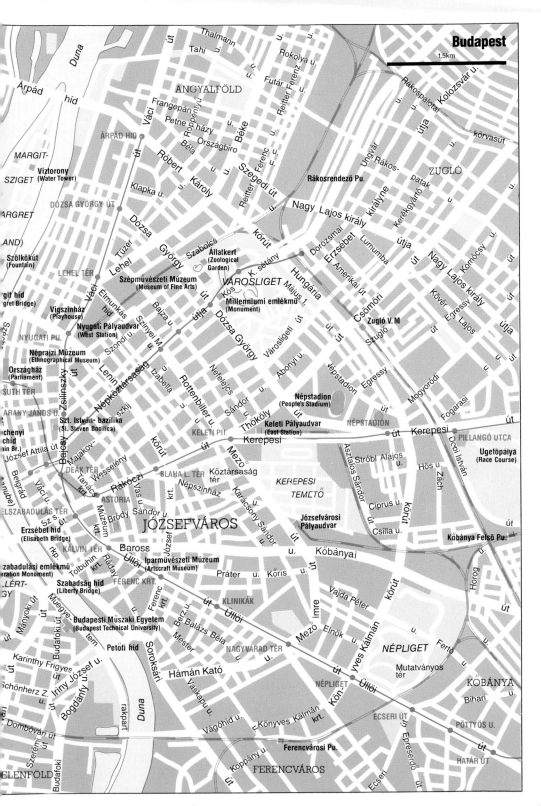

Budapest

1,5km

Duna

Árpád híd

ANGYALFÖLD

Thalmann u.

Tahi u.

Rokolya u.

Futár Ferenc u.

Reiter Ferenc u.

Rákospalotai

Kolozsvár u.

útja

körvasút

Frangepán u.

Petne házy

Roppentyű

Béla

Országbíró

Béke

Szegedi út

Reiter Ferenc u.

Ungvár

Rákos-

Rákosrendező Pu.

patak

ZUGLÓ

Komócsy

u.

ÁRPÁD HID

Váci

Róbert Károly

Klapka u.

MARGIT-
SZIGET

Víztorony
(Water Tower)

MARGIT

DÓZSA GYÖRGY ÚT

Dózsa György

Nagy Lajos király

királyne

Kerékgyártó

Kövér Lajos

Nagy Lajos király

útja

(AND)

Szölkőkút
(Fountain)

Tüzér

Lehel

Szabolcs

Szépművészeti Múzeum
(Museum of Fine Arts)

Állatkert
(Zoological
Garden)

K. sétány

Kós

Dorozsmai

Erzsébet

Lumumba

Amerikai út

útja

Egressy

gret híd
gret Bridge)

LEHEL TÉR

Vác

Elmunkás híd

VÁROSLIGET

Hungária

Május 1.

Csömöri

út

Vigszinház
(Playhouse)

Szinyei M.

Baiza u.

útja

Dózsa György

Millenniumi emlékmű
(Monument)

Városligeti u.

Zugló V. M

NYUGATI PU.

Nyugati Pályaudvar
(West Station)

Szondi u.

Abonyi u.

Szugló

u. út

Néprajzi Múzeum
(Ethnographical Museum)

Lenin

Izabella

Nefelejcs

Népstadion

Mogyoródi

Országház
(Parliament)

Zsilinszky

út

Népköztársaság

Rottenbiller u.

Sándor

Egressy

Fogarasi

SUTH TÉR

szkj.

Thököly

Népstadion
(People's Stadium)

NÉPSTADION

út

ARANY JÁNOS U.

Bajcsy

Szt. István- bazilika
(St. Steven Bocilica)

KELETI PU.

Keleti Pályaudvar
(East Station)

út

Kerepesi

PILLANGÓ UTCA

chenyi
chid
ain Br.)

József Attila út

Majakov-

körút

Kerepesi

Asztalos Sándor

Stróbl Alajos
u.

Hős u.

Dcai István

Ugetöpalya
(Race Course)

DEÁK TÉR

Tanács

Wesselény

Zách

Belgrád

Váci u.

Rákóczi

krt.

BLAHA L. TÉR

Vas u.

Köztársaság
tér

KEREPESI
TEMETŐ

Ciprus u.

körút

út

ELSZABADULÁS TÉR

Sz s. út

ASTORIA

Múzeum krt.

Bródy Sándor u.

Népszinház

Karácsony Sándor

Józsefvárosi
Pályaudvar

Csilla u.

Kőbánya Felsö Pu.

Erzsébet híd
(Elisabeth Bridge)

KÁLVIN TÉR

Baross

József

u.

Kőbányai

zabadulási emlékmü
ration Monument)

Tolbuhin

Ráday

Üllöi

Iparművészeti Múzeum
(Artscraft Museum)

Práter u.

Kőris

Vajda Péter

körút

Horog

LÉRT-
GY

Szabadság híd
(Liberty Bridge)

FERENC KRT

Ferenc krt.

Berzs u.

KLINIKÁK

Üllöi

út

Mező

Imre

Elnök u.

út

Mányoki u.

Müegye-

Budafoki út

Budapesti Műszaki Egyetem
(Budapest Technical University)

Balázs Béla

Mester

NAGYVÁRAD TÉR

Mező

yves Kálmán

NÉPLIGET

Fertö

Karinthy Frigyes
út

Irny József u.

Petöfi híd

Soroksári

Hámán Kató

Kön u.

Mutatványos
tér

KÖBÁNYA

Schönherz Z.
u.

Bogdánfy u.

Duna

rakpart

Vaskapu u.

NÉPLIGET

Üllöi

Bihari

u.

Dombóvári út

Vágóhid u.

Könyves Kálmán

krt.

ECSERI ÚT

PÖTTYÖS U.

Szeremi

Budafoki

Ferencvárosi Pu.

Epreserdő

út

HATÁR ÚT

ELENFÖLD

Koppány u.

FERENCVÁROS

Ecseri

BUDAPEST

Those halcyon days when Budapest was romantically compared to Paris and life for the Western tourist was so cheap that even those with modest incomes could afford a meal in the best restaurants, with elegant waiters and live music, are a thing of the past. The fall of the iron curtain and the triumphant march of capitalism has turned most of the old stereotypes upside down and nowadays Budapest, with its plethora of 24-hour stores, street vendors, homeless people and wild honking traffic, is more reminiscent of New York.

Nightlife, which used to be restricted to a handful of clubs with corny entertainment, or a few bars that dared to remain open beyond midnight, has come alive. Places such as Tilos az A, offering cheap booze, light fare and alternative music and theatre until the small hours, have opened up.

There is a down side, too. The high cost of living, coupled with wages that are tailing inflation, have encouraged criminality; prostitution, illegal under the old system, has penetrated most districts. Budapest is sometimes referred to as the Bangkok of the West.

Yet some things never change. Budapest is the seat of government, the centre of Hungarian industry and commerce, the great turbine that powers the country. It remains the Mecca for provincial Hungarians looking for the yellow brick road on its weary pavements. It is the cultural heart of the nation, now improved through contacts with the world beyond. And it still possesses some of the late-19th century flair that attracts nostalgic Westerners. Artists of all types flock to certain cafés. As the grime of 40 years of neglect is removed from one monument after another, the great city of the days of the emperor and king is beginning to re-emerge. Budapest's famous humour is also making a comeback following several gloomy years in which the country shifted gear, and it is that humour that has enabled its citizens to weather the many storms.

The Mongols came raging through in 1241, followed by the Turks in 1541 and the Habsburgs in 1686. In 1848, the Hungarian revolution broke out in Budapest. In 1919, the Romanians marched in. During World War II, invasion came from Gestapo, the Wehrmacht, the Hungarian Nazis (Nyílas), and the Russians, whose tanks returned in 1956. In peace time, there were several occasions when the city flourished economically and culturally, for instance under Mátyás "Corvinus" Hunyádi (1458–90) or after the Compromise of 1867.

Buda: The city is actually composed of three historically independent communities, which were merged in 1872: Pest on the east bank of the Danube, and Buda and Óbuda on the west.

Preceding pages: painting in Serbian Orthodox church, Ráckeve; Mátyás Church reflected on the Hilton Hotel; Bishop Gellért watches over Buda and Pest. Left, fortress district. Right, the Lanchid or Chain Bridge.

The motorway route from the west to Budapest almost forcibly leads you to the Buda bank of the Danube, where **Castle Hill** and **Gellért Hill** rise up out of the city. If you follow the road at the foot of these hills along the Danube, you will arrive at the milestone in **Clark Adam tér** from which all distances in the country are measured. On the east side of the square the **Chain Bridge** (Lánchíd) leads to Pest, and on the west side a tunnel goes through the Castle Hill. An antique-looking cable car – *budavári sikló* – overcomes the difference in height between river bank and Castle Hill in a few minutes. You can also go up on foot via countless steps and little stairways. Once at the top, you will be well rewarded for the rigours of the steep climb.

From Castle Hill, the eye is drawn to the Danube and its bridges – you can see almost all of them from here – the white cruise vessels, Margaret Island

on the left, the imposing Parliament building on the Pest bank with its greenish-brown dome, and on the river promenade, the "Corso", three conspicuous and modern luxury hotels. Pest spreads out like the sea to the usually misty horizon.

The first castle in Budapest was built on the southern part of the Castle Hill in the early Middle Ages (1255) by Béla, after Pest had been ravaged by the Mongols. It was destroyed several times—in the Turkish wars, during the revolution of 1848–49 and in World War II – and rebuilt. Today it houses several museums.

Mátyás Church: The north side of the central east wing of the castle is adorned by the famous King Mátyás Cascade by Alajos Stróbl – a fountain which shows King Mátyás hunting. Next to it is the Lion Gate. The centre of Castle Hill is dominated by **Mátyás Church** (*Mátyás templom*), built in 1255–69. Originally called the Church

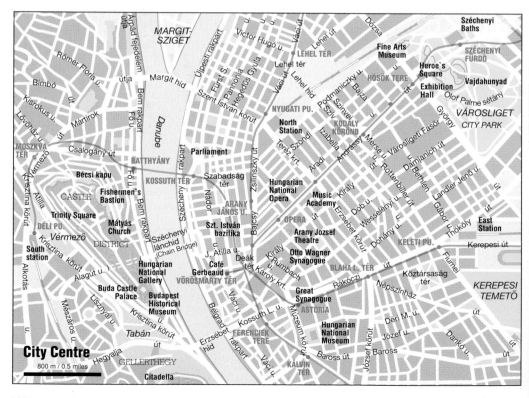

of Our Lady, its popular name comes from King Mátyás (Matthew), who, during his reign (1458–70), extended and decorated it. Its present-day appearance dates from the renovation of 1873–96. The raven which can be seen above the church is a reminder of Mátyás, whose nickname "Corvinus" came from the symbol on his coat of arms (*corvinus*=raven).

Only a little light penetrates the dark-coloured windows of the church. Once your eyes have adjusted to the light, you will see the exquisitely decorated pillars, walls and ceilings. There are stone capitals in the crypt and gallery of the church, statues of saints, monstrances, reliquaries and ceremonial robes. The robe embroidered by the popular Empress Sissy (Elizabeth) on the death of her son can be seen, as can a piece of her platinum-embroidered wedding veil. Unfortunately, at the time of writing, there were no foreign language descriptions for the exhib-its, so you are advised to ask one of the elderly women who take care of the treasures and who are only too willing to impart information.

Around the church there is a fairground atmosphere. Hundreds of tourists from a myriad of countries stroll among the historic sites and the souvenir stalls. In front of Mátyás Church, the Fishermen's Bastion (Halász-bástya) rears up. It is a *fin de siècle* monument to the brave fishermen who defended Buda in the Middle Ages, and is one of the most popular subjects for photographers. Behind the Fishermen's Bastion the Miklós Tower, a late-Gothic remnant of a former Dominican church, forms part of the glass façade of the Hilton Hotel. The successful integration of this historic monument into a modern hotel complex results in a delightful contrast, further strengthened by the reflections and distortions of the Fishermen's Bastion in the glass façade.

Parliament Building, dominating the Pest bank.

The **Vienna Gate** (Bécsi kapu) forms the northern boundary of Castle Hill, offering a good view of the Buda hills. The square in front of it (Bécsi kapu tér) is dominated by the mighty building of the **Hungarian State Archives**. In the nearby Kapisztrán tér is the Gothic **Magdalene Tower**, which belonged to the Church of Mary Magdalene, and which was ruined by bombs in 1944–45. Today it houses an art gallery.

On the eastern edge is the approximately half-mile long Bastion promenade (Tóth Árpád sétány), along which you can see cannons and mortars dating back several centuries.

The streets and alleys to the north and east of Castle Hill are decidedly peaceful when compared to the lively crowds around Mátyás Church and the Fishermen's Bastion. The houses are almost all jewels of classical or baroque style. It is almost always worthwhile peeking into their doorways and courtyards; often you can find medieval parts of the buildings here, such as Gothic alcoves. This has always been a popular place to live, and nearly every house here has been lovingly restored at some time, but today those who live here are mainly members of the government.

There are many cafés and restaurants inviting you to take a rest, in particular the famous pâtisserie, **Ruszwurm** (Ruszwurm cukrászda). The dining room, decorated throughout in the Biedermeier style, is small, but with a bit of luck you can find a seat on the worn green plush upholstery. Ruszwurm is the oldest *cukrászda* in Budapest, but its cakes and gateaux are always fresh.

Gellért Hill: You can also climb Gellért Hill via steps and snaking paths, along which you will pass the monument (1902) to Bishop Gellért, who was thrown from this point into the Danube by pagans in 1046.

The Fishermen's Bastion

The summit is crowned by the **Citadel**, built by the Habsburgs after the suppression of the revolution of 1848–49. The barracks, where German troops made a desperate last stand in 1945, today boasts a restaurant with 1,500 seats and a big hotel. Bullet marks in the walls are signs of the final throes of the struggle.

The Liberation Monument, hallmark of Budapest, rises before the walls of the Citadel. This reminder of the liberation of Hungary from German occupation was created by the Communist government but was originally commissioned by the Regent Horthy in memory of his son who died in an accident.

At the foot of Gellért Hill, right by the Pest entrance to the Liberty Bridge, is the famous **Gellért** hotel and spa. It is a veritable temple of bathers, with its pillars, mosaics and domes of coloured glass. The place has a sophisticated atmosphere, everything is in excellent and expensive taste. Several women keep a strict eye out for anyone without an entrance ticket trying to get a glimpse of the bathers. Things are quite different in the nearby **Rác** baths. Here the passage of time has left noticeable traces, and there is no sign of any previous glories or splendours. Helpful bath attendants offer you special bathing shoes and usher you into the hot and humid vaults where half-naked bathers relax and soothe their bodies in hot pools.

Pest: Cross the **Liberty Bridge** (Szabadság híd) and the way on the Pest bank leads to the University of Economics. In the vicinity, the **Market Hall** (between Vám ház körút and Sóház/Pipa utca) is an attraction in itself, it's a steel-framed brick building dates from the end of the last century. Here you will find all kinds of fresh vegetables, pulses and meat. The display of plenty is surprising and worth seeing, but above all it is the

Statue to commemorate the joining of Buda and Pest.

peddlers who give the place its unique atmosphere.

Instead of using the Liberty Bridge, you can also cross from Buda to Pest on the Chain Bridge, whose conception goes back to Count István Széchenyi. It was inaugurated in 1849. Roosevelt tér is the Pest bridgehead. To your left is the **Hungarian Science Academy**, another brainchild of Széchenyi built in neo-Renaissance style in 1862-65, after the count's death. The right hand side of the square is occupied by the glass and concrete Atrium-Hyatt and Intercontinental hotels. If you follow the axis of the Chain Bridge, the József Attila út, and turn left, you will come to **St Stephen's Basilica** (Szent István bazilika). Building work was begun in 1851 but the dome collapsed in 1868. The basilica was completed between 1873 and 1905 under the direction of Miklós Ybl, who was also responsible for the **State Opera House**. The mosaics in this gigantic dome are by Károly Lotz, the figure of St Stephen on the high altar is by Alajos Stróbl, two extremely prolific artists whose names recur continuously not only in Budapest but in much of Hungary as well.

Wending one's way northwards through the pompous streets of Lipótváros (Leopold city), one reaches Szabadság tér, site of Hungarian Television, the American embassy (where the rebel Cardinal Mindszenty lived in exile between 1956 and 1971), and a monument to the Red Army. Just beyond the latter looms the central dome of the Parliament which, at 315 feet (96 metres) , is exactly the same height as the cupola of the basilica, not a coincidence some say: secular and religious power in the country are thus equal. On closer inspection this neo-Gothic edifice reveals itself as being immense, especially considering the size of the country it serves. It is 879 feet (268 metres) long, 380 feet

Portraits for sale, Vörösmarty tér.

PORTRÉ

(116 metres) at its widest point, and there are allegedly 12 miles (20 km) of staircases inside. The exterior walls are decorated with 233 statues; internally, and the numerous frescoes were produced by some of Hungary's most important artists, including Mihály Munkácsy and the afore-mentioned, indefatigable Karoly Lotz.

The Parliament was the work of the late-19th century architect, Imre Steindl. Construction began in 1884 and officially ended in 1904, whereby one should mention that air pollution and extreme weather has meant almost continuous repairs to the limestone building. That is why at least one part of it always seems to be shrouded in scaffolding. Guided tours can usually be arranged through most tourist offices.

Kossuth tér, where Parliament stands, is in itself an impressive sight. Two statues in the middle show Lajos Kossuth, leader of the 1848–49 revo-lution and (on horseback) Ferenc Rákóczi II, who led the ill-fated War of Independence (1703–11). To the north and south of the Parliament respectively are the statues of Count Mihály Károly, and the poet József Attila.

Shopping fever: Between József Attila út and Kossuth Lajos út lies the main shopping area of Budapest, most of it a pedestrian precinct. **Vörösmarty tér**, the square dedicated to the most important romantic poet, is filled with countless local people and tourists, street artists (musicians, clowns, breakdancers and portrait artists) and pigeons. The bustle of the crowd is infectious, money for the street artist is easily parted with and several dishonest black-market money-changers find rich and easy pickings among the unwary few.

The **Váci utca**, centre of the Budapest shopping district, begins at Vörösmarty tér. It is a chic street, not just

with regards to the architecture. Everyone is kept busy here with the commercial activity of fashion boutiques, travel agents, perfumeries, cafés, restaurants. Here stand Hungarian temples of consumerism in the most modern style, elegant department stores, boutiques with the most fashionable clothes. For those with hard currency it is all relatively inexpensive. And there are Western shops as well: window-shoppers regularly flock to the Salamander shoe shop or line up for hours outside the jammed Adidas store. Near a Hungarian fast-food place offering genuine Hungarian hamburgers made of pork with paprika, McDonald's peddles its standard fare while at the same time helping to confront the visitor with Budapest's typical east-west melange of scarcity, long queues and consumer fever.

The shopping continues on Kossuth u. at the end of Váci u. and then carries on as far as the Eastern Railway Station on Rákóczi út. The department stores of Blaha Lujza tér are always full of Hungarians, which for someone exploring city life is quite an experience (just to the left of the main avenue you will find the famous **New York,** or Café Hungaria as it used to be known). Should you make it as far as the station, go the extra few steps to the **Kerepesi Cemetery** (*temetö*), the nation's final resting place for VIPs and IPs.

Kossuth u. intersects with Múzeum and Karoly körút at the old Astoria hotel. The **National Museum** (*Nemzéti Múzeum*) is to the right, and Budapest's old and slightly ramshackled Jewish quarter begins beyond Károly körút. The recently restored **Great Synagogue** on Dohány u. was built in the 1850s by the Viennese architect, Ludwig Foerster, and has a seating capacity of 6,000. The little Jewish museum in the front section unfortunately fell victim to an extensive rob-

Cyclists in Heroes' Square.

146

bery in 1993. A very moving memorial to the victims of the Nazi porams stands behind the synagogue, a weeping willow of metal on whose leaves are engraved the names of the dead and missing. Károly körút continues to Deák tér, the traffic hub of the city, and shortly thereafter begins Andrássy út, Budapest's 1½-mile (2.5-km) long showy thoroughfare.

Culture fever: The broad **Andrássy út** saw the construction from 1844–75 of the Hungarian State Opera House. The entrance faces the statues of Franz Liszt and Ferenc Erkel, composer of the "national" opera *Bánk Bán*. All this splendour was supposed to show the Austrian rulers of the time who had the last word in cultural matters. A great variety of small and colourful theatres have sprung up in the vicinity of the Opera House: Mikroszkóp, Thália, Vidám, Radnóti; the Fövárosi Operetta House which offers "family entertainment"; right next door to the Moulin Rouge with its cheeky (and expensive) revues. In Jókai tér is a puppet theatre for young and old.

Let's be serious: The Millennial Monument in **Heroes' Square** (Hösök tér) marks the end of the Népköztársaság útja. It was built in 1896 to mark the millennial celebrations commemorating the conquest by the Magyars, and shows, on a pillar 118 feet (36 metres) high, the Archangel Gabriel, surrounded by tribal chiefs at the foot of the pillar, with their leader Árpád in the centre. The significance of the monument is underlined by the Tomb of the Unknown Soldier, watched throughout the day by two poker-faced soliders, in front of the pillar and the statues of Hungarian kings, princes and statesmen right behind it. There they all stand in a semicircular row of columns, from St István to János Hunyádi and Lajos Kossuth, and look down doubtfully on the giant square filled with tourists, acrobatic roller-

Winter fun in the park.

skaters, teenage skateboarders and cyclists.

The area around the Millennial Monument offers many opportunities for entertainment and relaxation. Behind the Museum of the Visual Arts is a large park, the **City Park** (Város-liget), the biggest park in the city. At its northwestern edge, right next to the entrance to the **Zoo**, the famous restaurant **Gundel** still retains a touch of the old elegance of times past. This is the birthplace of the well-known delicious thin pancakes *á la Gundel*, which you find throughout Hungary. The luxury establishment has survived all the city's troubles and maintained an excellent reputation. However, a visit to the Gundel, one of the oldest restaurants in Budapest, can be quite costly.

Those with a smaller budget may want to console themselves over missed culinary opportunities at the **Vidám Park's** year-round amusement park. Another way of spending a few

pleasant hours is in the thermal waters of **Széchényi Baths**, a stupendous neo-baroque complex with an outdoor pool and full spa facilities. Here the water rises from a depth of 4,121 feet (1,256 metres) and feeds steam baths, hot baths and saunas.

The romantic castle of **Vajda-hunyad** stands on an artificial island in the middle of Stadtwoldchen's pond, where you can boat in summer and ice-skate in winter. By the way, you don't have to swim across the lake in summer, as there are bridges to the island that guarantee dry feet. The castle, an architectural cross-section of Hungary with a strong Transyl-vanian flavour, houses in one part a museum of agriculture. The castle itself is a copy of the former palace of János Hunyadi in Vajdahunyad, now in Romania. All the other parts of the castle are copies of historic Hungarian buildings, giving rise to this imposing mixture of kitsch and opulence.

Exhibits in the Museum of Applied Arts.

Opposite the Parliament and still on Lajos Kossuth tér, is the neo-baroque **Ethnographic Museum** (Néprajzi Múzeum), built between 1893 and 1896 as the seat of the Royal Court. The neo-classical building next door still serves an important political function: it houses the Ministry of Food and Agriculture.

Between the Margaret and the Árpád Bridges, in the greyish-brown Danube, lies the famous **Margaret Island** (Margitsziget), an almost exotic world apart, which has inspired poets and philosophers, composers and kings to perform great deeds. You can only reach the island by car from the Árpád Bridge; otherwise it is closed to private motorists. Buses are the only motorised traffic on the island, otherwise use a horse-drawn trap or bicycle to get around.

The most noticeable building, due to its height of 187 feet (57 metres), is the **Water Tower** above the open-air stage. In the tower of a restored Premonstratensian church with a south wall and windows dating from the 12th century hangs one of the oldest bells in Hungary (14th/15th century). It was found in 1914 under a tree uprooted by a storm.

A little further to the south are the ruins of a convent of Dominican nuns. King Béla IV had it built after the Mongol invasion of 1241. He placed his daughter Margaret there, to be brought up as a nun fulfilling a vow for deliverance from the Mongol purge. The island, previously known as Hare Island, was named after her. There is further evidence of the past near the centre of the island, south of the Rose Garden – the ruins of a 13th-century Franciscan church.

This, the largest park in Budapest, is just as interesting for nature lovers and sports fans as for those interested in historic buildings. The former can enjoy tulips, acacias, weeping wil-

Frescoes by Károly Lotz, National Museum.

lows and chestnut trees as well as several botanical gardens. In the Japanese Garden, a hot spring steams away above an artificial cliff. In the Rose Garden, there isn't a rose in the world that's missing, or so they say. Sports enthusiasts will find swimming pools, well-kept tennis courts and boathouses, as well as many opportunities for jogging.

Turks and Romans: If you leave Margaret Island at its southern end via the Margaret Bridge and go back to Buda, don't miss two reminders of Hungary's Turkish past. Near the Buda bridgehead, on Turbán ut/Mecset utca, is the **Tomb of Gül Baba**, a famous dervish known as "Father of Roses" because he brought roses to Hungary. The small park surrounding his simple tomb has been planted with roses.

In Fö utca 82–84, are the **Király Baths**, built by the Turks in 1556. Under the four squat green domes, the tallest crowned by a golden crescent, is an octagonal pool at the top of four flights of steps. You can also trace Buda's Roman past with a visit to the military and civilian amphitheatres on the corner of Korvin Otto út/ Nagyszombat út and behind the railway underpass on Szentendrei út, respectively. Even more interesting are the ruins of the Roman civilian town of Aquincum with their museum. It was built on the site of a Celtic settlement in 1 BC. Finds from the excavations can be seen in the museum; the most precious are the bronze parts of a water organ. The houses of Óbuda are not as old, but they also bear witness to the past. In this rather poor area the houses are small and pressed together, the walls have blackened over the years. Street battles of the 20th century and the passage of time have left their marks.

Behind the entrance portals are unrestored backyards and courtyards. Yet the more human architecture of **City transport.**

the old apartment blocks enables greater social contact than in the conspicuously monotonous housing projects on the city fringe. Here grey anonymity rules, while in the older houses a village-like community life is possible. People swap news across the courtyards, babysit for their neighbour's offspring, dry their washing amid odours from the kitchen below, while grannies and pet canaries keep one another company on the balconies. A close look will uncover hidden delights: little statues, tiles, wrought iron work, the careful marking of flood levels and elaborate stucco and mosaic work.

Museums: There are many museums in the city – from the **Pharmaceutical Museum** (Tárnok útca) to the **Transport Museum** (Városliget körút), and they offer national and international, historical and modern collections. There are three museums in the Castle alone: the **Ludwig Collection**, a comprehensive display of contemporary art, the **Hungarian National Gallery** (*Magyar Nemzeti Galéria*) in the wings B, C and D, and the **Budapest Historical Museum** (*Budapesti Történeti Múzeum*) in wing E.

In the **National Gallery** are works by Hungarian painters, graphic artists and sculptors, from the Middle Ages to the present; the Gothic altars are particularly worth a visit. If you want to buy the works of living Hungarian artists, contact the Art Gallery in Táncsics utca 5, which is not far from the castle.

In the **Historical Museum** you can see some remains of the medieval royal castle. The vaults reveal the impressive walls of the dungeon and the castle church (don't miss the sanctuary of the castle chapel dating from the 14th century). Here you will find the Gothic statues from medieval Buda, and ceramic-tiled stoves of the 14th and 15th centuries.

Budapest passer-by.

Táncsics utca no. 7 is the **Music History Museum** (Zenetörténi Múzeum) which contains, apart from many historic instruments (most impressive is a 1790 Parisian pedal harp, decoratively carved and painted), a Bártok exhibition and a coin collection.

The **Hungarian National Museum** (Múzeum körút 14–16) was founded in 1802 by Ferenc Széchenyi. The neo-classical building was built by Viennese architect Michael Pollak (Mihály Pollák in Hungarian) and completed between 1837 and 1847. Its gigantic pillared hall, the massive chandeliers and the wide staircases make it worth visiting for the architecture alone.

But the wonderfully rich and varied collections are the real reason for visiting the museum. They have recently been completely reorganised to form a permanent exhibition of compelling interest entitled "The History of the Hungarian State – from the Foundation of the State up to the 20th century". There are jewels, craft work, furniture, arms and armour, paintings, garments, posters, films, even a piece of the "Iron Curtain", all splendidly displayed. Also on show, under strict guard, are **St Stephen's Crown**, the coronation mantle, the royal sceptre, the orb and the sword. The crown and insignia were returned to Hungary in 1978 by the US government. They were stolen by the Wehrmacht at the end of World War II and eventually reappeared in the US.

The **Museum of Applied and Decorative Arts** (Iparmüvészeti Múzeum), Ullöi út 33 is an architectural jewel of the turn of the century built by Ödön Lechner. Its exhibits offer a good impression of Hungary's handicrafts, from faience and ceramics, to embroidery, leatherwork and marquetry.

One of the most important museums in the world is the **Museum of Fine Arts** (Szépmüvészeti Múzeum),

Restaurant on Margaret Island

Dózsa György út 41 – a vaguely neo-classical, eclectic building designed by Albert Schickedanz and Fülöp Herzog. There are Egyptian, Greek and Roman collections, together with collections of modern sculpture and drawings. The paintings on the first floor provide an opportunity for tourists to see works by almost all the well-known artists from the 13th to the 19th century. Opposite, on the other side of Heroes' Square, is the **Art Gallery**, where monthly exhibitions show modern works of art.

You should take a look at the Ethnographic Museum, Kossuth Lajos tér 12, if only because of its architecture (pillared hall several storeys high, beautiful stained glass windows, ceiling frescos). Apart from objects from Hungarian peasant life, the collections also include relics of non-European tribes.

Although Budapest has a wealth of interesting sights to offer, the most important part of the town is not large, in contrast to the entire city area, which occupies 12,850 acres (5,200 hectares). If you have fairly strong legs and comfortable shoes, you should be able to visit many areas. The excellent public transport system links all parts of the city cheaply and efficiently and is an invaluable aid to exploration, though it is best to avoid the rush hour. There are plenty of taxis too, though they are no longer as inexpensive as they once were.

The Metro was the first underground on the mainland of Europe, built to model that of London, and opened just in time for the 1896 millennial celebrations. There are three lines: line 1 from Vörösmarty tér to Heroes' Square and under the City Park, line 2 going east from the South Station in Buda (Déli pályaudvar) under the Danube, and line 3 which goes in a north–south direction from Árpád Bridge to Kispest.

Liberation Bridge.

COFFEE HOUSES

Once upon a time, Budapest was known as the "city of coffee-houses". After the turn of the century, astute business people opened coffee-houses one after another, and coffee merchants, speculators and adventurers did not shrink from investing their money in such enterprises. This was where the literary circle met.

Poets penned their verses, joined by journalists, actors, small-time singers and operetta starlets. Southern cattle-traders and street-walkers came to listen. On the tables, in the famous bamboo racks, were dozens of newspapers and journals. Friendly, quick and efficient waiters served coffee, soda water, and eggs for breakfast.

Unfortunately, this eclectic and opulent coffee-house world of the art nouveau era has almost completely disappeared. The only genuine coffee-house still functioning today is the **New York** – on the ground floor of the **Press Building** in the **Elisabeth Ring** (Erzsébet körút). It opened in 1894 and has retained the splendour of the turn of the century despite having been rebuilt several times. Frescoes and mirrors adorn the walls, as do portraits of the artists who patronised the place, and drawings of the literary society that once met here.

Something of the same feeling can be found in the spacious surroundings of the café in the venerable **Astoria Hotel**, once the haunt of political plotters and shady functionaries.

At No. 29 Andrássy út is the **Café Müvész** (Artists' Cafe). It is the most splendid of those coffee-houses that have survived along the lower part of the radial road, the one with the most patina. Artists from the opera house opposite, elderly retired bankers and respectable old ladies visit the rooms

Elegance from a former era.

154

of this coffee-house, furnished with sculptures and adorned with mirrors.

If you reach Vörösmarty Square, haunt of street musicians, via the old Metro route, you will arrive at the entrance to one of the most elegant and historic coffee-houses in the city – the **Gerbeaud**. The first coffee-house by this name was founded in 1858. Now, restored to its former glory, the coffee-house has splendid examples of art and craft,plus masterpieces of interior decoration and period furniture.

Often spelled "Zserbó" in the Hungarian fashion, this coffee-house and pâtisserie is a popular meeting place for the remainder of the former upper middle classes, for the groups of new entrepreneurs with their clipped hair, snazzy briefcases and mobile phones, for Hungarians from the West who return for a visit or to live, and, nowadays, for foreigners hungry for local fare and house specialities.

The service may not always match up to the atmosphere or the utterly delightful cakes, but an afternoon in the Gerbeaud will give a better insight into Hungarian life than many a tour down a damp and unfamiliar street.

In the 1930s, the increasing tendency towards functional architecture was reflected in a series of elegant and generously proportioned cafés, but over the years they have been either redecorated or closed.

The capital of Hungary was also praised as the city of *eszpressós*. From the 1930s, one *eszpressó* after another opened its doors and by the 1950s, many new establishments joined the first-generation *eszpressós*. They included Mocca, American, Parisien, Joker, Intim and Darling. The *eszpressós* gave the city a singular flair. Nevertheless, the trend to use catchy English names came to an end. In neon lights, above the new *eszpressós* revolutionary names reminiscent of radical slogans Plan, Prosperity, Spartacus appeared.

These *eszpressós* of the post-war years still exist. However, little remains of the 1950s style. The red and green neon lights have gone, and so too have the little coffee cups and the lemonade.The best places to recapture something of their atmosphere are the **Ibolya eszpresszó** on Ferenciek tere 4 and the **Majakovszkij** on Király utca 103 in the 7th District.

Buda has its share of classic coffee-houses. **Ruszwurm**, rather too close for comfort to the Hilton Hotel, is a tiny establishment in an old building on Szentharomság utca. Inevitably, and because of its convenient location, Ruszwurm has become something of a tourist trap, still basking in the fame of its pastries which were once delivered to connoisseurs in far-off Vienna.

At the foot of Castle Hill, in the parish room of St Anne's Church on Battyhány tér, **Angelika** is a haven for locals and visitors alike.

ost-war
szpressó.

PRESSZÓKÁVÉ

AROUND BUDAPEST

As for trips into the countryside around Budapest – after three days at the most of "serious" sightseeing, the soul longs to relax, the lungs long for fresh air and the feet are tired of asphalt. The area around Budapest has plenty to attract the visitor – delightful landscape, art and culture, flora and fauna. There are so many things worth seeing that you will need to make a selection.

Lake resorts: leave Budapest on the M7 motorway (Route E96) in a south-westerly direction. The drive to Székesfehérvár – 32 miles (50km) or so – leads through hilly countryside, meadows, orchards and vineyards.

In Érd, on the outskirts of Budapest, is one of three minarets, evidence of the former occupation of Hungary by the Turks. Just before Székesfehérvár, on the left, is **Velencei tó**, a lake which achieves its characteristic appearance from its many reed beds. On the southern shore are a number of water resorts.

Székesfehérvár is one of the oldest towns in Hungary, and one of those rich in tradition. The former Roman settlement of Gorsium, to the south, served as the spiritual centre for Pannonia early in the first millennium AD. Árpád, leader of the conquering Magyars, camped here after crossing the Danube. His descendant, St Stephen (István I), chose Székesfehérvár to be his residence (1000–38) and had the royal basilica built in 1016. For almost 500 years it remained the place where Hungarian kings were crowned and buried. Gradually, Buda gained political significance, but the mythical aura of Székesfehérvár remains to this day, despite destruction and industrialisation, and despite the constant flow of heavy pedestrian and vehicular traffic.

Székesfehérvár's present-day im-

Preceding pages: headquarters of the pioneering Danube Steamship Company Below, angler at Lake Velence.

portance lags far behind its medieval status. However, this town is still impressive and you can still feel something of the spirit of history, especially as the shape and size of the medieval town remain unchanged to this day. The great majority of the buildings were destroyed during the Turkish occupation and only one of interest, St Anne's Church, remains. Not all the churches, the baroque buildings, the well-arranged museums and the narrow streets can overcome the bitterness felt about the orgy of destruction that must have swept through the town.

Town centre attractions: In the centre, which is closed to traffic most of the time, is the main square **Szabadság tér** (Freedom Square). From here, via the narrow, rising streets, you can reach the heart of the town, the square of Prince Géza. Here is the Gothic **Chapel of St Anne** (1470) mentioned above, the only surviving medieval building in Székesfehérvár. Next to it lies the **Cathedral**, founded by King Béla IV. In both towers you can still see parts of the Gothic windows. A Byzantine church once stood in the middle of the square; today only an outline remains in the pavement.

Go back to Szabadság tér, once dominated by the mighty royal basilica. It is hard to repress a slight shudder when standing on the ground of the ruins of what was the most important building in medieval Hungary. Nowadays, the southwestern tower of the basilica lies under the fountain in the square, the transepts are under the road. In the **Garden of Ruins** (Romkert) behind the square, the apse, a few pillars and the tomb of King István I can still be seen.

To the southern side of the square stands the town hall, its main entrance adorned with the figures of Justitia and Prudentia. The unclothed equestrian figure facing it is a memorial to

Bishop's Palace in Székesfehérvár.

the Hussars. Opposite the town hall is the **Hiemer House** (Jókai u. 1), which has stood here since the beginning of the 18th century. It has particularly delicate rococo stucco work and a bay window, but is in need of restoration. Close by is a baroque Franciscan church (1720–42) with its monastery buildings. The eastern side of the square is bounded by the **Bishop's Palace** (1800–01) one of the most notable buildings of the period.

To the north of the square, in Március 15 út, is the baroque **Cistercian Church** with its two towers and its monastery buildings. It was built from 1745 to 1751 by the Jesuits and is well worth visiting. After the dissolution of the latter order in 1773, the church passed into the hands of the Pauline monks, and from 1813 on, it has belonged to the Cistercians. Unique in Hungary, the furnishing of the sacristy is carved out of oak and lime wood and dates from between 1754 and 1767. You can enter the sacristy from the side entrance to the church in **St John's Passage** (János köz). This architectural treasure survived World War II thanks to the parish priest of the time. He protected the sacristy with sandbags, even at the cost of damage to the nave. Opposite this church, on the other side of the street, is the **Black Eagle Pharmacy** (Fekete Sas Patika), a pharmaceutical museum with baroque carved furnishings (1758). The oldest of the medicine jars on view dates back to Jesuit times.

The Lake: Follow highway No. 70 and leave Székesfehérvár in the direction of Velencei tó. Rare water birds live in the reed beds and islands, and because of them the area is a nature reserve. The lake is a paradise for fishing. There are carp and eels, sometimes catfish. In the summer boat trips leave the Touring Hotel in Agárd almost every hour. The lake, "grandchild of Balaton" to the Hungarians, is very shallow and the water warms up quickly in summer. The two most popular resorts on the southern coast are **Agárd** and **Gárdony**.

Travelling on to Budapest, don't miss a visit to Martonvásár. In this beautiful little palace Beethoven was often a guest of the Brunswick family. The park is believed to have inspired his composition *Moonlight Sonata*, which he wrote here, and a blackbird is said to have "whispered" the theme of the third movement of the *Violin Concerto* to his ear. There is also a small Beethoven museum in the palace, which has now become an agricultural research institute of the Hungarian Academy of Sciences.

A trip to the south: If you want to leave Budapest from the south, you should avoid the two major roads M5 (motorway in the direction of Kecskemét) and E15 (No. 4, in the direction of Szolnok). To get to know the countryside, minor roads are a better bet, as long as they are marked on the map and tarmacked. Apart from horse-

Székesfehérvár's Garden of Ruins.

160

drawn carts, you hardly meet another vehicle on these roads which are often so narrow that a centre line would be ineffective. It is so peaceful that often the chirping of birds is the only sound to be heard. This area marks the start of the famous Nagyalföld, the Great Plain. In the village of **Ocsa**, many straw-thatched houses cluster around a mighty basilica dating from 1560. A stork's nest crowns a telephone pole.

Here the local people have a darker complexion than their counterparts in Budapest. Middle-aged female peasants wearing headscarves and gumboots cycle past, and the farmers ride horse-drawn carts along the sandy side of the road.

Further south, to the east of Apaj, you can still find the "genuine" puszta, quite flat and with steppe-like vegetation and the famous wells. Scattered across this region are herds of sheep and goats, and you could meet a proud horseman in traditional finery.

Gödöllö and Hatvan: For this excursion, leave Budapest in a north-easterly direction on the motorway M3. After 19 miles (30km) you will reach Gödöllö with its baroque palace. This palace, built in 1744–50 for Prince Grassalkovich, was presented by the Hungarian government to the Habsburgs, who used it as a summer residence from 1867 to 1918. In this spacious palace (currently under restoration) the Empress Elizabeth ("Sissi") recovered from the Viennese court life that she found so unpleasant.

Near the palace chapel, which today serves as the parish church, a memorial for the dead of World War I has been built. After a long period of degradation, during which time outbuildings were used by the Soviet army and the palace itself was converted into an old people's home, restoration is at last taking place. Much of the palace can now be seen in its former glittering state and there are plans to restore

View of Székesfehérvár

the extensive parkland to its original glory.

Diagonally opposite, in the inner courtyard of one building, a weekly market is held. Here you can study the difference between the big city and the countryside. Most of the produce on sale is grown by the farmers themselves, and the neighbouring stalls offer home-made bottled fruit and concentrated fruit juice as well as hand-carved wooden spoons.

Gödöllö is also the seat of a famous **Agricultural College** – you can find it in the middle of the industrial area situated within the splendid buildings of the former Premonstratensian school. On the way out of the town, to the left in the direction of Hatvan, the road leads past a baroque church. Along the footpath leading to the church the Stations of the Cross are depicted, and at the start of this path you pass through a carved and painted gate. A sign by the church warns of the danger of the building collapsing. There is a small chapel in the cellar, underneath the nave of the church, which is decorated with many bright, colourful ceiling frescoes.

After six miles (10km) you come to **Aszód**, which had own baroque palace (1767–72), that is also in danger of collapsing. The palace dates back to the Podmaniczky family, who produced several mayors of Budapest in the 1800s. Nowadays it is used as a garage, workshop and storehouse and is not open to visitors. On the hill above is a small baroque church.

In front of the palace a sign points to the right to the museum, but if you hope to find information about the palace or its former inhabitants, you will be disappointed. The former schoolhouse (1771) has been used to house the **Petöfi Museum**. The famous Hungarian poet Sándor Petófi (1823–49) went to school here between 1835 and 1838. Inside the mu-

Some of the country's 3 million sheep.

seum, the story of the town of Aszód is told from prehistoric to medieval times. Extracts on the economic and social development of the region, costumes from the area and documents from Petófi's life are also on show.

A third palace, also in the same condition, is to be found in **Hatvan**, 34 miles (55km) from Budapest. However, the park around it is fenced off, so little can be seen from the outside. This palace also goes back to the Grassalkovich family. Marriage put it into the hands of the Hatvány family, whose roots go back to the times of King Mátyás, and after whom the town is now called.

Budapest – Tata: Leave Budapest in a northwesterly direction along the motorway in the direction of Tata. On the way, you could make a short diversion via **Zsámbék**, with its Romanesque church and monastery ruins dating back to the 13th century. The church's two towers have be-

Storks are both valued and protected.

come a focal point in the area. Just before Tata is **Vértesszölös**, the oldest and most extensive excavation site of a prehistoric settlement in Hungary. It was here in 1963 that the bones of the pre-human archanthropus were discovered in a former quarry. Their bones, tools, the animals they hunted, and the remains of their campfires are all exhibited in an open-air museum.

Tata, a charming town with many springs and lakes, was already a summer resort for King Zsigmond and King Mátyás. Along the Öreg-tó, (the Old Lake) which is endowed with warm springs, lies a large park with the church ruins of Vértesszentkereszt, dating from the 13th century. Ruins of the **Öregvár** (Old Castle), dating from the 14th and 15th centuries, can also be seen by the lake. The castle was destroyed by the Turks and by the Austrians. Its restored rooms house the Kuny Domokos Museum which has a collection of ceramics which will please lovers of faience. In Kossuth tér is a mid-18th century church with two towers, and a former palace belonging to the Esterházy family and dating from 1769, off Rákóczi u., today serves as a wing of the municipal hospital.

On the other side of the lake, on Ady Endre u., is the baroque Miklós Mill, dating from 1770 and built by Jakob Fellner. It houses the Museum of Ethnic Minorities' ethnographic exhibition revealing the life, history and handiwork of the various nationalities (notably Germans) who have settled in the region over the centuries.

For the trip back to Budapest, travel along highway No. 10 to gain an impression of **Tatabánya**, a mining town which supplies almost half of Hungary's demand for lignite. From the top of a hill a great bronze bird surveys the town: it is the *turul*, a legendary hybrid of eagle and falcon that allegedly guided the Magyars into the Carpathian Basin.

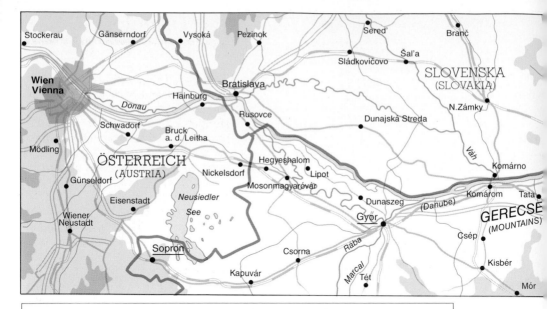

THE DANUBE

Hungarian name: Duna.
Length: 1,775 miles (2,857km), second longest river in Europe after the Volga.
Drainage area: 315,446 sq. miles (817,000 sq. km).
Source: Confluence of the rivers Breg and Brigach, both rising in the Black Forest, at Donaueschingen (Germany).
Mouth: On the Black Sea near Izmail through a wide delta, which lies mainly in Romania and also in the Ukraine.
Countries on the banks: Germany, Austria, Slovakia, Hungary, Serbia, Romania, Bulgaria and Ukraine.
Tributaries: More than 300 including Iller, Lech, Isar, Inn, Wörnitz, Altmühl, Naab, Regen (Germany), Traun, Enns, Leitha (Austria); Váh (Slovakia), Rába (Hungary), Drava, Tisza, Sava (Serbia), Iskar (Bulgaria), Olt, Siret, Prut (Romania).
Industry: Because of its shallowness, the Danube is not as suitable as the Rhine for heavy transport. Before World War II, quantities of grain were transported up the Danube to Western Europe from Hungary, Yugoslavia and mostly from Romania. Once into Romania, traffic on the river is much greater. There are several huge hydro-electric power stations along the banks, including the vast Gabčíkovo-Nagymaros scheme, a source of dispute between Hungary and Slovakia because of its environmental impact. Ever since

the completion of the Rhine–Main–Danube Canal in the early 1990s, Rotterdam has been linked with the Black Sea.
History: As early as 7th century BC, Greek sailors reached the lower Danube and began a brisk trade. Later, the river formed the northern border of the Roman Empire, with its military camps Vindabona (Vienna), Aquincum (Budapest) and Singidunum (Belgrade). The Ottoman Empire secured its rule in the Balkans by a series of fortifications along the southern banks of the Danube. Not until the Turks were driven back could the river take up what had been its leading role in medieval times – that of an international trade route between East and West.

Treaties between the adjoining countries on the use of the Danube have existed since 1616. Those signed in 1838 and 1840, between Austria, Great Britain and Russia, guarantee the free flow of river traffic. These were confirmed by the *Peace of Paris* in 1856 and supervised by an international commission based in Galati in Romania until 1945.

Yugoslavia and the Eastern Bloc states signed the Belgrade Convention in 1948, thus removing the right to decide matters on the Danube from those states of countries lying outside the river course. Austria agreed to the convention in 1960, Germany did not, and foreign ships use the former West German part of the Danube according to bilateral agreements.
Source: *Brockhaus Enzyklopädie*

Preceding pages, Danube tributary near Szentendre.

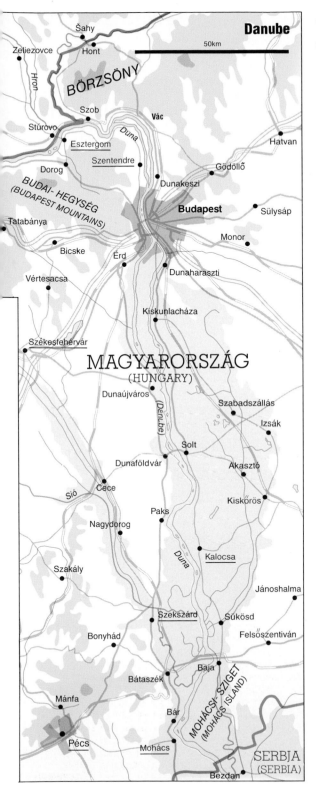

The map shows the region around the Danube with labels including: Šahy, Zeliezovce, Hont, Hron, BÖRZSÖNY, Szob, Vác, Stúrovo, Duna, Esztergom, Hatvan, Szentendre, Dorog, Gödöllő, BUDAI-HEGYSÉG (BUDAPEST MOUNTAINS), Dunakeszi, Tatabánya, Budapest, Sülysáp, Bicske, Érd, Monor, Vértesacsa, Dunaharaszti, Kiskunlacháza, Székesfehérvár, MAGYARORSZÁG (HUNGARY), Dunaújváros, Szabadszállás, (Danube), Izsák, Solt, Dunaföldvár, Akasztó, Cece, Sió, Kiskőrös, Paks, Nagydorog, Duna, Kalocsa, Szakály, Jánoshalma, Szekszárd, Sükösd, Bonyhád, Felsőszentiván, Baja, Bátaszék, MOHÁCSI-SZIGET (MOHÁCS ISLAND), Mánfa, Bár, Pécs, Mohács, SERBJA (SERBIA), Bezdan. Scale 50km. "Danube"

THE DANUBE

If you want to travel from Vienna to Budapest – and back again – on the Danube, you can do so by Austrian or Hungarian jetfoil. Water sports enthusiasts and river travellers can make the trip in their own boats, as long as the required paperwork is obtained.

The outward journey: Remaining in Austria for the first 37 miles (60km), you sail passed the massive old imperial fortress of Hainburg to the mouth of the March river. The Danube flows into Slovakia through the Dévin Gate between the rocky reef with the Slav fortress of Devín and Austrian Braunsberg. On the left bank is Bratislava, the capital of Slovakia. Under the name of Pozsony, it was also the capital of Hungary during the 150 years that the Turks ruled the central region of Hungary, which included Buda and Pest.

The actual Slovak stretch of the Danube is quite short – 14 miles (22km). Only an unobtrusive watchtower signals the change of sovereignty on the right bank. For the next 99 miles (160km), the Danube forms the border between Slovakia and Hungary.

You will notice one special feature of the Danube: the further you are from its mouth the lower the number of kilometres on the markers along the river. The reason is that the Danube is the only river in Europe whose length is not measured from its source to its mouth but vice-versa.

Between Slovakia and Hungary, the banks offer the same view for a long stretch. The river, flowing quietly, is bordered by thick woodlands, into which various broad and narrow side channels lead. There they form overgrown jungle-like islands or spread out into lagoons, havens for wild ducks and cormorants.

There are few villages near the river and hardly any people in sight. The only exception on the Hungarian side is **Gönyü**, a sleepy place which can only with some exaggeration be labelled as the harbour of Györ. Behind the dike, you can see the roofs of low houses, and a few weathered boats on the banks. Elsewhere in this desolate country between the water and the forests, only the occasional white house or an excavator removing gravel and mud from the riverbed and piling it into whitish-yellow heaps act as reminders of human presence. Here and there, silt is deposited on both banks and has raised the river-bed of the Danube, so that the surrounding countryside appears to be lower than the river.

You don't reach "civilisation" again until you get to **Komárom** (on the Hungarian side) and Komárno (on the Slovak). In earlier years, the two towns – then unified – belonged to Hungary and played a key role as a defensive fortress in the Turkish wars and in the revolution of 1848–49. Today they are divided into two distinct areas, but joined by a bridge for trains and road traffic. The only sight worth seeing are the ruins of the old fortress standing in the river.

Komárom is associated with one great name – from the world of light music. On 30 April 1870, Franz Lehár, son of a musician from Moravia, was born here. He composed *The Merry Widow*, and was also responsible for the second golden age of Viennese operetta.

Just past Komárom, the scenery along the Danube banks changes. On the Hungarian side, the thick woods thin out, the foothills of the Gerecse Hills come close to the river, and there are villages once again dotted along the river. Finally, the great dome of the basilica at Esztergom rises from the rocky plateau in front of the Pilis Hills. If you want to visit Esztergom, however, you shouldn't travel along

Ferries shuttle regulary across the Danube.

the Danube, as the boats don't usually stop between Vienna and Budapest. If you come by car from the direction of Vienna, you should leave highway No. 1 behind Györ and drive straight to Dorog on highway No. 10.

Ancient capital: At the time of the Árpád kings **Esztergom** served as the capital of Hungary. As the seat of the Archbishop of Esztergom, who bears the title Primate of Hungary and is head of the Hungarian bishops' synod, the town still retains its significance today.

The Hungarians describe the neoclassical **Basilica** as the biggest church in the country. The dome, supported by four pillars, has an inner height of 235 feet (71½ metres). The guides never forget to mention that the church is the fourth biggest in the world.

The whole building, begun in 1822 and completed in 1856, is 387 feet (118 metres) long and 131 feet (40 metres) wide. The roof of the entrance hall, which faces the land, bears eight Corinthian pillars, 72 feet (22 metres) high. The Basilica was consecrated on 31 August 1856. Franz Liszt composed the *Gran Mass* for the occasion.

The main attraction of the Basilica, is the older Bakócz Chapel. It was built on the south wing as a side chapel and named after Tamás Bakócz, one of the most famous Archbishops of Esztergom. Constructed for him between 1506 and 1511, its walls are of red marble. The chapel, once part of the medieval church of St Adalbert, even survived destruction by the Turks during their retreat in 1683. When the Basilica was being built in the previous century, it was taken apart and incorporated into the new building.

The no longer extant church of St Adalbert was the first church on Castle Hill and dated from the 11th century. It bore the name of the first Bohemian bishop of the diocese of Prague, who converted Prince Géza of the Árpád

Below, the ruin of the "friendship" bridge between Esztergom and Slovakia. Right, glass art in Café Nostalgia in Szentendre.

dynasty and his son István, the first King of Hungary. The latter was alleged to have been crowned in Esztergom, too, with the crown sent to him in the year 1000 from Rome by Pope Sylvester II.

More of the former **Royal Palace**, which was later the residence of the archbishops, has survived than of the church of St Adalbert, and Hungarian archaeologists are constantly discovering new parts. The visitor can admire several beautiful Romanesque portals dating from the 12th and 13th centuries, for instance, at the entrance to the castle chapel. Some of the rooms of the palace have also survived or restored, such as the so-called Vaulted Hall, which is probably the oldest living space surviving in Hungary.

Apart from Castle Hill, the Basilica and the Royal Palace, there are other interesting sights in Esztergom which shouldn't be missed. The Archbishop's Palace, between Castle Hill and the Danube, houses the **Museum of Christian Art**, the most notable art collection outside Budapest. Among its exhibits are valuable paintings and wood carvings dating back to the 15th and 16th centuries representing the work of artists from the entire Danube region including Hungary. Italian artists are also featured.

While visiting Esztergom, don't fail to visit the baroque, rococo and classical houses on Széchenyi tér and in the surrounding streets. Above all, there is the 17th and 18th century Town Hall.

Six miles (10km) below Esztergom, on the left bank, the River Ipolja flows into the Danube from the Slovak mountains. The Slovak-Hungarian border follows the river in northerly direction. From this point on, the Danube is purely Hungarian.

The Danube Bend, probably the most beautiful stretch of scenery on its Hungarian course, lies between

Esztergom, where the archbishop presides.

Esztergom and Visegrád. The landscape is at its most impressive near Visegrád, where the Börzsöny and Pilis hills force the river into a fairly narrow gorge. The view from the castle of Visegrád down into the valley is just as stunning as that from the Hotel Sylvanus behind it.

Visegrád today is merely a small town on the Danube, but in the 14th and 15th centuries it was one of the residences of the Hungarian kings. St Stephen's Crown and the Royal Insignia were kept from time to time in the castle above the town. The kings of the house of Anjou started using Visegrád as a royal residence in the first half of the 14th century. King Zsigmond of Luxembourg extended the palace at the foot of the castle. However, it was under the "Renaissance King" Mátyás Corvinus and his wife Beatrix of Aragon, in the second half of the 15th century, that Visegrád had its period of glory. According to the chronicles, the huge palace here had fountains spouting wine, endless opulent rooms and other extravagant amenitites befitting a rich and powerful king.

The powerful **Solomon's Tower** was part of the lower castle, and it was obvious that traffic on the Danube and the road along the river was to be controlled from here. It is connected to the upper castle by a half-ruined wall, along which you can climb up to the castle. It is rather more comfortable to follow one of the two roads leading up the hill east and west of the ruins. Both roads offer a changing panorama of the Danube valley, its villages and the hills of northeastern Hungary.

Past Visegrád, the Pilis rise to heights of 2,461 feet (750 metres). These hills are mostly covered with forest, and there are only a few villages in the valleys. Once upon a time they served as royal hunting grounds. Today the

A boat takes on the appearance of an island at Visegrád.

hunters are mostly well-heeled foreigners who come to shoot stags, deers, boars and moufflon.

Diagonally opposite Visegrád, on the other side of the Danube, is the village of **Nagymaros**. During Visegrád's prime it is believed the nobility had several palaces here, but nothing remains of them today. Nowadays the village is well-known for other reasons. In the summer the people of Budapest pick their raspberries here, and the name of the place is a buzz word for environmentalists. Despite their protests, a dam and locks were built at Nagymaros for the Slovak power station at Gabcíkovo. But an interesting by-product of the resistance to the dam was the consolidation of the opposition in the late 1980s which contributed to the fall of the Communist regime in Hungary. The Hungarians have since pulled out of the project, which is expected to change the face of the landscape along its stretch of the Danube considerably. Slovakia has pressed ahead and as a result relations between the two countries have soured.

A few miles away from Visegrád-Nagymaros is the actual Danube Bend. Here the river turns abruptly to the south. At the same time it splits into two channels. The easterly one, used by international shipping, flows past Vác. On the other, favoured by water sports enthusiasts, lies the picturesque town of **Szentendre**. In between is Szentendre Island, 24 miles (38km) long and about two miles (3km) wide. Many people in Budapest have a weekend house here, and come to enjoy the sandy beaches.

City of churches: Viewed from the river or the island, **Vác** looks quite cosy. The pretty silhouette of this baroque town is not disturbed by any industrial or harbour complex. Only 21 miles (34 km) from Budapest, Vác has always been overshadowed by the

Memorial to the patron saints of Hungary.

172

capital and still is today. Its historic roots are deep. By the 11th century, István I had made it a bishop's seat with a cathedral (which, did not survive the turbulent centuries). Today's **Cathedral** on the expansive tree-lined Konstantin tér is considered one of the greatest examples of classicism in Hungary. Work began in 1790, based on a design that was the result of collaboration between three architects and one very independent-minded building contractor, which didn't help with the harmony of the building. The main façade, with its mighty Corinthian pillars, may be impressive, but the towers and domes do not appear to grow from the building naturally. The interior features such interesting sights as the frescoes in the choir, the *Affliction of Mary* and the *Triumph of the Trinity* in the dome, both by the Swabian-born painter Franz Anton Maulbertsch.

The Cathedral is the focal point of Vác, the so-called "city of churches". Opposite is the baroque bishop's palace, with its well proportioned but much neglected park leading down to the Danube. Downstream, only a few minutes away, on **Géza Király tér**, where the medieval castle of Vác once stood, is the Franciscan church, another baroque building.

If you leave Konstantin tér and go north, you will come first to **Szentháromság tér**, which owes its name to a pillar of the Trinity and a two-towered Piarist church. Both date from the baroque period. The most valuable piece in the church is a tabernacle, adorned with polished Venetian mirror glass.

At the edge of Vác is the former Dominican church on the southern side of **Március 15 tér**. This square was in former times and still remains today the centre of the old town. Evidence of its status are the Town Hall, a baroque palace dating from 1764

with a balcony above the entrance, a row of mainly single-storey buildings from the second half of the 18th century and – under the flower beds in the centre of the square – a good-sized wine cellar.

Vác has yet another sight to offer: at the northern exit of the town is a late baroque triumphal arch, which Bishop Migazzi, who supervised the construction of the cathedral, had built in 1764 for a visit by Maria Theresa. It does look rather strange today, surrounded by small suburban houses. So does the gloomy prison next door, surrounded by high walls topped with barbed wire.

Seven churches of Szentendre: The most interesting place on the right arm of the Danube is Szentendre, only 12 miles (18km) away from Budapest and linked to the city by a commuter rail service. There is nothing to equal this little town in Hungary, neither in history or in atmosphere. Its skyline is dominated by seven churches: four Serbian Orthodox, two Catholic and one Reformed. Once there were six Orthodox churches here, all with Serbian names which the surviving ones still bear today. For it was Serbs who settled here, fleeing from the Turks at the end of the 17th century. Together with some Dalmatian and Greek families, they made 18th century Szentendre into a market-place for trade from the southeast. The impressive merchants' houses around Marx tér, with their capacious warehouses are evidence of the vast wealth that was once accumulated here. The Greek Orthodox Merchants's Cross stands in the middle of the square. It was erected in 1763 by the "Privileged Serbian Trading Company".

Later, when trade with the southeast had found other routes, artists from Budapest discovered the town and stayed here, at least for the summer. Already by the turn of the century, well-known artists such as the impressionist Károly Ferenczy had settled in Szentendre. His works, as well as those of his children, hang in a museum named after him. Béla Czóbel, Jenö Barcsa and Lajos Vajda are other great names from the world of Hungarian painting who are linked with Szentendre. There is also a permanent exhibition of the works of the famous ceramics artist Margit Kovács in the vaults of one of the old merchant's houses now a museum named for Kovács. The artist's work was greatly influenced by folk art of the day and the way it was used for everyday objects.

City approaches: The point where the two Danube channels surrounding Szentendre Island meet again marks the northern boundary of the city of **Budapest**. The right bank is called *Római part* (Roman bank) and *Rómaifürdö* (Roman baths) – a sign indicating that you have reached Aquincum, the erstwhile capital of the Roman province of Pannonia.

The view of Óbuda (Old Buda) is at

Sunbathing by the banks of the Danube.

174

first obscured for the traveller on the Danube by the Óbudai-sziget (Old Buda Island). It is uninteresting for tourists, as most of it is covered with wharves. In any case, the view from the river hardly offers any insight into this possibly oldest section of Budapest. In the last few years it has become a new housing area with highrise apartments, new highways and department stores.

The Hungarian metropolis finally greets the Danube traveller at **Margaret Island**. You can now see the view for which the city has become famous: to the right, in front of the background of the Buda Hills, is Castle Hill with Mátyás Church, the Fishermen's Bastion, the Hilton Hotel and the restored castle, which has several museums. Behind it is Gellért Hill, dropping steeply down to the Danube, crowned by the fortress and the Liberation Monument.

Along the left bank lie the official buildings – the massive complex of the neo-Gothic Parliament, the Hungarian Academy of Sciences and Arts, then the new hotels and the Vigadó concert hall, and a sea of houses in the background.

After the **Chain Bridge**, the oldest bridge in Budapest, you are at the foot of the castle, in the heart of the capital. On the left (Pest) bank, up and downstream from **Elizabeth Bridge** (Erzsébet híd) is **Belgrade Quay** (Belgrád rakpart). This is where all boats moor and where passengers go through customs and immigration.

Gellért Hill is both mentioned in Christian legend as well as in the German Danube legends. The former tells of the Swiss bishop Gerhardus (Gellért), who was placed in a barrel studded with spikes by pagan Hungarians and cast into the Danube from the top of the hill. The German Danube legends tell of the beautiful Lau, the water queen, who, ignoring the

Waiting for a bite.

warnings of her husband, the Danube King Ingold, joined the witches' feast, a Danube version of *Walpurgisnacht*, on Gellért Hill. She was saved from Satan when Dr Faustus wrapped her in his magic cloak.

Csepel Island, 29 miles (47 km) long, marks the point where the Danube leaves Budapest. Only its northernmost point still belongs to the capital. It contains the largest Hungarian heavy industrial concern, the steel and metal works of Csepel, whose work-force has repeatedly taken a decisive part in the politics of the country – in the 1956 revolution for example. Also on the island is the Hungarian international free port and the biggest inland port.

South of Budapest: Fluvial traffic uses the broader western Danube channel, which winds its way once more through riverine landscape. The banks are thinly populated. Access to Csepel Island from the west is via ferries. The first Danube bridge below Budapest is at Dunaföldvár, 44 miles (70 km) south of Budapest.

However, the left-hand Danube channel, which goes around Csepel Island from the east, is more "civilised". Several bridges lead to the island, and its banks are lined with villas, weekend chalets and well-kept gardens. It is also popular with fishing and water sports enthusiasts. On the western shore of the island's southern tip lies the town of Ráckeve. Here stand a palace of Prince Eugene, built by Lukas von Hildebrandt, and the oldest Serbian Orthodox church in Hungary dating back to 1487.

The trip between Budapest and the Serbian border is by no means as full of variety as that between Vienna and Budapest. The land to the right and left of the river is barely cultivated, and there are only a few towns on the banks. For this reason the Hungarian Danube Shipping Company runs no

Interior of the country's oldest Orthodox church, built in 1487 in Ráckeve.

hydrofoils or hovercrafts on this stretch, either scheduled or chartered. Only the Russian, Romanian and Bulgarian passenger ships travel this stretch on their way to and from the Black Sea, but they make no stops. Freight traffic is even more intensive on this part of the river, as the industries of Csepel Island and the oil refinery and power station of **Százhalombatta**, as well as the iron and steel works of Dunaújváros still get most of their raw materials from the countries of the former Soviet Union via the waterways.

A socialist paradise: Thirty-one miles (50 km) south of Budapest, is **Dunaújváros**, a new town created after World War II. Where once the little village of Dunapentele lay, stand iron and steel works surrounded by some 30 other factories and housing developments.

Dunaföldvár, another 12 miles (20 km) to the south, deserves a mention

for having the only bridge over the Danube between Budapest and Baja. Originally there was a ford over the Danube, protected by a castle of which a square tower still survives. Today's bridge is an important link between Transdanubia and the Great Hungarian Plain. For tourists in Dunaföldvár there is a hotel, a spa and a camp site. And, if the will of the tourist industry in Tolna district prevails, Dunaföldvár will have a harbour in the next few years. Beyond Dunaföldvár, the river turns east and flows through a landscape almost devoid of people. For 19 miles (30 km), with the exception of two small villages, there are no towns or villages on the river bank. Then you reach **Paks**, site of the only nuclear power station in Hungary.

A further 9 miles (15 km) downstream from the ferry at **Gerjen**, you can make a diversion to the town of **Kalocsa**, 6 miles (10 km) from the Danube, the ancient bishopric between

Icons in the Serbian Orthodox church at Ráckeve on Csepel Island.

the Danube and the Tisza. It is also known as one of the capitals of "red gold", i.e. paprika, and is a folk art centre famous for its ceramics and embroidery.

Another 5 miles (8 km) downstream is the popular holiday region of **Fadd-Dombori**. It lies along a channel, over 4 miles (7 km) long and 1,312 feet (400 metres) wide, which is part of the old bed of the Danube.

Szekszárd, a town of 35,000 inhabitants, lies 8 miles (12 km) away from the Danube, but belongs to it for several reasons. It is considered the gateway to the **Gemence Forest**, which stretches for 16 miles (25 km) southwards along the right bank of the Danube, and is the biggest game reserve in the country.

Part of the area is closed, as the Hungarian government invites important guests to hunt here. However, the average citizen can also enter this jungle-like growth on the Danube flood-plain, with its network of causeways and its quiet lakes surrounded by fields of reeds, remnants of the old river course, and bright glades. Ancient willows and poplars, oaks and rowans make up the trees of this forest, which is also the habitat of deer, roe deer and wild boar. You can even ride across a porion of the forest in a narrow-gauge train.

For water sports fans, it may be useful to know that the **Sió Canal** flows into the Danube here. It comes from Lake Balaton and is only navigable by smaller pleasure boats for a few miles past the confluence, being too shallow further up. With canoes, however, you can risk a trip to Siófok on the southern bank of Lake Balaton and in the opposite direction.

Between Szekszárd and the Gemence Forest lies the **Sárköz**, an area famous for its folk traditions and costumes. There are four communities lying on this slight elevation that

Something on the line.

178

rises gently up out of the land, other wise flat as a table top. For years these communities formed a world of their own, in which old customs survived for longer than in other countries. Today you can only admire the colourful traditional costume, with its dominant reds, in the peasant house (and museum) of **Decs**, or in the workshops of the Sárköz co-operative, which make the black and white embroideries and the red, black and blue skirts for export.

Journey's end: Baja and Mohács are the last towns through which the Danube passes before it leaves Hungary. **Baja**, a friendly town, is remarkable for the fact that the visitor can find everything he or she will need – a hotel, a restaurant, a camp site and a swimming pool – directly opposite the main square.

This square is called Béke tér, one side of which opens out on to the **Sugovica**, a tributary of the Danube.

In the square is the town museum, which was named after István Türr, a general on Garibaldi's staff in the war for the unification of Italy.

Baja has two Serbian Orthodox churches and a high school which uses German as its primary language. Once the Turks had been driven out of southern Hungary in the late 18th century, German and Serbian farmers were invited to move in. For this reason, the area is still referred to as "Swabian Turkey" in Hungary (many settlers came from Swabia in southwest Germany). In Szekszárd there is a German theatre company which performs in all the places where "Swabians" live today.

The name **Mohács** is linked to one of the greatest catastrophes in the history of Hungary. Here, on 29 August 1526, the Turks destroyed the Hungarian cavalry. King Louis II lost his life, and the central part of the country, including Buda and Pest, came under Turkish rule for 150 years.

The present memorial of the battle is at **Sátorhely**, an impressive creation by several Hungarian artists, 4 miles (7 km) to the southwest of the town. The museum contains exhibits that were recently discovered on the site of the battle.

Mohács is also known outside the immediate area for its black peasant ceramics and the **Busójárás** (Busó Procession). This has a Serbo-Croat origin and takes place every year on the last Sunday of the carnival season (i.e. the Sunday before Ash Wednesday). From Mohács Island, crowds of bizarre and strangely dressed figures enter the town, wearing painted masks and horns and making a great deal of noise. According to some, it is an occasion to usher in spring, while others say it is to celebrate the expulsion of the Turks.

Only 9 miles (14 km) separate Mohács from the border with Serbia. But if you have time, why not stay a little longer in Hungary?

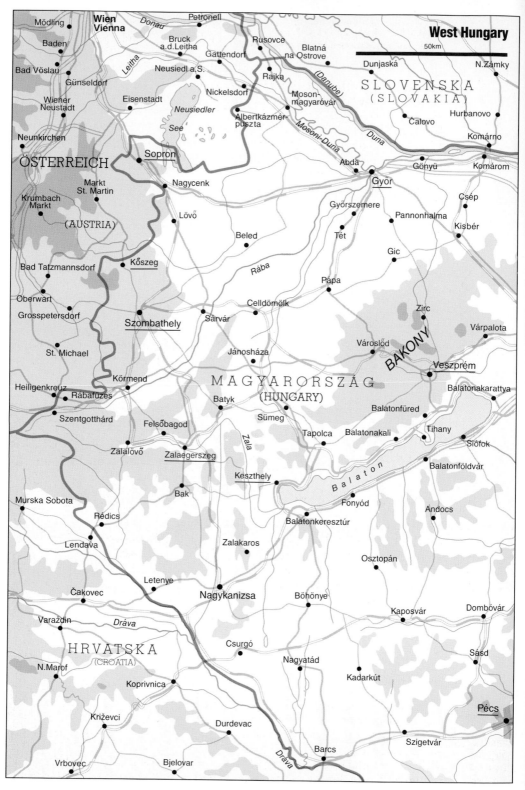

West Hungary

50km

Mödling · Wien Vienna · Donau · Petronell

Baden

Bad Vöslau · Günseldorf

Wiener Neustadt · Eisenstadt

Neunkirchen

ÖSTERREICH

Markt St. Martin

Krumbach Markt

(AUSTRIA)

Bad Tatzmannsdorf · Kőszeg

Oberwart

Grosspetersdorf · Szombathely

St. Michael · Körmend

Heiligenkreuz · Rábafüzes

Szentgotthárd · Felsőbagod

Zalalövő · Zalaegerszeg

Murska Sobota

Rédics

Lendava

Čakovec · Letenye

Varaždin · Dráva

HRVATSKA

(CROATIA)

N.Marof

Koprivnica

Križevci · Durdevac

Vrbovec · Bjelovar

Bruck a.d.Leitha · Gattendorf · Rusovce · Blatná na Ostrove

Neusiedl a.S. · Rajka · Nickelsdorf · Moson-magyaróvár

Leitha

Neusiedler See · Albertkázmér-puszta

Sopron

Nagycenk

Lövő

Beled

Rába

Sárvár

Jánosháza

Batyk

Sümeg

Tapolca

Zala

Bak

Keszthely

Balatonkeresztúr

Zalakaros

Nagykanizsa · Böhönye

Csurgó · Nagyatád

Kadarkút

Barcs

Dunjaská · N.Zámky

SLOVENSKA (SLOVAKIA)

Čalovo · Hurbanovo

Komárno

Abda · Gönyü · Komárom

Győr

Győrszemere · Csép

Pannonhalma · Kisbér

Tét

Gic

Pápa

Celldömölk · Zirc

Várpalota

Városlőd · BAKONY · Veszprém

MAGYARORSZÁG (HUNGARY)

Balatonakarattya

Balatonfüred

Balatonakali · Tihany

Balatonföldvár

Balaton

Fonyód · Andocs

Osztopán

Kaposvár · Dombóvár

Sásd

Szigetvár

Pécs

Mosoni-Duna · (Danube) · Duna

182

GATES TO THE WEST

The following official crossings on the Austrian border are the main entry points to Hungary: Nickelsdorf/ Hegyeshalom, on the direct route from Vienna to Budapest; Klingenbach/ Sopron, the route to Vienna for those who live in west Hungary south of Lake Fertö, and Heiligenkreuz/ Rábafüzes, the quickest route from Graz to Budapest, which offers the easiest access to the resorts around Lake Balaton.

Budapest via Hegyeshalom: The main flow of traffic from the West undoubtedly goes via Nickelsdorf/Hegyeshalom, especially since the completion of the M1 motorway all the way from the border to Budapest.

Once the border-crossing ritual is out of the way, it's a good idea to get moving again as fast as possible. There isn't much to see near the border, either in Hegyeshalom or in Moson-magyaróvár, formed from the union of two towns, Moson (formerly Wieselburg) and Magyaróvár. Wieselburg is of particular interest to amateur historians. In 1809, a truce was reached here between Napoleon and the Austrian Empire, which was a precursor to the Peace of Schönbrunn. Also, Wieselburg was one of the four western Hungarian districts (Pressburg, Wieselburg, Ödenburg and Eisenburg) from which the new Austrian state of Burgenland was once created. The district of Eisenburg has been, since the end of the monarchy, part of the district of Györ-Sopron.

Between the rivers: In Mosonmagyaróvár the European routes E5 from Vienna and E15 from Bratislava join up and go on to Györ and Budapest. Lovers of unspoilt nature should, however, avoid the main road and make a small diversion northwards into the Szigetköz (Little Gravel Island), a 106 sq. mile (275 sq. km) flood-plain be-tween the main channel of the Danube and a side channel, the so-called "Little (or Moson or Wieselburg) Danube". Even after the regulation of the main flows of water, the area, crisscrossed by many waterways, has retained much of its original charm. You retrun to the main highway via Hédervár, Asványráró and Mecsér. Cross the highway and 3 miles (5km) further on you will come to the most prominent site in this region – **Lébény-miklós**. The church (completed in 1208) of the former Benedictine monastery, together with the cathedral of Pécs and the churches of Zsámbék, is undoubtedly one of the most important Romanesque buildings to be seen in Hungary.

Like Ják and Zsámbék, the three-aisled basilica of Lébénymiklós with its three semi-circular apses is one of the so-called family churches, built in the early 13th century by an aristocratic sponsor and later given to a

monastic order. The troubles of history have left their mark. In the 15th century imperial troops burned monasteries and churches to the ground. (The whole of western Hungary has been attacked time and time again by German and Austrian troops; no wonder that Hungarian feelings of friendship towards their neighbours in the west have had their limits). Barely rebuilt, the church fell victim to the Turks in 1529 and again in 1683. Then the Jesuits took it over – until their dissolution in 1777. A hundred years later, the church was restored once more and returned to its original form.

The western wing is particularly impressive, with its mighty twin towers (the tops of the towers date from the last restoration) and its precious portal, which is perhaps only exceeded in beauty by the south portal on the side of the former monastery graced by the statue of an angel.

Back on the main highway, **Györ** is a mere 9 miles (15 km) further on. This important industrial city is the administrative and economic centre of the Kisalföld, the Little Plain. Györ, capital of the district Györ-Sopron, lies at the confluence of the Little Danube, the Rába and the Rábca. This land has been settled for centuries. After the Celts and the Romans, the Avars built their circular fortress (*gyürü*, hence the Hungarian name Györ; the river Rába gave the town its German name of Raab. However, the Turks, who burned the town to the ground in 1529, gave it the fitting name of *janik kula*, or burned town).

In Hungary the conversion to Christianity was the means, if not the precondition, of the making of the nation. It was not by chance that the coronation of the first king of Hungary, King – and Saint – István I, in 1000 coincided with the creation of an independent archdiocese of Hungary. The two events heralded the removal of

The museum in Györ, once a place of execution.

the Pannonian lands from secular imperial authority and from the spiritual domination of Salzburg. The Hungarian princes of the church, precursors of the struggle for national identity, made a decisive contribution to establishing the power of the state.

These thoughts are appropriate when standing on the castle hill of the old bishops' fortress in Győr, with the ensemble of cathedral and castle in front of you, the symbol of the unity of spiritual and secular power in the Middle Ages. The bishopric of Győr was founded in the early 11th century. On the site of an old Roman *castrum* a fortified place was prepared to serve as a bishop's seat – clear evidence of that the prince of the church, who ruled the city as its overlord, had political and spiritual responsibilities.

The Bishop's Castle had the opportunity of proving its mettle in the turbulent years of the Turkish wars. It changed owners several times, until the Habsburgs finally prevailed around 1600. However, the castle remained a garrison for more than 100 years after the expulsion of the Turks – the fortress was not dissolved until 1788. Some 50 years earlier, though, the castle was given a baroque facade, a concession to the peaceful years of the 18th century.

Surrounded by faceless industrial suburbs, the old town, its buildings protected by the government, gathers around the **Cathedral Chapter Hill**. The wealth of old houses with their 17th, 18th and early-19th century façades is surprising. At the top of the hill, dominating all except the old Sforza Bastion, is the harmonious castle and cathedral complex.

The Cathedral of Our Lady dates back to the time when the bishopric of Raab was founded in the early 11th century. Destroyed several times, the church was remodelled in baroque style in the mid-17th century and re-

The Győr ballet troupe.

ceived a neo-classical façade in the 19th century. The reliquary of Saint László, king of Hungary, one of the greatest masterpieces of medieval goldsmithery (circa 1405) is kept in the Gothic Hédervary Chapel. The treasure chamber of the cathedral contains a wealth of gold and silver liturgical objects.

Next to the cathedral is the fortified **Bishop's Castle (Püspökvár)**. Its baroque character dates from rebuilding in the 18th century. One tower has 12th century foundations, and the late Gothic Dóczy Chapel dates from 1481. The single-towered **Carmelite Church** (1721) is probably the most beautiful baroque building in Győr. Among the museums in the town are the **Castle Museum** and the **Janós Xantus Museum** which houses an extensive ethnographic collection.

Early Christians in Hungary: Twelve miles (20 km) south of Győr, on highway No. 82 to Veszprém, is **Pannon-halma**, the oldest monastery in Hungary. This Benedictine Abbey on the 328 feet (100 metres) high St Martin's Hill was founded in 996 by Prince Géza, father of King István I. It was here that Christianity in Hungary originated. In the archives of the monastery there is also the first authentic document in the Hungarian language, the charter of the Benedictine Abbey of Tihany on Lake Balaton, dating from 1055. The monastery is dedicated to St Martin of Tours, the patron saint of France, of beggars and of geese. The saint was born a "Hungarian" in 317 in the Roman garrison town of Savaria, modern Szombathely.

The oldest surviving part of the abbey church is the crypt, dating from the 13th century, with the abbot's throne, which popular wisdom has named the throne of István I. The recently restored late Gothic cloister was not built until the reign of King Mátyás Corvinus. The abbey com-

Observer in a window in the old town of Sopron.

plex in its present form dates from the early 19th century; the tall classical tower of the dome can be seen from a great distance. Buried in the crypt of Pannonhalma, beside her second husband, the Hungarian Count Lonyay, lies Princess Stephanie, daughter of the King of Belgium. The widow of the Austrian heir to the throne, Rudolf, who killed himself in 1889 in Mayerling. She survived him by more than 50 years and died in 1946.

Klingenbach to Sopron: Day after day, particularly at weekends, an avalanche of cars rolls from the west across the border post at Klingenbach. The Austrians are going shopping in Sopron. Few visitors have an eye for the beautiful buildings. Food seems more important than art. If you don't happen to be on the usual shopping and (heavy) drinking tour, you may find the general lack of interest quite pleasant. You can get to know the beauties of this town in relative peace and quiet.

Sopron, formerly Ödenburg, lies just past the Austrian-Hungarian border between the Sopron hills in the west and Lake Fertö in the northeast. Encircled by rows of 19th- and 20th-century houses, the horseshoe-shaped old town of Sopron lies like an oyster in the shell of a wall dating back to the Romans. The foundations of the latter are currently being excavated. The old town is a protected area. It has the richest collection of historic and artistic buildings in Hungary.

The hallmark is the **Fire Tower**. Roman stones were used in the medieval foundations (the Roman name for Sopron was Scarbantia); the central section with its arcade (don't miss the beautiful view) dates from the Renaissance; the top of the tower and its baroque copper roof are 17th century. Next to the tower, in the town hall, is an informative exhibition describing the town's history. The tower is at the end of Fö tér, the main square, which is lined with beautiful houses dating from the 15th to the 17th centu-

ries, among them the Gothic Fabricius House, the Storno House with its Renaissance façade, the Gambrinius House and the house of the Angel Pharmacy.

The baroque **Trinity Column** (c. 1700) in the centre of the square is considered one of the most remarkable in Hungary. On the corner of the square and Templom utca is the Church of St Mary (dating from 1280), the most impressive sacred building in Sopron. It is a three-aisled Gothic church with a slender tower 141 feet (43 metres) high, which is considered the most beautiful Gothic church tower in the country. In the 16th century three Hungarian queens were crowned here. In the adjoining former Franciscan monastery, the Gothic hall of pilasters awaits your presence. Nowadays it serves as an exhibition hall.

In Templom utca and the alleys of the old town which run parallel to it, Új utca (New Street) and Kolostor

utca, nearly every house is worth a closer look. The Middle Ages still seem to survive in the narrow, twisting alleys. You feel magically transported via a time machine to some earlier century. The whole quarter is being lovingly restored. Notable are the two medieval synagogues in Új utca, the former Jewish street. Both were turned into private houses after the expulsion of the Jews (1526).

On a hill beyond Lenin körút, on the highest point of the town, lies **St Michael's Church** (14th century). In the cemetery is the oldest sacred building in the town, the Romanesque-Gothic Jacob's Chapel.

Six miles (10 km) from Sopron, near Lake Fertö, is **Fertörákos** with its former residence of the Bishops of Sopron, a delightful little baroque palace. The real attraction of the village is the Roman quarry, which was in use until 1945. Here the cut Leitha limestone was used to build St Stephen's Cathedral and the Ringstrasse buildings in Vienna. The mighty limestone blocks standing upright form massive vaults vaguely reminiscent of Egyptian temples. One of these "halls" has been turned into a theatre. Every summer musical performances take place against this magnificent background as part of the Sopron Festival.

Further along this local road is the little spa of Balf, then further still the great Baroque palace at Fertöd, the "Hungarian Versailles". Built in the 1760s by the most flamboyant of all the Esterházys, Prince Miklós "The Magnificent", Fertöd was a rival in splendour to the court at Vienna, with its own opera house and Haydn as court musician.

On Highway 85, **Nagycenk** was the home of the "greatest Hungarian", as Count István Széchenyi (1792–1860) was known, even in his lifetime. Just as his slightly older contemporary, the

Benedictine abbey of Pannonhalma.

Habsburg Archduke Johann, did with Styria, the Count in Hungary strove to put his country in touch with modern times. From around 1820, his liberal and moderate programme of reforms supported the liberation of the peasants, opposed the privileges of the nobility, supported science and research and also a free economy. He founded the Hungarian Academy of Sciences and created the basis of the modern system of Danube navigation. Budapest has him to thank for the Chain Bridge. Széchenyi was a great patriot – he was the first to deliver a speech in Hungarian in Parliament – and yet he could not, in the long term, prevail against the "hawks" supporting Lajos Kossuth.

Nagycenk Palace was, until 1945, the residence of the Count's family. It was built in the mid-18th century and rebuilt in 1834–40 – the classical façade dates from these years. Even the rooms of the palace themselves, which don't show any of the ostentation often associated with palaces of the Hungarian nobility, are evidence of the restrained, moderate spirit of the "greatest Hungarian". An interesting exhibition in one of the palace wings is devoted to him. The palace was the first building in Hungary to have gas lighting; water closets and bathrooms were installed here 20 years before they arrived in the Hofburg Palace in Vienna.

Köszeg and Szombathely: Nine miles (15 km) past Nagycenk, the road to Köszeg turns off to the right. A short stop in **Sopronhorpács** should suffice to admire the magnificent arch at the entrance to the Romanesque village church. Romanesque buildings are surprisingly common in western Hungary, often in small places where they are quite unexpected, for instance in **Csempeszkopács**.

Köszeg, the old border fort of Güns, is a picture-book small medieval town.

Keeping the faith in Oriszentpéter.

It has a defiant-looking castle with a moat and a largely intact town wall. Pressed up against the wall is the old town.

Time stands still when you enter Jurisics tér through the **Heroes' Gate** (Hösi kapu), built in 1932 and a replica of a typical Gothic city tower. The broad main square of the little town is surrounded by beautiful houses. Unfortunately they have only been partially restored with the necessary care. In the middle of the square are two churches, one beside the other: **St Jacob's**, a Gothic building, later remodelled in the baroque style, and the early baroque **St Emery's Church**.

The oldest parts of the castle go back to the 14th century. It has only recently been restored to its former glory. It houses the **Jurisics Museum**, a reminder of its great moment of fame when it was the fortress of Güns and the heroic defence in 1532 under Miklós Jurisics against the Turks. Ever since, the bells in Köszeg have been ringing daily at 11am.

From Köszeg it is not far, in a southerly direction, to **Szombathely** (formerly Steinamanger). This is the capital of the district of Vas and, after Györ, the biggest town in Transdanubia, as western Hungary is also known. It is a friendly, well-kept, pleasant place with some nice town houses in the pedestrian area in the centre. As the Hungarian name makes clear (*szombat*=Saturday, *hely*=place, an obvious reference to the market held here), the town was and still is a trading centre for the surrounding area. This was once the site of the important Roman town of Savaria, where Septimus Severus was proclaimed emperor in AD 193, and in AD 317 St Martin of Tours was born.

You can see impressive discoveries in the **Garden of Ruins** right behind the cathedral. Here the remains of St Quirinus' Basilica, built with stones

Left, signs of the times. **Below**, farmyard with peppers.

from the governor's palace, have been unearthed, as have a splendid mosaic floor and a Roman crossroads. Somewhat disappointing, in another part of the town, is the reconstruction of a temple of Isis.

The monolithic, sterile Szombathely Gallery, serves as a modern backdrop to the ruins. and has impressive collections, especially the contemporary ones. Opposite the gallery the Béla Bartók music school is housed in a typically Moorish-style synagogue built in 188. During the reign of Maria Theresa Szombathely became a bishop's seat, and large, impressive buildings – the cathedral, the bishop's palace, the former seminary – were built in the mid to late 18th century Zopf style, a typical hybrid of late baroque and classicism.

However, most people don't come to Szombathely for the sights, but for other, more prosaic reasons. What Sopron is to the Viennese and Lower Austrians, Szombathely is to the Styrians and Austrians from Burgenland – a Mecca for shopping, a paradise of low prices. The bargain applies usually to food, but does not necessarily exclude services such as hairdressing, beauty salons, dentists; even handmade shoes, suits and shirts are in demand. The spas of the district also make a profit out of price cuts, and the good value of their services attracts many clients from the West. Perhaps the most famous spas in Transdanubia are **Bük** and **Sárvár.** Bük forms a rough triangle with Köszeg and Szombathely. Its hot spring is the most prolific in Central Europe, and even feeds a small lake. A very spacious swimming hall allows for bathing throughout the year. Bük also sports one of the few golf courses in Hungary. While Bük has a tradition of spa treatment, Sárvár is a newcomer. Its hot springs were only discovered 25 years ago. For this reason, the spa has

Back from the market.

the most modern equipment and the highest standards of comfort based on Western expectations. Sárvár is 15 miles (25 km) to the east of Szombathely, on the main road to Sopron.

On the way to Lake Balaton: Compared to the elaborate border posts in Nickelsdorf and Klingenbach, the border crossing at Heiligenkreuz is small fry. But even here you can find yourself in a queue lasting many hours – a sign of the importance of Hungary's most southerly gate to the West for through traffic. As European routes go, E66, highway No. 8, is rather narrow, but in good condition.

Just beyond the Austrian border, a road branches off to **Szentgotthárd**, the site of the victory over the Turks at Mogersdorf, also known as St Gotthard on the Raab, in 1664. The detour – a mere 3 miles (5 km) – is hardly worth it. Apart from a rather nice baroque church, there's nothing else to see.

There is another detour, after a further 15 miles (25 km), which really is worth making. Here you travel northwards on a side road to **Ják**, undoubtedly the most important architectural monument in the region. The church of the former 13th century Benedictine abbey is possibly the finest Romanesque building in Hungary. The great church with its mighty twin-towered façade was rebuilt in the original style after fire damage early this century. Particularly impressive is the great grabbed portal with its over-flowing wealth of figural decoration. The deep, rounded inner arches give way to shallower pointed arches. The decoration of the outer walls of the three round apses is of special interest, particularly the stone frames of the round arch windows, with their false arcades and the remains of figural ornamentation.

E66 leads you to the town of **Körmend** shortly after the turnoff to Ják. The palace of the Batthyány-Strattman princes is a massive baroque building with four corner towers dating from earlier times. Another treasure from the Romanesque period is the little village church in **Csempeszkopács**, 6 miles (10 km) to the north on highway 87, which meets up with the E66 15 miles (25 km) past Körmend. The tiny single-nave church with its round arch apse and a façade tower shows the influence of Jáks, is a jewel among Hungarian churches.

Before you reach the turning, you pass the town of **Vasvár** on the E66. Under the name of Eisenburg, it once saw better times. Here the (premature) Peace of Eisenburg was signed in 1664, which took the sting out of the victory over the Turks at Szentgotthard and led to an anti-Habsburg conspiracy. Before Eisenburg said farewell to history, it still provided, together with Pressburg, Altenburg and Ödenburg, the name for the youngest Austrian federal state, existing on what had been West Hungarian territory – the Burgenland.

Left, young "lion-tamer" at Ják. **Right,** St George's Basilica.

AROUND LAKE BALATON

Hungarians call Lake Balaton the "Sea of Hungary". It really is quite impressive. Its area of 230 sq. miles (595 sq. km) makes it the biggest lake in Central and Western Europe.

It is also Hungary's biggest tourist attraction, next to Budapest. This results in a heavy influx of tourists during the summer months, with the usual side-effects of local price rises and a shortage of accommodation, even at campsites. The ecological consequences of this seasonal population growth can be severe, ranging from vehicle pollution to a thin layer of suntan oil on the lake.

Nevertheless, the lake is worth even a brief visit. Its grey-green water is very warm in July and August, up to 82°F (28°C). The scenery on the northern bank, with its volcanic mounds, vineyards and wide bays is picturesque, and the south bank, with its sand dunes and shallow water, is ideal for children. There is a tradition of sailing on Lake Balaton and private motor boats are banned. In the winter, in the intense cold on the thick ice, sledges share Lake Balaton with skaters.

Lake Balaton is 48 miles (77 km) long. It runs from southwest to northeast and divides Transdanubia in two. The lake is itself divided in two by the peninsula of Tihany; the eastern section is smaller, but broader and deeper, the western is bigger and narrower. Between Tihany and Szántód, where there is a car ferry, it is less than a mile (1½ km) wide. If you want to drive around the lake, you will need to make a journey of 122 miles (197 km).

Technically speaking, Lake Balaton is a "shallow water" lake. The average depth is a mere 12–13 feet (3.5–4 metres). It is deepest in the narrow part near Tihany, 35 feet (11 metres).

Because Lake Balaton is shallow, it is warmed up relatively quickly by the sun's rays. However, it cools down just as quickly in bad weather. In general, you can be sure in summer of enjoying your swim along the densely packed beaches.

Lake Balaton is well known for the sudden storms that can appear, mostly from the northwest. Sailors have to be on the lookout for strong squalls. When the storm baskets at the mooring places are at half-mast, that counts as a storm warning. Yellow rockets warn of strong winds and smaller vessels, rowing boats and yachts should stay near the shore. Red flares warn of a real storm and are a signal for all vessels to head for the harbour.

The winds are also the reason for the tidal effect that can be seen in the narrows of Tihany. It can happen that a strong southwesterly can press the water back into the eastern half of the lake. When the wind dies down, the water flows back. The reverse phenomenon can also be seen.

Sailing centre: Sailing on Lake Balaton is a tradition going back more than 100 years. All types of boats can be found here, from the smallest dinghy to larger yachts. **Balatonfüred**, on the north bank, is the sailing centre. Here, around the middle of last century, steamships began to make trips around the lake. May signals the start of the season. There is a sailing school in Balatonfüred, and others in Siófok, Balatonszemes and Tihany.

Most of the towns on the banks of the lake are served by the motor boats belonging to the Balaton Boat Company. In the western part of the lake they will take you from shore to shore in about 25 minutes, in the eastern part a crossing takes 40–50 minutes.

However, the picture of Lake Balaton would be incomplete without fish. There are supposed to be 42 different kinds in the lake. The most famous is *fogas*, a kind of pike-perch. Fishing enthusiasts sit patiently waiting for the great *fogas* catch, but many of

Preceding pages: fishery, a dying industry. Left, sunset on Lake Balaton.

them say that the only fogas they ever caught is hanging in the wardrobe at home – *fogas* in Hungarian also means coat-hanger.

Getting there: If, coming from the West, you want to travel directly to the lake, the best approach is to cross the Austrian-Hungarian border at Klingenbach-Sopron and then follow the Hungarian highway No. 84 south via Sárvár and Sümeg. To avoid weekend traffic jams at Klingenbach, try using the border crossing of Mannersdorf-Köszeg. Then you can continue to Keszthely via Szombathely and Zalaegerszeg. If you want to approach Lake Balaton near Tihany and Balatonfüred, you can cross the border at Nickelsdorf-Hegyeshalom and continue your journey via Györ and Veszprém.

To reach Lake Balaton from Budapest, use the motorway M7 or the highway 70. The former passes Lake Velence to the north, the latter goes by Martonvásár, where Beethoven's "immortal beloved" lived, and Székesfehérvár, the old city where the kings of Hungary were crowned. Both routes lead to Siófok, the main town on the south bank of the eastern part of the lake.

The south shore: The landscape is generally flat and the cultural sites not as diverse as the northern shore. But it does have its benefits. The northeast winds from the **Bakony Forest** stir up the shallow water, and the waves wash sand and silt to the shore creating long sandbanks. These now serve to delight children.

A string of bathing resorts has developed behind the sandbanks. Between **Siófok** and **Balatonberény** (a stretch of some 40 miles/65 km), one resort practically runs into another. In the last few years any open spaces remaining between the old farming and fishing villages, with their villas and summer houses, have been

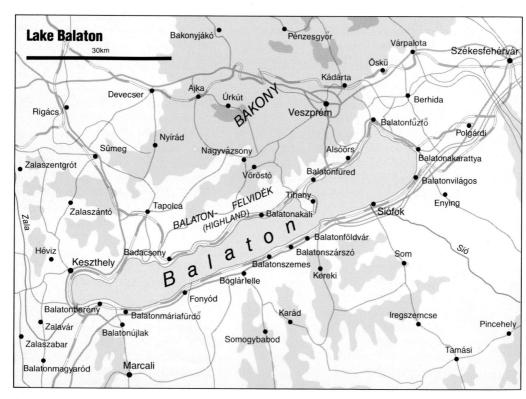

built up. Countless *eszpresszós,* ice-cream parlours, *csárdas* (inns) and other tourist haunts and resort phenomena "adorn" the streets.

The southern shore has one further attraction. From here you get a splendid view of the bizarrely shaped hills and basalt cliffs of the north shore, evidence of the region's volcanic origins.

Apart from its beach, Balatonberény has a notable 15th century village church, and in the surrounding villages there are still some interesting old farmhouses with thatched roofs and pillared verandahs. Take a look, for instance, at the typical farmhouse at Csillagvár utca 68 in Balatonwszentgyörgy. This little home, built in 1836, is one of the few remaining traditional constructions in the area and houses a collection of exhibits illustrating the local way of life in times past. Further along the street is the old Csillagvar, a castle where the rich local history is documented. It stands in the grounds of what is today a bird sanctuary.

The 4-mile (7-km) stretch from **Balatonmariafürdö** to **Balatonfenyves** (where there is a shady pine wood behind the beach) is a recreation park. **Balatonboglár** is one of the oldest resorts on the south shore. From the tower on the Várhegy you have a view of the vineyards and orchards. The village of Buzsák, some 12 miles (20 km) south, is worth visiting to see the traditional arts and costumes.

Fonyód, the town before Balatonboglár, also has its "hill" and the old village lies between the two peaks. Fonyód has the second largest harbour on Lake Balaton, with a 1,522 feet (464 metres) long pier, and the second longest beach (after Siófok).

Between Balatonboglár and Balatonföldvár, there are a number of institutionally-owned chalets, but there are also beautiful stately homes,

Anglers at the pier hope for the big catch of the day.

reminders of an earlier era, and *csárdas* (inns). It is worth taking a look at the red village church in **Balatonlelle**.

Further east you wil reach the area of **Siófok**, the biggest town on the southern shore. It also has the longest beach on Lake Balaton. It follows the shoreline for 10 miles (16 km). Here you'll find the biggest, most modern hotels, some are actually built right by the lake, while others are located a short distance away.

One man born in Siófok later became famous as a master of light entertainment: Imre Kálmán, whose name is linked with the golden age of operetta. The house where he was born no longer exists, but on the site, in Kálmán Imre sétány 5, there is a museum devoted to him. It contains exhibits on the life and work of the creator of such warhorses as *Countess Mariza* and the *Csárdás Princess*.

In Siófok the navigable river Sió, which links Lake Balaton to the Danube, leaves the lake. The Romans had already learned to value this connection. They regulated the flow of the river and under Emperor Galerius (3rd century) they built locks, the remains of which can still be seen today.

The north shore: Coming from the direction of Budapest, you will catch your first glimpse of the north-eastern part of Lake Balaton between Siófok and **Balatonkenese**. It is impressive. The surface of the water stretches out before you, and in the distance you can make out the outline of the hills beyond Balatonfüred and the Tihany peninsula. It is as if you were standing by the seashore.

If you turn off the motorway M7 or the highway 70 northwards, onto the highway 71, the coastline is not particularly attractive at first. Neither Balatonkenese nor Balatonfüzfö on the northeastern corner of the lake are among the major resorts of Lake Balaton. The loess shore is rather **Down the slide, into the lake.**

monotonous, and Balatonfüzfö is more of an industrial town than a holiday resort. However, between the towns you come across two peculiarities of the countryside around Lake Balaton. On the hills above Balatonkenese a rare plant can be found. In May it produces hanging bunches of white honey-scented flowers, and is popularly known as "Tatar bread" (the botanical name is *crambe tataria*). During the Mongol invasion of the 13th century, people are supposed to have dug up the roots, which grow 5 feet (1½ metres) deep, roasted and eaten them as a substitute for bread.

The loess ridges themselves, up to 131 feet (40 metres) high, are studded with dark holes, the entrances to the "Tatar caves" in which the local population is supposed to have sought refuge during the Mongol invasion and later during the Turkish wars.

Balatonalmádi, protected against the north winds by the heights of the Balaton hinterland, has been a bathing resort since the second half of the 19th century. In little wooden houses, some of which still exist, visitors followed the Kneipp system of hydrotherapy. Nowadays the 12-storey Hotel Aurora dominates the scene. On a hill in the Vörösberény district of the town there is a church with a rather rare feature for this area. It is fortified and surrounded by a stone wall, like those often found in Transylvania or northeastern Hungary (today the eastern part of Slovakia). The Reformed church dates from the 13th century.

Though **Veszprém** is not on the lake itself, it usually forms part of a tour of this region. It is about 8 miles (13 km) north of Balatonalmádi. Its history stretches back to the earliest period of Hungarian statehood, when it was founded as the first bishopric by King István (Stephen) I. The bishops of Veszprém had the sole right to crown the Hungarian queens. Nothing remains of the first castle and cathedral. What was left following the departure of the Turks was thoroughly dealt with by the Austrian army during the War of Independence at the beginning of the 18th century. The reconstruction of Veszprém was thus accomplished under the aegis of the Austrian baroque.

The Castle Quarter, which has been restored and is now a protected site, stands clustered around a single street on the ridge of a hill that overlooks the rest of the town. The entrance is marked by a pretty fire tower that dates back to 1817. The glockenspiel, however, has been computerised and its sound, though cute, is a little too synthetic for the dignity of the *genius loci*. The Heroes' Gate was built in 1936 on the site of the old town gate houses a small museum.

Beyond is the Piarist church, a fairly simple structure with a single tower. The neighbouring Bishop's Palace is set back and reflects more of the pomp of the baroque age. It was planned by

Bell of 1930, on a boat in Balatonfüred.

the great Jakob Fellner and executed between 1765 and 1776 using stones from a royal castle that once stood on this spot. Fellner also worked on the Gizella Chapel (named after the Bavarian wife of István I), which can be found at the northern end of the palace. On reaching the central square of the Castle Quarter of Veszprém you will see, in good baroque style, a typical statue of the Trinity. The little well here is perhaps one of the few remnants of medieval Veszprém. The two other churches, the one Franciscan (with a single tower) and St Michael's Cathedral (with the two towers) were both rebuilt in the early part of this century in neo-Romanesque style. The cathedral's history dates back to the early 11th century, when Hungary tied its fate to the Catholic Church, but of course that is merely on paper.

The end of the Castle Quarter is marked by the old bastions, which offer a splendid view over the rest of the town and its surrounding area. István I and his wife, Gizella, are honoured here in *effigio*. The statues date back to 1938, the 900th anniversary of the death of the founder of the Hungarian state.

The Balaton Riviera: At **Felsöörs** and **Alsóörs** you reach that part of the coast known as the **Balaton Riviera**. The vegetation is lush by Central European standards, and narrow paths wind up the hills, leading into vineyards. Popular white wines are made from the grapes grown here.

In **Felsöörs** you can see a medieval church built of red sandstone, with a richly decorated portal and a somewhat bizarre tower with an impressive roof. **Alsóörs** is important for fish production in Lake Balaton. The fish breeding farm here was built in the 1950s. In the pike-perch breeding season pine, juniper and other twigs are tied to ropes 2,000 feet (610 metres) long, that are then laid out in the

I spy with my little eye.

202

lake. The fish lay their eggs on those twigs. Then the ropes are drawn out of the lake and the twigs with the eggs are immediately transferred into pools. As soon as the young hatch, they escape into the lake via a special channel. Also in Alsóörs is the oldest stately home on the shores of Lake Balaton. It was built around 1500 and is now known as the "House of the Turkish Tax Collector", either because of its turban-shaped chimney, or because a tax collector lived there during the Turkish occupation.

The "capital" of Lake Balaton: Lying 6 miles (9 km) further west, **Balatonfüred** is undoubtedly the resort with the most tradition on Lake Balaton. However, the town doesn't owe its reputation to the lake, but to the hot springs which contain carbon dioxide. Their medicinal powers were discovered by the German geographer Martin Zeiller in 1632. In the 18th century the first permanent bath

houses and drinking pavilions were built, the sanatoria followed in the 19th century. The biggest, built in the Secessionist style, was named after the Empress Elizabeth, today, it is one of the best-known hospitals for sufferers of heart and circulatory diseases.

The "Heart Hospital", as it is known, is flanked on the east by **Gyógy tér**, the centre of Balatonfüred. On its northern side, the square is bounded by the complex of the trade union sanatorium. Every year, in the great hall of the town's cultural centre, the "Anna Ball" takes place on 26 July. It is the social event of the season in Balatonfüred and dates from the 19th century, when the Horváth house, a late-baroque building on the western borders of the square, was the meeting place of the political and cultural elite of Hungary. The first ball was held in 1825 in honour of the daughter of the house, and the event still survives.

In the centre of Gyógy tér is the

A cruise vessel on Lake Balaton stands by for passengers.

classical drinking pavilion, dating from 1800 and named after Kossuth. It is fed by one of five hot springs which rise out of the volcanic ground.

Poets: There are three memorials between Gyógy tér and the shore promenade: to the Hungarian poet Sándor Kisfaludy, to the great reformer István Széchenyi and to the Indian poet Rabindranath Tagore. Kisfaludy's poetic work was strongly influenced by the Balaton landscape. Széchenyi helped to revive the economy of the Balaton region in the 1840s. He started steamship travel on the lake in 1846, and his yacht *Himfy* on made sailing on Lake Balaton fashionable. The "Blue Ribbon" competition which takes place every two years on the lake is held in honour of his initiative.

As for Tagore, who spent some time in Balatonfüred having his heart condition treated, he is not only remembered in the memorial but in the Tagore Promenade (Sétány) along the lake.

Up until 1972 it was lined by rows of poplar trees, but these all fell victim to a sudden whirlwind. The poet also left this verse next to a lime tree which he planted:

> *When I am no longer on this*
> *earth, my tree,*
> *Let the ever renewed leaves of*
> *spring*
> *Murmur to the wayfarer*
> *The poet did love while he lived.*

If you are interested in buildings of the late baroque and classical periods, take a stroll along Blaha Lujza utca between Gyógy tér and the odd round church. Here you will find a pharmacy dating from the year 1782 and the Kedves pâtisserie from 1795. Don't forget the little villa of the "Nation's Nightingale", the singer-actress Lujza Blaha, who delighted Hungarian audiences around the turn of the century.

The English, by the way, took early note of Balatonfüred. The doctor and travel writer Richard Bright visited

The Benedictine abbey of Tihany.

the town at the time of the Congress of Vienna, and in 1835 John Paget spoke of Balatonfüred as a spa which deserved an international reputation.

Boat-building on Lake Balaton is also bound up with an English name. In 1881 Richard Young founded a small boatyard. At first the yard built only sailing boats; motor boats were produced in the 1920s, and in the 1950s – following nationalisation – the bigger passenger vessels and car ferries that sail regularly on the lake were also built here.

Tihany offers the most picturesque scenery on Lake Balaton. This peninsula runs far out into the lake, its slopes covered with verdant growth, occasionally broken by bizarre shaped rocks, the whole crowned by the twin towers of a baroque abbey church, surrounded by little farmhouses and fishermen's cottages, although most of these today have become shops, cafés and restaurants serving tourists.

In order to really appreciate the view of Tihany, you should approach it from across the lake, on one of the passenger boats from Balatonfüred, or by ferry from the opposite shore. Tihany looks lovely from where the boat moors at the slightly curved mole of the harbour, beneath the abbey.

Evidence of the volcanic past of Tihany are the geyser mounds – petrified remains of the activities of hot springs half a million years ago. The only other places where you will find so many mounds are in Iceland and Yellowstone Park in the US. The most spectacular of them – it glows golden in the sunset – is near **Hármashegy**, to the south of Belsö-tó. This is the Inner Lake, 85 feet (26 metres) above Lake Balaton, another reminder of the area's prehistoric past.

Royal burial ground: Tihany is old ground, not only geologically, but also historically speaking. Here King András I, the "most Christian bearer

One of the volcanic mounds on the northern shore.

of the sceptre", as the charter calls him, founded a monastery in 1055. It was supposed to become the burial ground for the Hungarian kings. However, only the founding king is buried in the Romanesque crypt, the only surviving part of the 11th century building. Hence the inscription in the crypt: "This is the only royal tomb in the 1,000-year old Kingdom of Hungary that was passed down to us in its original form." The squat, unadorned pillars bearing the massive vault are not the only impressive features in the crypt. The narrow tomb of the king also has a touching quality. The tombstone is cut from white limestone, with a twisted staff and a simple cross chiselled out at one end.

The baroque church above the crypt, with its two towers that can be seen from a considerable distance, was built between 1719 and 1754, i.e. after the Turks had been driven out of Hungary. The first building was destroyed by fire in 1736, but the abbot at that time, Agoston Lécs, persevered.

The church's splendid but at the same time completely harmonious interior is particularly effective. Various furnishings are of interest, including the pulpit, the altars, organ and choir and the decoration of the sacristy. They are the work of the Austrian artist Sebastian Stuhlhoff, a woodcarver who worked here in the 18th century for more than 25 years.

The ancient history of Tihany and the times when Hungary still had close contact with the Eastern churches is reflected in a system of hermits' cells in the basalt-tufa cliffs that drop down to the lake to the east of the church. They date from the abbey's foundation. King András invited monks from Kiev to settle here. The king had spent part of his youth at the court of the Prince of Kiev, Jaroslav the Wise, and married his daughter Anastasia.

More recently, the last emperor of

Veszprémfajsz, one of the many "hills of Calvary".

the house of Habsburg-Lorraine, Charles I, spent his final night on the soil of his former empire here in the abbey. Following the failure in October 1921 of his second attempt to retain at least the title of King of Hungary, he was interned in Tihany and, on 31 October, taken to the Danube harbour of Baja. Here he boarded the British warship *Glow-worm*, which took him on his journey into exile on Madeira.

On the road to Badacsony: To the east of Tihany the bays are mostly full of reeds, the beaches narrow, and the railway and highway 71 run parallel to the shoreline in several places. Hotels are scarce, but there are several campsites. A few interesting sights can be seen between Tihany and Badacsony, including some strange heart-shaped tombstones of white sandstone in the churchyard of **Balatonudvari**.

Some 19 miles (30 km) to the west of Tihany, the landscape suddenly takes on a dramatic appearance. The massive hill of Badacsony rears up and protrudes into the lake like the foothills of a mountain range. It stands like a sentinel at the entrance to the plain of Tapolca, out of which rise more bizarre-looking volcanic hills.

On the gentle lower slopes of Badacsony grow the vines which produce several white wines prized both in and outside Hungary – green Sylvaner and Hungarian Riesling, to name but two. Further up the gentle slope becomes a rocky cliff stretching steeply towards the plateau on the summit, which is thickly covered with a dark crown of forest. Viniculture has a long tradition on the slopes of Badacsony, and there is a legend that no vintner could become mayor of any of the villages on the slopes if he had let a stranger pass by his cellar without offering a glass of wine. Today the vine-growing business is usu-

Below, 12th-century church in Oskü. Right, façade of the Festetics Palace in Keszthely.

ally carried out in co-operatives. But, there are small private wine cellars, too, where the vintners store the wine made from their own vineyards.

Among the vineyards are a number of pleasant country houses and a wine museum in which visitors can taste and buy local wines to take home and enjoy at their leisure. Two houses stand in memory of the poet Sándor Kisfaludy and his wife Róza Szegedy, both of whom spent many years here. The **Kisfaludy House**, today a popular restaurant offering a magnificent view of the lake, once housed the poet's wine press. His wife's house contains a literary museum which, besides the poet who was inspired by Lake Balaton's landscape, also celebrates other Hungarian literary figures of Transdanubia. Living Hungarian writers can stay in the castle in nearby **Szigliget**, which formerly belonged to the Esterházy family and is now an artists' retreat. In **Badac-sonytomaj**, one of the four villages surrounding the hill, there is, near highway 71, a church built of basalt. It was erected in 1932, and with its two bell towers it is supposed to be the only one of its kind in all of Europe. Another important excursion in the area around Badacsony is a visit to **St George's Mountain** (Szent György-hegy), 1,358 feet (414 metres) high. Its main attraction is the "great organ" on the eastern edge of the hill, a wall of 98 to 131 feet (40 metres) high basalt columns, lined up like church organ pipes.

Last stop: Before you arrive in Keszthely, make a quick stop in **Bala-tongyörök** to see its lovely beach and, most of all, the **Belvedere** (Szép-kilátó). This is a promenade offers a splendid view of all that this part of Lake Balaton has to offer; the vineyards and the bay of Szigliget, the castle ruins on the former volcanoes in the plain of Tapolca, the mass of **Autumn in Lake Balaton.**

Badacsony and in the mist the fine lines of the southern shore.

In the town of **Keszthely**, sloping gently down to the lake, the first thing you will notice is the palace with its generous proportions. Its southern wing dates from baroque times (1745), but its present appearance dates from the period 1883–87. It was created by the Festetics counts and the town has developed outwards from it. In front of the palace is the statue of Count György Festetics (1755–1819). He was a man of the Enlightenment, and both the palace and the town owe much to him. In his palace he created the **Helikon Library**. Today it has some 60,000 volumes and forms one of the most valuable collections in the country. The library hall with its classical coffered ceiling is the main attraction of the palace.

In Keszthely Count György Festetics also founded the **Georgikon** in 1797. It was the first advanced agricultural college in Hungary, and the modern agricultural college has developed from it. Filled with the spirit of Ancient Greece, he began the Helikon meetings of poets, which were of great importance for the cultural rebirth of the Hungarian nation. It comes as no surprise, then, that in Keszthely, the big park near the lake, and the modern hotel on the shore bear the name of that mountain which in Greek mythology is the home of the Muses.

Also of interest in Keszthely are some baroque houses in **Szabadság utca**, which leads down to the lake. In house No. 22 Karl Goldmark, the composer of the opera *The Queen of Sheba*, was born. Apart from the one near the Hotel Helikon, there are two more beaches in Keszthely, one further west, one in the direction of Fenékpuszta.

In **Fenékpuszta**, 5 miles (7½ km) south of Keszthely, you will also find the ruins of the Roman fortress of Valcum. Among the attractions here

Hungary's own little sea: Lake Balaton.

are the foundations of an ancient Christian basilica and the classical stables and accommodation of the stud farm of the Festetics family. About 4 miles (6 km) northwest of Keszthely lies the spa of **Hévíz**, whose reputation, extending far beyond Hungary's border, rests mainly on its gigantic thermal lake, the largest in Europe.

In summer the water temperature rises to 93°F (34°C), and in winter it seldom falls below 78°F (26°C). The changing rooms and bath-houses, built on stilts extending out into the lake, were originally conceived by Count György Festetics at the end of the 18th century, although they have been rebuilt since. How long Hévíz will continue producing thermal water is uncertain as a nearby bauxite mine has caused the water level to sink.

Zalavár: For those interested in history, a visit to **Zalavár** is certainly recommended. It is about 12 miles (20 km) south of Keszthely, in the (now-

adays mostly drained) marshland around the Kis-Balaton (*Kis*=little) and the little river Zala. There isn't much to see here, apart from the foundation walls of a small 9th century church.

However, the area does have its historical significance. Zalavár is in fact the Mosapurc, mentioned in Bavarian chronicles, where the Slavs of Pannonia were converted before the invasion of the Danube region by the Magyars. It was in Mosapurc, the residence of Slav princes, where the historic confrontation took place between the missionaries of the Archdiocese of Salzburg, who proclaimed the teachings of Christ using Latin language and liturgy, and the Slav apostles Cyril and Methodus, who preferred to preach in the Old Slavic language and celebrate the mass according to the Byzantine liturgy. The later schism of the church between East and West, between Byzantium and Rome, and between the Orthodox and Papal churches – with all its secular consequences – originated in Zalavár, a sleepy little place today.

The Upper Regions of Lake Balaton: During 150 years of Turkish rule in central Hungary the border between the Ottoman and the Habsburg Empires ran through the hills of the northern shore of Lake Balaton. Both sides had their border fortifications here but today, little remains of them. For during the great revolt under Ferenc Rákóczi against the emperor in Vienna in 1703–11 they served as bases for the Kuruz or rebel troops. The imperial forces destroyed them during – and especially after – the collapse of the revolt.

One of these border forts against the Turks was **Nagyvázsony**, about 16 miles (25 km) to the north of Tihany. Its horseshoe-shaped barbican, the mighty outer fortifications of which once protected the castle from attack, and the 92 feet (28 metres) high fortified tower are still in good condition.

Left, "a yo-ho-ho and a bottle of pálinka!"

The name of Pál Kinizsi, a general under Mátyás Corvinus, is linked with Nagyvázsony. The fact that Hungary was relatively untroubled by the Turks during this time, i.e. the second half of the 15th century, is due to the military skills of this man. However, he is remembered among the people for his legendary brute strength. A picture in the castle portrays just how strong Mátyás was – he is depicted lifting a burly Turk with his teeth, and with a sword in each hand performing some kind of warrior dance.

The upper regions of Lake Balaton are also an idyllic rider's paradise. Some Hungarian travel bureaus arrange riding excursions lasting several days here. In Nagyvázsony, the baroque palace is a riding hotel with a riding school. Every two or three years, equestrian games are held here, with riders dressed in period costumes.

On the road between Nagyvázsony and Veszprém is the *csárda* (inn) of Nemesvámos. Lying on the border between two districts, it was, only 200 years ago, a famous "Betyár csárda".

The Betyárs were young people who had either tried to escape military service, or were in some way in conflict with the landowners or the law in general, and who had taken refuge in the forest. They had to earn their living by highway robbery. As they often robbed the wealthy and left the poor alone, they were very popular, and there are numerous songs and stories in praise of them. In the inn at Nemesvámos they were fairly safe, for whenever the gendarmes of one district approached, they could quickly escape to the other.

The *csárda* also has the privilege of being featured in architectural history, because of its open-arched passages on the ground and the upper floors, which make it a good example of rural architecture of the late 18th century.

The bleak mid-winter at Balaton-kenese.

NORTHEAST HUNGARY

Compared to Lake Balaton, Budapest or the puszta, northeast Hungary cannot claim to be a great centre of tourism. It is probably because many people believe that this part of the country, with its ranges of low and medium-height mountains, is not "typically Hungarian". In fact, this region has delightful scenery, historic towns and castles such as Eger and Sárospatak, natural phenomena such as the stalactite caves of Aggtelek, and a wine which has become a European legend: Tokay.

If you want to visit the Börzsöny, the most westerly of the hill ranges going from Budapest, the best place to start is **Vác**. The town lies on the left bank of the Danube, 21 miles (34 km) to the north of the Hungarian capital, and is linked by the first railway ever built in Hungary.

Vác is often called the "city of churches" and their many towers rise above the single-storey 18th-19th century baroque and classical houses on the rising slope of the Danube bank. The basilica dominates everything. It is a classical building dating from the late 18th century, and a number of builders and architects worked on it, resulting in a lack of harmony.

The Börzsöny hills: Seen from the river promenade of Vác the hills look impressive, although they hardly reach 3,000ft (900 metres). Overall, the Börzsöny are sparsely settled, barring the villages on the southern slopes facing the Danube, that are nowadays often visited by tourists and day-trippers from Budapest. There are very few villages on the northwest slopes, towards Slovakia – the border runs along the Ipoly river. The landscape is accordingly unspoilt.

To find out more about the traditions and the history of this isolated region, visit the Börzsöny Museum in Szob (only 19 miles/30 km) away from Vác. Before you arrive, you come to **Verőcemaros**, where there is a ceramics museum named after the artist Géza Gorka. From here, you can also travel about 6 miles (10 km) into the forest on a narrow-gauge railway. From Királyrét, the terminus of the little track, several paths lead up to the surrounding summits.

The largest town on the Börzsöny's western slopes is **Nagybörzsöny**. In the Middle Ages, it was the centre of a flourishing mining industry. The plain Gothic Miner's Church and St Stephen's Church (one of the few surviving Romanesque churches in Hungary, surrounded by a stone wall and dating from the early 13th century) are both reminders of the town's former days of greatness.

The most famous town on the eastern side of the range is **Nógrád**. Protected by a massive castle, it played an important role in the Turkish wars and changed hands several times.

Undulating Cserhát: To the east of the Börzsöny range lie the hills of the Cserhát, an undulating landscape rising to a mere 2,139ft (652m). The valleys are broad and fertile, and for this reason – in contrast to those of the Börzsöny – densely populated. The people living in this part of Hungary are known as Palots. Some ethnographers see them as the remnants of a separate group which came into the country before or with the Magyars, others consider them Hungarians with their own customs clearly influenced by Slovak culture.

The traditional art, both past and present, of this ethnic group is best seen in the Palot museum in the little town of **Balassagyarmat** on the Slovakian border. Central to the collection are objects made of wood – drinking ladles, for instance, with decoratively carved handles and clothes and linen chests, with stories depicted on their sides.

Traditional costume here is colourful, and the towering headdresses of the girls are often decorated with glittering beads, not seen elsewhere in Hungary. Worth seeing, too, are the Palot houses in the museum garden, spacious, dark painted wooden buildings on a stone foundation, covered by a densely thatched roof.

Palot village: One complete village of these Palot houses still exists. It is called **Hollókö** and lies at the feet of a ruined castle some 22 miles (35 km) southeast of Balassagyarmat. It is under a preservation order and most of its houses belong to intellectuals from Budapest, who have pledged themselves to take look after the buildings. Most of the original population, however, have sold their "old" houses and have moved to the "new" village, where they can build and furnish without government interference.

Some of the houses offer simple accommodation at reasonably low prices. There are also small restaurants with fine basic fare. One of the Palot houses has been turned into a museum, but it is not nearly as complete as the one in Balassagyarmat.

In 1988 Hollókö, as well as the castle of Buda, was put on UNESCO's "Cultural Heritage of the World" list as a rarity to be preserved at all costs. Now this little village in the hilly Cserhát, its structure unchanged since the Middle Ages even though most of the houses were built after the fire of 1909, is on the same list as the Great Wall of China, the Leaning Tower of Pisa and the Acropolis in Athens.

On the way from Balassagyarmat to Hollókö, you pass through Szécsény, a larger village with a church rebuilt in the baroque style but with a sacristy that still retains its earlier Gothic form. Of the castle only one corner tower and the wall of a bastion remain, both included in the **Palace of Forgách**, which today houses the local museum. In 1705 the famous Hungarian parlia-

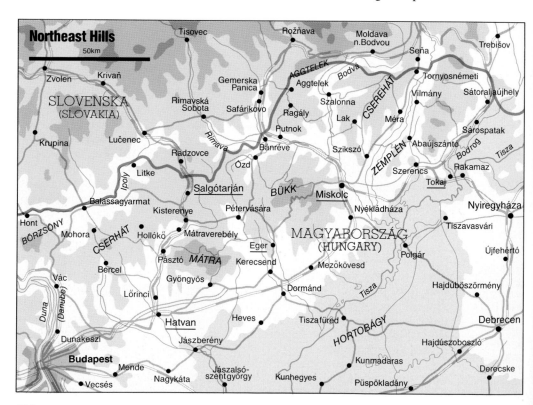

ment was held in Szécsény, during which the "Confederation of Hungarian Lands" chose Ferenc Rákóczi to be their ruling prince.

There is nothing of historical importance about **Salgótarján**, today the centre of the district of Nógrád. It is a "model socialist town" of 40,000 inhabitants and an important industrial centre with lignite mines, steelworks, glassworks and high-rise apartments.

To the south of Salgótarján lie the **Mátra Mountains**, which deserve the name "mountains" if only because they boast the highest peak in Hungary, the 3,327feet (1,014 metres) high **Kékestetö**. From the tower of the **Institute of Telecommunications** on the peak you have extensive views, including a good portion of Hungary's Great Plain. For the Hungarians who do not have much choice when it comes to mountains, the Mátra Mountains are a popular tourist attraction as they are only 62 miles (100 km) from

Hungary's small mountain ranges make a lasting impression.

Budapest. **Parádfürdö** is one of the oldest resorts in the country. The local rulers were once the Karóly family, whose most famous member must be Count Mihály, who took the reigns of the first Hungarian Republic in 1919. His stables, in the middle of this long town, still serve their old purpose, in addition to housing a coach museum. On the eastern side of town is a pretty Palot house that gives a good idea of how people used to live.

Bull's Blood town: Between the Mátra Mountains and the Bükk range is **Eger**, the most interesting city of northeast Hungary. It has a turbulent history, a varied architecture, and a name linked with a famous red wine: *Egri bikavér*, Eger Bull's Blood.

Eger is famous in literature, too. The novel *The Stars of Eger*, by Géza Gárdonyi, a popular work which has been translated into several languages, deals with the heroic defence of the castle of Eger in the year 1552 against

a superior Turkish force. Under the command of captain István Dobó, 2,000 men, supported by their women-folk, defended the citadel against a Turkish army of nearly 100,000. The Turks failed to capture the town until 1596. They stayed for 91 years and left their mark with a 131-foot (40-metre) minaret, the most northerly in the former Ottoman empire. It is a decorative construction standing on a 14-sided base. There is also a bastion of the castle and the walls of some baths, now included in the baths district near Petöfi tér.

The castle courtyard contains the restored Bishop's Palace with a Gothic arcade on the ground floor. A museum has reminders of the brave defenders of the castle against the Turks, among them is the tombstone of István Dobó. The actual castle museum on the upper floor contains a revised version of the founding charter of the bishopric dating from the second half of the 13th century. However, Eger as the seat of a bishop, was one of the 10 bishoprics founded by King – and Saint – István (Stephen) at the beginning of the 11th century. Only stumps remain of the walls of the former diocesan church, the three-aisled 12th-century Romanesque **St John's Cathedral**.

Baroque centre: A visit to the dilapidated barracks, built in the second half of the 16th century, gives a further impression of the fortification of Eger. Much less martial-looking is the centre of the town at the foot of the castle, around Dobó István tér.

Apart from the classical basilica in Szabadság tér – which is the second largest church in Hungary, after Esztergom cathedral – the style of the town is baroque.

The prominence of baroque lines has to do with both the Bishop's Palace, a U-shaped building, and, with the former archepiscopal Lyceum, now a teachers' training college. It is

Eger, the seat of a bishopric founded by St Stephen.

a square complex of buildings, built between the years 1765–85 by the great master of the late baroque, Jakob Fellner. Art historians consider it the most important mid-18th century building in Hungary. The sheer size of the building is impressive. Each of the four wings is 279 feet (85 metres) long and 69 feet (21 metres) high. They flank an inner courtyard and are crowned by a 10-storey tower with an observatory.

The showpiece of the building is the library hall with the lively ceiling fresco by the Bohemian painter Johann Lukas Kracker. It depicts the Tridentine Council with 132 figures, including Emperor Charles V. The ceiling in the north wing of the former chapel has a fresco by Franz Anton Maulbertsch, one of his last creations.

In **Kossuth Lajos utca** the Grand Prior's House, today the district library (No. 16), the offices (No. 9) and the Lesser Prior's House (No. 4) are worth mentioning, both for their design and also for their magnificent wrought iron gates and balconies.

You shouldn't miss visiting the **Minorite Church** on István Dobó tér, built (1758–73) according to plans by the great baroque architect Kilian Ignaz Dientzenhofer. Its main façade with the curved central section, the pair of pillars flanking it and the curved gable, together with the twin towers reaching towards the heavens, displays an extraordinary harmony, which is reflected in the interior. The painting above the high altar is also the work of Johann Lukas Kracker. The square dominated by the Minorite Church was the medieval market square. It still gives the impression of being at the centre of things, as many of the town's narrow alleys lead to it. The dramatic statues of István Dobó and the town's defenders can't detract from the square's quaintness.

Finally, another traditional aspect

Burning charcoal in the Bükk mountains.

of Eger are the wine bars in the town and the cellars on the outskirts, where private vintners will pour you a quarter litre – not only of Bull's Blood, but also of white wine, Riesling, muscatel and the dessert wine *Leányka*.

Bélapátfalva is the sole surviving monastery church in Hungary. Surrounded by lime and chestnut trees, it lies wholly isolated on the northern fringe of the Bükk range. French Cistercian monks began the building in 1232. The main façade with its Romanesque pillared portal dates from this period as do the stocky pillars that divide the three aisles, the ogive vault that they support, and the rose window under the triangular gable. The Gothic church was not completed until the end of the 13th century.

Szilvásvárad, which once belonged to the Margrave Pallavicini, is a popular place for excursions. Among its attractions is a Lipizzaner stud farm and museum depicting the history of these horses, for which the Spanish Riding School in Vienna is renowned. There is also the romantic landscape with its deeply cut valleys, waterfalls, fish-ponds and ancient caves. The most beautiful impressions of the Bükk scenery, however, can be gained along the narrow road from Szilvásvárad to Lillafüred and Miskolc.

The road winds uphill with many bends, to the high plateau of the range. The landscape is stern and lonely, made up of meadows and forests with mighty beech and oak trees, of juniper bushes and limestone rock, without a trace of human habitation.

Lillafüred, on the eastern side of the range, is a popular resort renowned for its fresh air. The big Hotel Palota, famous in the inter-war years, was turned into a trade union hostel in Communist times, but is a conventional hotel once again. It lies in the middle of a large park bordered by thick forest. The nearby **Lake Hámor**,

Village church of Szalonna manifests simplicity.

where you can row, has many footpaths around its perimeter. On the right bank of the lake is a strange building, which looks like three piled up limestone cubes. This is the original ironworks (Öskohó) of Ujmassa, the core of the Lenin Metalworks, which turned Miskolc into the most important industrial region of Hungary with more than 130 companies.

Third city: Before reaching Hungary's third largest city, Miskolc (population 210,000) you pass the castle of **Diósgyör**, with its four massive corner towers, which nowadays are almost hidden behind the high-rise apartment blocks. It is one of the few diamonds to be found in this rough industrial town. First mentioned in a 13th-century chronicle, Diósgyör grew from the lesson learned after the Mongol invasion of 1241. The Golden Horde succeeded in taking the undefended valleys, but such boggy places as Székesfehérvár and hilltop fortresses such as Pannonhalma resisted. After the Mongols left, King Béla IV decided to build a string of fortified places in case they should return. Castrum Geuru, occupied by a local nobleman and governor for years, was one of these edifices.

In the 14th century, the castle changed hands several times. Offspring of the original family, the Erny, rebelled against the king, Charles Robert of Anjou, and found themselves on the losing side. Diósgyör was handed over to the voivode of Transylvania, but later became the property of the Ban of Croatia.

Royal visitations: Successive Hungarian kings (Louis of Anjou, Sigismond, Mátyás Corvinus, Wladislaw II Jagiello, Louis II of Habsburg) used Diósgyör as a kind of pied-à-terre in a well-protected spot on the Hungarian map, but during the occupation of Hungary by the Turks the castle was made into a fortified border post and

The castle of Diósgyör, one of many 13th-century fortifications.

the luxury for which it had become known rapidly vanished. Attempts were made to restore it, but it reverted to its utilitarian function.

As the Turkish threat faded, tensions between the Austrians and the Hungarians broke out, leading to divisions and counter-divisions of Diósgyör which stood, ironically, near the line dividing Royal (Habsburg) Hungary and Transylvania under Count Thököly and his Kuruz armies. Tired of this stronghold of cantan-kerous Hungarians, the emperor finally had it "and all the people in the immediate surroundings" destroyed.

Open-air theatre: The ruins stood for more than 200 years before anyone other than local masons looking for stone, or perhaps a tax official, noticed it. The Millennial celebrations revived interest in this bastion of Hungarian history. Based on plans by István Möller, excavations started in the 1930s and resumed in the 1950s. The

castle became a museum and open-air theatre in 1968. Too much had been plundered and destroyed, to warrant restoring Diósgyör to its former glory. The documents, however, do suggest what it must have been like, while the massive crenellated towers and their walls tell of its dramatic story.

Miskolc itself has few interesting sights. The oldest building in the city is the Reformed Church on the slopes of the hill of Avas. It is a Gothic building going back to the 13th century. At first it was a three-aisled church, it was converted to a hall church between 1470 and 1489. The old ribbed vault was not replaced by the coffered wooden ceiling until later. In the 16th century the church was taken over by the Calvinists. It is surrounded by an old graveyard, where burials have been taking place since the 11th century. Next to it is a bell tower with a wooden Renaissance gallery beneath the pointed roof.

The hot springs of **Miskolctapolca** (4 miles/7 km – from the centre) are radioactive and maintain a temperature of 84°F–88°F (29°C–31°C.) Hot springs also supply a cave-basin, which is the second largest in Europe after Badgastein.

Underground labyrinth: The new industrial areas of Kazincbarcika and Ózd, which have largely developed since the last war, are not particularly attractive to tourists. But the limestone caves in the *karst* of **Aggtelek-Jósvafö** at the Hungary–Slovakia border are a great attraction. Their underground passages are among the most complex structures of limestone caves in Europe stretching for 14 miles (22 km) well into Slovakia.

The biggest cave on Hungarian territory is the **Baradla cave**. It is connected to the **Domica cave** on the other side of the border. In Baradla cave there is the biggest stalagmite in the world, known as the **Observatory**. It is 82 feet (25 metres) high and 26 feet (8 metres) in diameter at its foot.

A married couple's grave marker, Aggtelek

The Aggtelek range and the hills of Cserehát (where the biggest artificial lake in Hungary, Lake Rakaca, lies) form a bridge to the **Zemplén Mountains**, the last link in the chain of the ranges of the northeast. Cserehát and Zemplén are divided by the Hernád river which flows from Slovakia.

The term "mountains" is a bit of an exaggeration for the Zemplén range, for it is only in the extreme north that it reaches the modest height of 2,933 feet (894 metres). Along its southern and southeastern slopes lies the vine-growing region of **Hegyalja**, and among the grapes grown are those for the world-famous Tokay wines.

On your way from Miskolc to Tokay, you will pass through **Szerencs**, a small town of 10,000 inhabitants. It once had a key role in the history of Hungary – in the 100 years or more between the early 17th and 18th centuries when the Hungarians often rose against the Habsburgs.

At the end of the 16th century, the castle of Szerencs fell in the hands of Zsigmond Rákóczi, the first member of this house to play a political role. He was a political ally of István Bocskai, who rebelled against the emperor in Vienna in 1604 to defend the rank and religious freedom of the Hungarian nobility. It was in Szerencs that Bocskai and, later, Zsigmond Rákóczi were elected as princes of Transylvania. Rákóczi was also buried in Szerencs – his red marble sarcophagus is in the Calvinist church.

Another great Hungarian rebel came from this area – Lajos Kossuth. His birthplace lies in the village of **Monok**, 8 miles (13 km) north of Szerencs. There is a museum in the plain house in which this leader of the 1848–49 revolution was born. Another important Hungarian politician was also born here, Gyula Nemeth, who steered the nation away from the Communist Bloc at the end of the 1980s.

Karst landscape near Aggtelek.

Wine, Wine, Wine: Tállya, 5 miles (8 km) to the east of Monok, competed from time to time with Tokay in giving the regional wine its name. Tokay finally won the tug-of-war. The Catholic parish church of the village has a painting over a side altar which is especially appropriate to the spirit of the place: the wine harvest of St Wendelin, where even God's angels are helping the saint. This painting is the work of Franz Anton Maulbertsch. **Tokay** lies at the end of a hill of loess, pushed out by the Zemplén Mountains like a peninsula into the Great Hungarian Plain. However, the Tokay wine doesn't just come from the vineyards close to town. The entire wine-growing area is known in Hungary as "Tokay-Hegyalja" and covers an area of some 12,355 acres (5,000 hectares), with 28 towns and villages, on the southeastern and southern slopes of the range.

The Hungarian kings after the Mongol invasion of 1241 strongly supported the wine industry and thus invited French and Italian vintners to settle in the country. It is said that even the Celts had vineyards here.

Tokay wine was described on Louis XIV's wine list as the "wine of kings and king of wines". It is served in Auerbach's tavern in Goethe's tale of Faust; Schubert sang its praises, and two personalities as different as Voltaire and Beethoven praised and drank it.

Renaissance landmark: Twenty eight miles (45km) to the northeast of Tokay lie a town and a castle which are both noteworthy for a number of reasons – **Sárospatak**. The castle's "Red Tower", a five-storey tower of massive proportions, dominates the site on the steep bank above the Bodrog river. The castle is considered to be the biggest and best preserved Renaissance castle in the country. In 1616 it fell into the hands of the house of Rákóczi, from which several princes of Transylvania were chosen, up to the time of Ferenc Rákóczi II, who leed the War of Independence against the Habsburgs from 1703 to 1711. Sárospatak was already known outside the borders of Hungary in the mid-17th century. The **Protestant College**, founded here in 1531, was the spiritual centre of Calvinism in Hungary and Transylvania, where young Protestant noblemen received their training. From 1650 to 1655, the great Moravian teacher and humanist Johann Amos Comenius lived and worked here. His ideas influenced education and schools until the 20th century.

It was also here that he completed his major work, *Orbis pictus*. Nothing dating from those times remains in the college in the centre of the city. On the site is a classical complex of buildings including a high school, a boarding school and a library. The **Comenius Exhibition** gives a full depiction of the history of the college and of student life in the single-storey baroque building in the courtyard.

The buildings of the castle around the trapeze-shaped courtyard do not quite blend architecturally, as the wings date from different centuries. The remaining Renaissance elements from the 16th century are, however, of great beauty – especially the stairs and the loggia with its four arches, which adjoins the second floor of the "Red Tower".

Another interesting sight is the big Gothic church with its beautiful tombstones. Considering Sárospatak's historical aura, it is quite apt that one of the two hotels (the Borostyán) should be in a former Trinitarian monastery of the 17th century.

No trip through northeastern Hungary is complete without a visit to **Hollóháza**. This is the northernmost community in Hungary, 27 miles (38 km) to the north of Sárospatak, close to the border with Slovakia. It has the second most important porcelain factory in the country, after Herend.

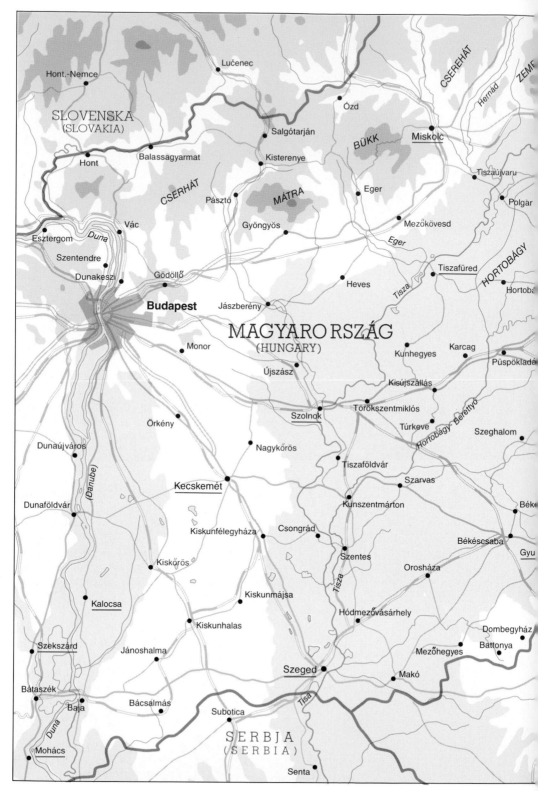

Hont.-Nemce
Lučenec
CSEREHÁT
ZEMP
Hernád

SLOVENSKA
(SLOVAKIA)
Ózd
Salgótarján
BÜKK
Miskolc

Hont
Balassagyarmat
Kisterenye
Tiszaújvaru

CSERHÁT
Pásztó
MÁTRA
Eger
Polgár

Vác
Gyöngyös
Mezőkövesd

Esztergom
Duna
Eger

Szentendre

Dunakeszi
Gödöllő
Tiszafüred
HORTOBÁGY

Heves
Tisza
Hortob

Budapest
Jászberény

MAGYARORSZÁG
(HUNGARY)

Monor
Kunhegyes
Karcag

Újszász
Püspökladá

Kisújszállás

Örkény
Szolnok
Törökszentmiklós
Túrkeve
Szeghalom
Hortobágy- Berettyó

Dunaújváros
Nagykőrös

Tiszaföldvár
Szarvas

(Danube)
Kecskemét
Kunszentmárton
Béke

Dunaföldvár

Kiskunfélegyháza
Csongrád
Békéscsaba
Gyu

Kiskőrös
Szentes
Orosháza

Kiskunmájsa

Kalocsa
Hódmezővásárhely

Kiskunhalas
Dombegyház

Szekszárd
Jánoshalma
Mezőhegyes
Battonya

Szeged
Makó

Bátaszék
Tisa

Baja
Bácsalmás

Duna
Subotica

SERBJA
(SERBIA)

Mohács
Senta

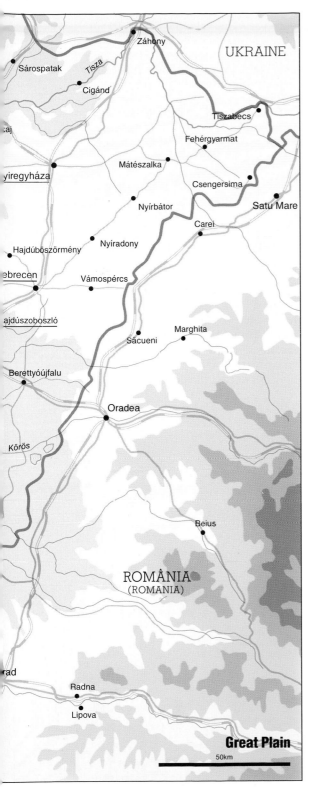

Great Plain

50km

THE GREAT PLAIN

The **Alföld**, the Great Plain, takes up more than half the area of Hungary. Its highest point (597 feet/182 metres) lies in the northeast, near Debrecen; the lowest (236 feet/72 metres) in the south, near Szeged.

Only by stretching your imagination can you conceive the vastness of the 12,800 feet (4,000 metres) high mountain range that is believed to have existed here a very long time ago. Earth movements caused it to sink to form today's basin, and a giant inland sea flooded it and levelled the ground. The present plain evolved out of the drying up of the sea. The Tisza, the largest tributary of the Danube and the second most important river in Hungary (and the one with the most fish) divides the area in two unequal parts just before it finally bends and follows a southern course.

Brahms's favourite: Let's start our trip by car, although it can also be made by the train running parallel to the road, in **Kecskemét**. The distance from the central milestone in Budapest is 53 miles (86 km), measured along the E5. "Kecskemét is the most beautiful town in the world", so said Johannes Brahms, praising this regional capital which has a population of about 100,000 and lies between the Danube and the Tisza. Kecskemét, expanding like some piece of rising dough on all sides over a gentle, hilly landscape, developed from a settlement that received its town charter in the 14th century. It was not destroyed during the 150 years of Turkish rule, as it was directly under the Sultan's protection.

The visitor is greeted by vineyards and apricot orchards, growing all around the town and into the suburbs,

Preceding pages: where the sunflowers – a main ingredient in some cosmetic products – always bloom in Hungary.

wrought from the sandy soil with great difficulty. The scent of a million apricot trees lingers. The olfactory nerves remember it for a long time, especially when sampling the famous *barackpálinka*, an apricot spirit.

The centre: Two large squares, Szabadság tér and Kossuth tér, together with the smaller Kálvin tér make up the centre. The former synagogue stands where Rákoczi út, an avenue leading to the railway station, joins Szabadság tér. It was built in 1864–71 according to plans by János Zitterbach jr. in a Moorish Romantic style with a "Persian tower and cupola". In the courtyard is the older, plainer synagogue dating from 1818. Also on the corner of Rákóczi út is one of the most beautiful buildings in town, the **Cifrapalota**, the "decorated palace", restored in 1983. Majolica tiles with colourful, stylised flowers adorn the façade. It was designed by Géza Márkus, a student of Lechner's. This palace is a fine example of Hungarian Secessionist style enriched with traditional ornamentation from Hungarian and Translyvanian folklore and even Islamic adornments brought by the Turks.

The majolica tiles with their gleaming metallic glaze are from the Zsolnay factory in Pécs. The Cifrapalota houses collections of drawings and paintings. In the southwestern corner of Szabadság tér is the Reformed Church, built in 1680–84 and crowned by a Renaissance tower. The interior, in late baroque style, dates from 1790, but the pulpit is pure rococo.

Kossuth tér with the **Kossuth Monument** joins Szabadság tér. It is dominated by the Town Hall. Ödön Lechner (1845–1914), the grand master of Hungarian Secessionist style, drew up the plans for this building, sparkling with majolica tiles and a beautiful wrought iron gate. It was built between 1893 and 1896.

City sights of Kecskemét, in the midst of the puszta: art nouveau architecture (left) and the former synagogue.

Kecskemét is reputed to be the "town of bells". The bells and carillons are often made of aluminium, a cheaper metal than bronze and one that is easier to transport. Aluminium also gives a beautiful tone. The Hungarians can rightly take credit for this small discovery.

Perhaps the most important, and at least in part the oldest, building in this square is the **Szent Miklós Church** opposite the town hall. It was already there in the 13th century, but was rebuilt in the baroque style in the 18th.

The **Town Theatre** is named after the poet József Katona, who was born in Kecskemét in 1791. The two architects Hermann Hellmer and Ferdinand Fellner, the most famous theatre architects in Europe, were responsible for the building. The **Trinity Column** in front of the theatre is a sign of gratitude donated by those citizens who survived the plague in 1739. The **Zoltán Kodály Institute** keeps alive the name of the composer who, together with Béla Bartók, did much to pave the way for modern Hungarian music. Kodály was born here in 1882. The building's origin goes back to a plan by the famous Hungarian architect and stage designer J. Kerényi, as does that of Museum of Naïve Art, the Toy Museum and several other houses.

After seeing so many of the sights of the town, you will need refreshment. Whether you go to **Kis-Bugac** in the north of the town, or to **Park-Étterem** in the southeast, to the restaurant of the **Arany Homok** hotel on Kossuth tér – you really should try one of the poultry specialities of Kecskemét: roasted goose liver, goose liver in garlic sauce, all kinds of chopped poultry dishes or roast duck. Then, treat yourself – and your digestion – to an apricot brandy, *barackpálinka*, which is drunk in style out of champagne glasses. Refreshed, you can now visit some of the town's 11 museums and

A old-time puszta excursion.

galleries, and enjoy the varied collections ranging from traditional folk to modern art and photography.

Picturesque drive: The quickest way from Kecskemét to Szeged is on the E5. A 6-mile (10-km) diversion to the east of Kistelek (about halfway between the two towns) takes you to one of the great monuments to Hungarian national feeling, the National Historical Memorial Park (Nemzeti Történeti Emlékpark). On display in the park is an extraordinary 360° panoramic painting called *The Arrival of the Hungarians* showing the proud Magyars taking possession of the land that was to become Hungary. An alternative route is along the highway No. 44, which takes you through a picturesque landscape dominated by the Tisza and the Körös, and where fauna and flora have not been affected by irrigation and river regulating schemes.

You cross the Tisza at Lakitelek and the Körös at Kunszentmarton. Here highway No. 45 turns off to the south via Szentes and **Hódmezövásárhely**. This town of 54,000 inhabitants was founded in the 13th century. It was named after the beaver (*hód*) which once lived in the lake south of the town, in the flood plain of the Tisza. The lake dried up because of the regulation of the river and the area is now a recreation park.

A walk through the "potter's town with the artesian well", often following road signs made of majolica, is worth your while. In the mid-19th century more than 400 potters were still at work here. Not until after World War II, with the coming of the age of plastic, was it possible for students of the Budapest Academy of Art to save the large number of jugs and bowls which did not fall victim to an epidemic of attic-clearing.

On the south side of Kossuth tér is the **Town Hall**, built in a classical style, with its lofty tower. Underneath,

Loyal farm help and one that survives the droughts in Hungary.

a bronze Hussar on horseback whirls his saber, charging to the attack.

The west side of Kossuth tér is bounded by the Hotel Béke, also a classical building with very attractive wrought iron work. The Old and the New Church, as well as the Greek Orthodox church, belong to the baroque period. It is worth noting at this point that the destructive Turkish wars completely devasted much of Hungary. Only fragments of the former period have survived.

To the south of the town highway No. 47 branches off and takes you to **Szeged**, Hungary's "Paprika Town". Because of its many hours of sunshine, it's also known as the "Sunshine Town". Archaeological finds show that people lived near the spot where the Maros flows into the Tisza in the Stone and Bronze Ages, and that Illyrians, Celts and Avars later lived here, too. Even Attila the Hun camped here.

A hesitant attempt to cultivate the puszta.

Szeged is first mentioned in documents dating from 1183, in this case as a salt trading post. In 1241 the Tartars destroyed the town. Following resettlement and rebuilding, it once more took on an important role and became a trading centre, later a centre of the peasants' revolt (György Dózsa, 1514), the Turkish Wars, as well as the struggle for independence under Ferenc Rákóczi II (1703) and the 1848–49 revolution. In Kárász útca is the house built in the classical style where Lajos Kossuth, whom the National Assembly had elected Regent of Hungary in April 1849, delivered a flamboyant speech that fired up the citizens of Szeged for the Hungarian cause. In August he resigned and fled to Turkey.

The flood of 1879 destroyed 95 percent of the town. It was rebuilt with international help. The names of the towns who donated funds were, as a sign of gratitude, given to sections of

the peripheral road marking the inner city on both sides of the Tisza. Szeged, rebuilt in a style more grandiose than before, now has its own calendar system before and after the flood.

The original structure of the town can be easily visualised – an inner and outer ring, with several linear and radial streets. When Cathedral Square was built, red brick came into its own. However, the most beautiful square is the park-like **Széchenyi tér**, with its statues and its fountain bearing an allegorical portrayal of the Tisza as bringing both destruction and blessing. Ödön Lechner extended what the flood left of the old **Town Hall**, a set of two buildings linked by a bridge of sighs and an ornamental tower.

Dom tér is, however, Szeged's largest square. The octagonal Demetrius Tower in front of the cathedral dates from the 12th and 13th centuries and is the oldest building in town. It was completely restored in 1985 and now serves as a baptismal chapel. However, the square is dominated by the red brick cathedral, a mighty neo-Romanesque building with twin towers, built between 1912 and 1929. The Virgin Mary, patron saint of Hungary, stands above the south portal, the 12 apostles at her side. The interior of the cathedral, with its white marble, statues of angels, gilded tabernacles and the grandiose altar, matches the outside. The only specifically Hungarian feature is the ceiling fresco in the choir. It portrays the Virgin of Szeged, wrapped in a peasant-style cloak, with embroidered Szeged "butterfly slippers" on her feet. The organ, which has five manuals and no fewer than 11,000 pipes, is only just behind that of Milan cathedral for size.

Festival venue: The cathedral itself becomes a marvellous theatrical background during the Szeged Summer Festival (opera, dance, plays). It delights an audience of about 6,000 with **The new synagogue in Szeged.**

every performance in the square, surrounded by buildings adorned with arcades. "*Szeged, híres város – Szeged, a famous town*" as the old folk song goes. This tune, which is played in fanfares, not only opens the festival each year, but is also played every midday by a glockenspiel housed in the Dom tér.

The Serbian Orthodox church is worth seeing. It is built in the baroque style (1773–78), has a splendid iconostasis and a tower in mid-18th century style. However, the most beautiful church in Szeged is in Mátyás király tér. It is the **Alsóvárosi templom** (Church of the Lower Town), built on the remains of a church from Arpád's time. Evidence of its origin is in the Romanesque window in the sacristy. Apart from that one feature, the building is in Gothic style – high narrow windows between the pillars. The tower stands on the north side of the choir in the Franciscan fashion.

Below, holding on to a memento. Right, sunset over the puszta.

The architect was one Brother John, who laid the last stone of the building in 1503. The high altar and the pulpit were made around 1700 in the baroque style. The "Black Madonna", a replica of the statue of Mary from Czestochowa, dating from mid-18th century, is not only an object of pilgrimage, but also, at the time of the melon harvest in summer, the reason for the church festival of Alsóváros.

Móra Park, with its cultural centre, lies near the northern bridge-head. It is bounded by the ruins of the castle, built by Béla IV (1235–70) after the Tatar invasion. Before its demolition in 1880, it served as a prison. Sándor Rózsa (1813–78), a famous Betyár, the Robin Hood of the Hungarians, spent 12 years of his life in the prison. However, the most prominent native of the town is Albert Szent-Györgyi, who discovered vitamin C in paprika. Szent-Györgyi was awarded the Nobel Prize in 1937.

GOING EAST

Highway 43 takes you 19 miles (30 km) to **Makó**, the "onion town" of Hungary. From here on almost the entire round trip will run for several hundred miles on very narrow roads. You'll swallow sand and dust, but at least you'll avoid driving in convoys on the main roads. It is a route which will have you longing for a bath, but you will have plenty of time for this in the spas. (The Hungarians, feverishly looking for oil, kept coming across hot springs, which they have put to good use.) However, you will have to be cautious on the country roads. Poultry, various quadrupeds and farm carts believe that the winding lanes belong to them. After 14 miles (22 km) of farming country typical of the Great Plain you reach **Mezöhegyes**, where there is a stud farm of Nonius horses.

Nonius, the sire of the breed, was born in Normandy and ended up as a prisoner of war. He helped to make Hungarian horse breeding world famous.

Bartók's muse: The narrow road that runs along the Romanian border takes you past Battonya, Dombegyház, Lökösháza, Kétegyháza to **Gyula** on the banks of the White Körös. Albrecht Dürer's ancestors came from this town. This was where Ferenc Erkel, composer of the Hungarian national anthem and the operas *Ban Bánk* and *László Hunyadi*, was born in 1810. In the garden of the **Harruckern Almássy Palace**, a baroque building with two flat corner towers, there is "Erkel's Tree", a sycamore in whose shade the master composed. Béla Bartók, too, spent some time here collecting folk songs.

The medieval castle, a massive, brick building with battlements, arrow slits and a square central tower, is to the eastern side of town, on the bend

Preceding <u>pages:</u> spoils of the hunt. <u>Below,</u> traditional rider's kit from the Hortobágy puszta.

of the Körös. For 130 years it was in Turkish hands. It is now used for more peaceful purposes, as a tourist attraction and as the setting for the local festival. If you happen to hear German spoken, it is not necessarily a tourist. It could well be the descendants of the Franconian farmers who settled here in the early 18th century.

Once you have seen the old Town Hall, the Greek Orthodox (Romanian) church and the Roman Catholic church – all three were built between 1775 and 1825 in baroque style – head for the small pâtisserie in Jókai utca 1. It has attracted local people and travellers since the mid-19th century. The house, in mid-18th century style, and also the interior decor reminds you of the old days. The spa will make you fit to travel on to Debrecen.

Centre of Protestantism: Once a federation of villages, **Debrecen** was united under a charter granted in the 14th century. It was and remains a major trading centre in Hungary. It developed gradually but continuously to its present position as the second largest town in Hungary and a centre of culture, much influenced by the Reformation. The present site of the town was already inhabited in the Stone Ages.

Before the Hungarians arrived in the 9th century, tribes of Scythians and Avars lived here. When Hungary was divided into three parts by the Turkish wars, Debrecen, a border town, was part of the area ruled by the invaders, but kept its autonomy. The people of Debrecen were free citizens of a city republic. This was fertile ground for the anti-feudal spirit of the Reformation. Thus Debrecen became a centre of Protestantism in Hungary. The Reformation spread rapidly, even though the Hungarian Assembly passed a law in 1521 stating: "Lutherans are to be exterminated."

Debrecen withstood reconversion

The farmers of eastern Hungary.

to Catholicism which came with the Habsburgs, who seized power after the retreat of the Turks. The cruel slogan of Cardinal Kollonich – "I will make Hungary a slave, then a beggar, and then a Catholic" – could not be realised here. Not even hard labour in the galleys could shake the faith of these people. A memorial in the garden of the Reformed Church honours them.

Debrecen held on not only to its faith, but to its role as a centre of trade and culture, and grew rich in this way. The main street, broadening out into squares, and with side streets branching off, runs from north to south. Petöfi tér with its fountain, in front of the station, is a good place to start. Your walk leads you past classical, romantic, eclectic houses which survived World War II (there was a tank battle lasting 12 days in Debrecen).

Independence site: On the corner of Béke útja/Piac utca is the former district house, adorned with stained glass windows and Zsolnay tiles. The oldest church, the **Little Church**, is in Révész tér. It was built between 1720 and 1727 on an oak foundation, and rebuilt in a neo-Romanesque style in 1876. Opposite the church is the **Town Hall**, built in classical style. Kossuth tér is the northern extension of the main street. It is bounded by the **Reformed Church**, a mammoth building in the classical style (1814–21). Ionic wall pillars divide the main façade, which is bordered by two square towers. This is where Kossuth proclaimed Hungary's independence on 14 April, 1849.

On the western side of the square is the opulent **Hotel Arany Bika**. It was built in its present Secessionist style according to plans by the architect Alfréd Hajós, twice Olympic swimming champion (1920–24).

Behind the Reformed Church and linked to it by a square stands the rectangular two-storey **Reformed College**, looking like an impenetrable fortress of the faith. Its history goes back to the 14th century. At that time it was the Latin school of the Dominican Order. In the 16th century this developed into one of the first Calvinist schools in Hungary and around 1750 it became the Reformed Theological College.

In his novel about childhood, *Légy jó mindhalálig,* the author Zsigmond Móricz, himself a pupil of the college, described this world of strict tradition and law, not at all a simple one for small boys. The library with its old codices and valuable manuscripts is the second largest in Hungary. The printing press founded in 1561 by Gál Huszár has survived. The present Alföld Printing Press, a huge concern, is its successor.

Two important political events took place in the oratory of this college. In 1849, Parliament met here under Kossuth's leadership, and on 12 December, 1944, the provisional

Flower power at carnival in Debrecen.

240

National Assembly met here as the Red Army drove the German forces out of Hungary.

There is also a rare object in the permanent exhibition of the college – a meteorite which landed to the southwest of Debrecen in 1857. In the **Déri Museum**, which can be reached via Perényi utca, is an Asian collection which is well worth a visit. If you want to stay in Debrecen for more than a day, look at the baroque and classical houses around Kálvin tér, and at **St Anne's Church** (1719–46), also in a pure baroque style, in Béke útja; but don't overlook the **Csokonai Theatre** in Liszt Ferenc utca with its Moorish-Byzantine elements.

Old post station: In Széchenyi utca is Debrecen's oldest surviving house. It dates from the year 1710 and belonged to the postmaster. It was a post station from the days of travel by horse-drawn coaches.

You can take a break from sightseeing in the **Nagyerdö** (the Great Forest) in the north, in baths, in the zoo and on boat trips. The university district is surrounded by the greenery of the Great Forest. Debrecen, despite its modern achievements, and though once a trading centre but now a tourist town, has remained in character and atmosphere "the biggest village in Europe".

For the past 300 years, travellers have agreed on this point. And whether you are in the well-equipped Hotel Arany Bika or in the Csokonai café (haunt of the literary world), you feel that Debrecen is the "secret capital of the other Hungary".

The Danube divides the country. To the east of the river the plain begins, its wide spaces reminiscent of Asia. "This country is one of contrast to the Catholic, conservative western part. It is Calvinist, active, the place which has brought forth the prophets of Hungary" (Dezsö Kerestury).

Even road runners sometimes stick to the Highway Code!

THE PUSZTA

The two cultural poles of East and West were made manifest in the 19th and 20th centuries in Debrecen, capital of Calvinism, and Pannonhalma, capital of Catholicism. The roots of this ancient polarity can be found in the two cultural spheres of influence which the conquering Hungarians joined in the 9th and 10th centuries – the Greek-Slavonic in the east, the Latin and the Holy Roman Empire in the west.

István I (970–1038) succeeded in bringing Hungarians faithful to Byzantium and eastern pagans under his rule; however, when Béla IV, 200 years later, settled heathen Kumans in the Tisza region, "forcibly" converted Hungarians soon reverted to paganism. Hungary's turning away from the West was complete. The historical chronicles (such as Simon Kézi's *Gesta Hungarorum*, 1238) supported the Eastern connection and named the Huns ancestors of the Hungarians. A movement towards the East was born. King Mátyás (1458–90) was known as Attila II by his court chroniclers, and Calvinist preachers were supportive of Eastern Hungarian tendencies.

Hungarian backwoods: The two most important politicians of the 19th century, Count István Széchenyi and Lajos Kossuth, were representatives of this dualism. Széchenyi came from the upper echelons of the Catholic Hungarian nobility, and wanted to achieve reforms in the "backwoods of Hungary" of his time on the basis of a statesmanlike system employing education and enlightenment. However, he wanted recognition for the House of Habsburg as well. Kossuth, from an east Hungarian, Protestant family of the lesser nobility, fought "with word and sword" for his ideal of severing Hungary from the Habsburgs. His aim was a Danube Federation, a project which fitted well with the revolutionary atmosphere current in Europe at the time.

Debrecen is the most Hungarian of all the country's towns because of its intellectual atmosphere. It is perhaps not suitable for mass tourism, despite all its efforts to attract visitors, among them the flower carnival on 20 August. It is, though, a rich mine of information for those looking for the "real" Hungary, and the courses at the summer university are a bonus.

A car trip to the **Nyírség** (birch country), the sandy regions reclaimed for agriculture, is not without its charm. Today there are fields of grain, sunflowers and sugarbeet, interspersed with woods and apple orchards. This area remained almost untouched even during the Turkish wars. Medieval settlement patterns, old village plans and buildings from the 13th to the 17th century have survived. Remember, however, that you are travelling through the poorest part of Hungary,

Left, the former Minorite church in Nyírbátor. Right, a restful chore for the industrious homemaker.

an isolated region considered to be nothing but the boondocks.

After 34 miles (55 km) along highway No. 471, you reach **Nyírbátor**. The name is linked to the 13th-century Báthory dynasty. The Báthorys (*bátor*=brave) have voivodes, princes and a Polish king (crowned in Krakow in 1576) in their family tree, and also the infamous "Bloody Countess" Elizabeth, who bathed in the blood of maidens in order to preserve her fair complexion. It was not until after the 80th murder that she was condemned to "perpetual imprisonment" and died in 1614.

The **Báthory Museum** in the former Minorite monastery, a baroque building dating from 1737–44, contains various family mementos, and a large ethnographic collection. Also on display are finds from the ancient bogland of **Báthoryliget**, a nature reserve with 98 feet (30 metres) tall oak trees and viviparous lizards. To protect their ecology, a special permit is needed to enter the boglands.

Two churches and a wooden bell-tower adorn the town. The **Reformed Church** was financed by István Báthory with booty taken from the Turks, built between 1484 and 1488, and largely destroyed by imperial Austrian troops in 1587. It was, however, completely restored in 1958. The ribbed vault above the nave and choir, supported by wall pillars, is very beautiful. Nowadays historians believe that this late Gothic church had some links with the royal builders of King Mátyás. The square wooden bell-tower with its narrow gallery and its four little corner towers is 200 years younger.

In contrast to this cool beauty, the **Roman Catholic Church** displays baroque splendour in its interior. It was built by István Báthory but was destroyed in 1587 by the Turks. An impressive feature is the Altar of the Passion in front of the organ loft. **Time for…**

Fourteen miles (22 km) further along highway 471 you reach **Mátészalka**. Here the Reformed Church, with its painted wooden ceiling, is a vehicle for traditional Hungarian art. The wagons, coaches and sledges in the museum show the means of transport in earlier times. The chronicles tell of 30 oxen needed to draw a wagon through mud and snow.

From here, head for the northeastern tip of Hungary, in the Tisza, Szamos, Kraszna and Túr region. It is mainly reclaimed swampland and provides the fattest oxen and the biggest plums.

Border town: If you follow the eastbound highway No. 49 which branches off to the east, you will come to **Csenger** on the Romanian border. This town joined the Reformation in 1540. The Protestant Church is decorated with glazed tiles, and has a coffered ceiling painted with pretty flower patterns. For lovers of such "peasant churches", an expression of the Hungarian soul – like the folk songs and tales – there is one in **Csenger-sima**, 4 miles (7 km) to the northeast. On the way back, turn off into highway No. 491 and then use the side road going north from **Fehérgyarmat** (here stands a Gothic Reformed Church, rebuilt several times in various styles). It meets highway No. 41 near Beregsurány and Nyíregyháza.

There are several interesting buildings along this route. Among them is the Romanesque church in **Csaroda** built in the mid-13th century with 14th century wall paintings, a painted wooden ceiling dating from the 18th century and a wooden bell-tower. The church in **Tákos** (just half a mile west), with its flower-patterned ceiling and painted pews – there is an inscription with the date 1766 – is one of the country's most beautiful peasant churches.

Nyíregyháza, destroyed by the Mongols in the 13th century did not

… a nap.

become important until towards the end of last century as the centre of an area dominated by agriculture. Some private houses dating from the 18th and 19th centuries, the district house and the Protestant church with its eclectic style are overshadowed by the town, which spreads out into the surrounding countryside. The spa of **Sóstó** (salt lake), 3½ miles (6 km) away, with its pools (the springs contain alkali and iodine) and oak woods covering 1,113 acres (450 hectares) attracts many visitors.

A short detour via highway No. 36 to **Tiszavasvári** is more pleasant than the main road back to Debrecen. Here a country road, running parallel with the railway and partly with the main canal, crosses the Hajdú ridge. Place names containing the element Hajdú point to the fact that István Bocskai (1556–1606), Prince of Transylvania, kept his promise to give land to the Haiduks, an army of herdsmen, mer-

cenaries and veterans, for their bravery in war. Bocskai also forced an agreement, in the "Peace of Vienna" of 1606, on religious freedom for Transylvania.

The fertile black earth produces wheat and sugarbeet, but underground there are natural gas fields. Hopefully, exploitation of the latter will not ruin the character of the landscape.

The puszta: A special travel experience lies in wait for you when you leave Debrecen and travel west through the Hortobágy Puszta to Tiszafüred, to the dam on the Tisza. *Puszta* means barren, or deserted. To the west of the Danube the word refers to houses and farm buildings, similar to homesteads. In the Alföld, it also refers to the vast grazing grounds and sandy steppes. The two areas left as nature reserves are Hortobágy Puszta and Bugac Puszta.

There had been attempts in the 17th century to hold the drifting sand by

Fulfilling a vow in the pustza.

planting acacias. However, it is only since 1945 that there has been a systematic planting of forests, with preference given to broad-leaved trees over conifers, along with a canal building programme. Underground lie not only medicinal and hot springs, but also oil and natural gas. With the exploitation of these reserves in the south and east of the region industrialisation is moving fast. It is due to these developments and to the progressive agricultural exploitation of the puszta, that the character of the landscape has changed considerably. Today it is dominated by machines and no longer by the vast herds of animals as in Bismarck's time, when he travelled through the Great Plain in 1852. He wrote to his wife about this "very eastern, but beautiful world" which was untouched in those days.

Another thing that belongs to the past is that need to travel, like Bismarck, with a troop of imperial Ulans

Nonius dressage in Hortobágy.

"as a protection against the Betyárs, robbers on horseback, wrapped in great furs, whose leaders wear black masks."

Today the tourist buses are accompanied by charming hostesses. In earlier years, the puszta was quite different. Then the herdsmen and their animals would head for home in December once snow fell. The *csikós*, the horse-herder, was the highest in the hierarchy of herdsmen. Next came the *gulyás*, the "cowboy", and finally the *juhász*, the shepherd, whose animals were forbidden to cross a grazing ground before the cattle.

"The cattle loathe the smell of the sheep so much that they would rather starve than graze after them," wrote Péter Veres. This puszta belongs to the past. The memory is kept alive by literature, Betyár tales and songs.

The romance of the steppe: The Hungarians, aware that their country is popular with tourists, are not satisfied with just putting their present in focus, they also display sections of their past, with all its glories and wretchedness. The life of the puszta is of course part of this.

The **Hortobágy Puszta**, the biggest single area of steppe grazing land in Central Europe, offers its area of 12,355 acres (5,000 hectares) for this purpose. Here horses graze in vast herds, and the herdsmen in traditional clothes – white linen shirt with wide sleeves, wide ankle-length trousers, broad-brimmed flat hat – display their horsemanship quite artistically before groups of amazed tourists.

A coach ride through the puszta, however, provides a genuine and authentic experience, for you will discover that the landscape is by no means monotonous. "On hot summer days, a mirage shows herds of cattle on the horizon. They appear to float on water, and the well-poles moving up and down show that water is just being drawn there." (Péter Veres)

This is still the home of the grey cattle with their wide, sweeping horns, tough animals who can endure great hardship. From the early Middle Ages until the last century, huge herds were driven in long treks to the slaughter-houses of Hamburg, Milan and Paris. Even the herdsmen's dogs are still here today: the little, mobile *puli* with its dark ragged fur, the shepherd's dog; the big *komondor* with its white and brown fluffy coat and the smooth-haired white and brown *kuvasz*, the faithful companion of earlier cattle herds, which could even get the better of wolves.

Birdwatchers will find a coach trip most valuable. Apart from the many kinds of water fowl (duck eggs provided welcome variety for the other-wise monotonous diet of the herds-men), herons, cranes and bustards, now rare in Europe, live here. In the woodlands there are hares, red deer and boar.

There are a number of attractions in the Hortobágy Puszta that cannot be overlooked. One of them is the 551-feet (168-metre) bridge (1827–33) which stretches its nine arches across the small Hortobágy river. Every 19–20 August the famous **Bridge Market** is held here where you can buy anything from soup to nuts, including souvenirs, of course. The group of statues, "People of the Alföld", is sur-rounded by the market and its activity. A *csárda* has been here since the 18th century. It offers good cuisine and accommodation.

There is also the **Herdsmen's Museum**; housed in a former toolshed its many exhibits give information about the herdsmen's lives of long ago.

The Tisza region: On highway No. 33 – if you're not stuck in a traffic jam – you'll reach **Tiszafüred** and the dam on the Tisza in 20 minutes. Not even the Danube has had to submit to so much in the name of economic profit-ability as the Tisza. It has been regu-lated, embanked, shortened, dammed up into a lake of 42 sq. miles (110 sq. km). The lake is a paradise for sailing,

surfing, fishing and other kinds of recreation, but this is no longer a se-cret. It is in danger of being filled with holiday villages and campsites and becoming, just like Lake Balaton, a victim of mass tourism.

Szolnok, the most important bridge-head on the Tisza, is the next stop on your itinerary. Highway No. 34 joins the E5 near Kenderes. After passing by the several fields which grow almost everything from grain to sunflowers, you'll see Hungary's rice-growing re-gion. In prehistoric times there was a ford at Szolnok, and the Romans set up a military camp here. Under the Árpáds, the city flourished, since it was a trading place for the salt shipped up the Tisza from the eastern Carpa-thians.

The **castle**, founded in 1506, was an important fortress for centuries. It fell to the Turks in 1552. Later, Szolnok was an administrative centre for the Turks for more than 130 years. After

Town Hall façade motif, Kiskun-félegyháza.

tho Turks had been driven out, the Habsburgs had the castle blown up, as the town had sided with Rákóczi's struggle for independence. Szolnok also played an important part in the 1848–49 revolution and in the workers' movement at the end of the 19th century. Szolnok's industrialisation rapidly increased its prosperity. Partially destroyed in World War II, it developed into a busy trade and shipping centre with its big harbour on the Tisza. The Pest-Szolnok railway link, opened on 1 September 1847, played a role in the process.

The only building really worth looking at is in Koltói Anna utca – the single-nave **Trinity Church**, named after the group of statues on the gable side. Those in need of recreation should go and relax in the **Tiszaliget** (Tisza Woods) on the left bank of the river. Here you can swim, take part in water sports and revive yourself with an excellent fish meal in the Fisher-

man's Csárda. The open-air swimming pool has space for more than 6,000 people. But if all of them should turn up, there's no point heading for it. Flee instead to your car, and drive on along the less crowded country road which crosses highway No. 44 at **Lakitelek** and takes you on to **Kiskunfélegyháza**. The area should already be familiar to you if you made the diversion on your trip from Kecskemét to Szeged. Hungarian place names containing the syllable *kun* are reminders of the 4,000 originally nomadic Kuman families which Béla IV (1235–79) brought into the country. They settled here, were converted to Christianity and founded towns.

Kiskunfélegyháza was totally razed during the Turkish wars, but regained some of its importance due to Maria Theresa's policy of settlement. It is worth visiting the Secessionist style Town Hall with its towers and majolica tiles, the pride of **Petőfi tér**.

Part of the the 500,000 Gypsy community.

Also interesting is the mid-18th century **Kiskun Museum** on the main street. In the courtyard is one of 80 windmills typical of the area up until the 19th century. The baroque Roman Catholic church and the rectory in Béke tér were built in 1750.

The road from the west of town to the village of **Bugac** in the midst of the puszta of the same name is a 9-mile (14-km) long concrete track. The village name appears for the first time in a document dating from 1381, when this land, partly covered by 66 foot (20 metre) high dunes and shaped by the constant wind into a sea of sandy waves, came into the hands of one Balázs Bugac. The area, covering a total of 42,007 acres (17,000 hectares), was cultivated, particularly after 1945, for forestry, orchards and vineyards. The straw-thatched *csárda* with its good food is an attraction for tourists. On summer weekends, sightseers arrive in buses, or on the little train from

Kecskemét, to enjoy thrilling demonstrations of horsemanship, admire old breeds of farm animal, or visit the yurt-shaped Herdsmen's Museum.

It is only 25 miles (40km) from Kiskunfélegyháza through the southern Kiskunság via **Kiskunmajsa** (medicinal and mineral springs, spa and hydrotherapy center) to Kiskunhalas. You, too, will not be able to resist the temptation to buy Halas lace. You can admire many examples of it in the **Lace Museum**. Celebrate a good buy with the wine of this region, Kadarka or Sylvaner. "In the glow of wine I couldn't care less about the rough world" – two lines of a poem by Petöfi, who was born in **Kiskörös**, reached after travelling 14 miles (22 km) north along highway No. 53. In the reed-thatched cottage, where the Hungarian poet of Slovak descent was born, are two rooms in memory of him.

A country road crossing the main Danube canal takes you south to **Kalocsa**, seat of an archbishop since the days of István I and the most colourful of all Hungarian towns. Kalocsa is the home of the *pingáló asszonyok*, the painting women. No piece of furniture, no wall is safe from their attention, they paint everything with vivaciously coloured traditional patterns – an orgy of colour, intensified by the strings of glowing red paprika hung up to dry outside the houses. Kalocsa and Szeged are centres of paprika production.

A contrast to this garish splendour of traditional art is the interior of the single-nave, baroque (1735–54) **cathedral**. The church was designed by A. Mayerhoffer. You will be familiar with his work from the Piarist church in Kecskemét. The altar-piece *Assumption of the Virgin Mary* is by L. Kupelwieser (1796–1862), who followed the style of the Nazerene school.

The **Archishop's Palace** has a library of more than 120,000 volumes. Among them is a Latin bible used by Luther with many notes in the margins.

Left, the attractive entrance to Kalosca station. Right, a poised Hungarian cavalry officer.

SOUTHWEST HUNGARY

From Kalocsa, a 27 mile (43 km) drive through the former flood plain of the Danube on highway 51 brings you to the southerly town of **Baja**, a major riverside settlement since the Middle Ages. The woods of the flood plain and the islands are an ideal spot for fishing enthusiasts, water sports fans and campers. You can crown your day with a fish speciality. If you should find perch rubbed with paprika, baked and topped with sour cream on the menu, don't let this delicacy pass you by. A good "sand wine", perhaps a Hungarian Riesling, will round off the meal. The wines are called sand wines because the vines grow in the sandy soil of the Great Plain. You are heartily invited to visit the vineyard in Baja and sample some of its wine.

The four churches of the town, among them a Serbian orthodox church, date from the 18th and 19th centuries, when the Habsburgs, as part of their policy of settlement and reconversion to Catholicism, invited mainly Catholic Southern Slavs to settle here. The **Museum of Folk Art**, housed in a classical building, is named after István Türr, who was born here. He was a general under Garibaldi, governor of Naples and, as an engineer, drew up the plans for both the Panama and Corinth canals.

Across the Danube: Drive in a westerly direction along highway No. 55 and leave the Danube behind you. You will cross part of the **Gemence Forest** and the **Sárköz**, crisscrossed by waterways, an area famous for its folk traditions. Many of the high-gabled farmhouses with decorative façades are protected by law. Near **Bátaszék** you have to decide whether to follow highway No. 56 south to Mohács or north to Szekszárd.

In **Mohács**, the most southerly town on the Danube in Hungary, the Hungarians fought the Turks in 1526 and suffered a defeat with dire consequences. The baroque poet Miklós Zrínyi wrote: "Our land, like a well-tended vineyard, was trampled down by a wild boar." *Busójóras*, a carnival procession featuring fearsome wooden masks and accompanied by music, symbolising the passing of winter and also the eviction of the Turks. It is a popular festival, with seasoned fish stew, washed down with strong drink, enlivening the celebration.

Szekszárd, a town on the Danube before the river was regulated, is known as the "town of seven hills". The hilly landscape and also the woods in the nearby flood plain make Szekszárd a peaceful holiday resort.

Already during Roman times this region was known for its wines. The Turks destroyed all the vineyards for religious reasons after taking the town in 1541. Today the most common wine is Szekszárd Kadarka, which was introduced in the 18th century by German and Southern Slav settlers. It was the favourite wine of Franz Schubert, and also refreshed Franz Liszt, who gave many concerts here. Cellars with great ambience in both the town and surrounding countryside serve this excellent wine.

The buildings worth seeing bear the hallmark of the 18th century. The wrath of the Turks left nothing of old "Sagard" standing, which had been built on a Roman settlement and was mentioned in documents as both town and seat of a Benedictine Abbey as early as the 11th century. Outside the gates of the town, in the former flood plain of the Danube, is the Gemence Forest. It is one of the most beautiful nature reserves in Hungary. If you don't want to walk through the reserve, enjoy the sights from the forest's 12-mile (19 km) long, narrow-gauge railway, or take a boat.

The road north out of Szekszárd joins highway No. 6 (coming from

Left,
a popular
meeting place
in Pécs—the
Hotel Nádor.

Budapest) after just over a mile (2 km). Continue south and you will pass through the Mecsek range on the way to Pécs.

This journey of 36 miles (58 km) takes you through Bonyhád, Hidas and Pécsvárad, which lie at the foot of **Zengö** mountain. At 2,237 feet (682 meters) its summit is the highest point of this range of forest-clad hills running from southwest to northeast. Here the climate is Mediterranean, and almond and fig trees flourish in gardens and by the roadside. The Turks introduced figs to the area. The summers grant you many hours of sunshine, and the weather is warm, but not scorching hot as it is in the Alföld; the winters are milder. You should stop at Pécsvárad and take a walk in the hills. Hiking trails are marked in yellow. For miles around, there is nothing but acacia groves, copses, and isolated whitewashed farms with green doors.

The **Castle of Pécsvárad** was a Benedictine abbey founded by István I. In the 14th and 15th centuries, it was developed into a fortress with fortified towers, a castle and strong walls. The abbot, Brother Georgius, had it demolished when it could no longer be defended against the Turks. The Archbishop of Cologne, Konrad Zinzendorfer, later took charge of the monastery and had it rebuilt in baroque style. The Romanesque church by the castle wall with its Byzantine frescoes in the apse survived, as did the massive gate tower dating from the 15th century with the Renaissance well-house.

A breath of the Mediterranean: Originally a Celtic settlement, **Pécs**, then known as Sopianae, was an important Roman town at the time of the Emperor Hadrian. Before the Hungarians settled here in 899 the town was inhabited by Germans and Franks and was known as Quinque Ecclesiae, Five Churches or, in German, Fünfkirchen.

The former mosque and the Trinity Pillar, Pécs.

The name referred to the five ancient Christian churches built here in the 4th and 5th centuries.

The town of Pécs was mentioned for the first time in the reign of King László I in 1093 as a diocesan town and a centre of trade with Byzantium. King Lajos I founded the first Hungarian university here in 1367. At that time it was the fifth university in Europe. The Turks conquered the town in 1543 but did not destroy it, they designed it according to their faith and prosperity. Mosques, prayer houses, minarets and an Islamic monastery were built. In 1686 the city fell to the Habsburgs, and rebuilding took place again – this time according to the faith dictated by Vienna. The Austrian baroque style arrived.

The town centre, oval-shaped, is just under a mile (1½ km) long and half a mile wide (½ km). Rákóczi út and its extension via Klimó Gy. u. to Felsö Malom utca surround the old

town of Pécs, now the town centre. The roads follow the line of the former city walls, built in the 13th century after the Mongol invasion. The narrow streets of the centre partly follow this curve. At the point where Esze T. utca joins Landler J. út is the former **Barbican**, an ancient medieval construction that was once part of the fortified wall, and served to defend the city gate. Széchenyi tér, intersection of the main roads going east-west and north-south, forms the core of the town. All roads going north lead towards the hills of the Mecsek, which are sometimes very steep, but often lead through a pleasant garden landscape. The highest point is the summit of **Misina** (1,719 feet/524 metres). This offers a beautiful view of the town, its tall towers, the green dome of the mosque and the reddish-orange roofs of the houses.

Pécs is possibly the most beautiful Hungarian city. This is not just be-

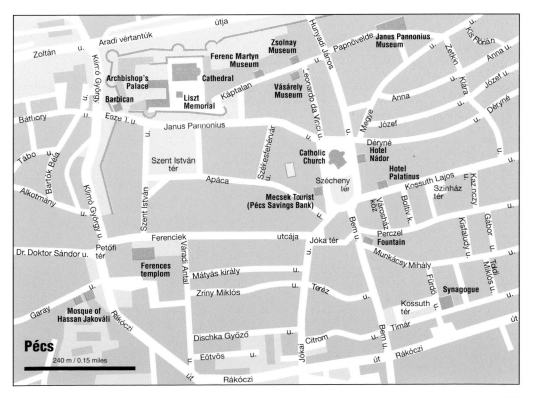

cause buildings from Roman, medieval, Turkish and Habsburg times have survived in considerable numbers, but also because nature, climate, culture, tradition, agriculture and mineral exploitation (coal, uranium, thorium) have combined in a fortunate symbiosis. City and landscape have done much to shape the open and friendly people. It is to be hoped that the Hungarians don't, for the sake of hard currency, give in to the pressures of mass tourism and ruin the idyllic centre with the fast-food outlets of hamburger and cheeseburger culture. This would alienate the city from its true character. Remember that the entire inner city has been declared a conservation area.

Mighty mosque: Széchenyi tér, the former market square, is dominated by a square building crowned by a mighty dome typical of the Middle East. This is the mosque of Pasha Kassim Gazi, the largest surviving building of the Turkish occupation in Hungary. It was built on the foundations and with the stones of St Bartholomew's Church.

In 1686, it was given to the Jesuits by Margrave Louis of Baden, the liberator of the city from the Turks. The minaret was removed and the mosque was altered to fit the baroque style. Following pressure from 20th century art historians, it was freed from these unsuitable impositions. Most important of all, the Turkish dome was exposed once more and covered with copper. Today this building, with both crescent and cross on its tower, serves as the inner city parish **Church of St Mary** for Catholics, and no one feels their faith weakened by ogives, fretted stone screens, the *mihrab* or prayer niche facing southeast, and the words from the Koran on the wall.

Besides the baroque Trinity square, Széchenyi tér also has an equestrian

Main post office façade, Pécs.

statue of János Hunyadi, the father of King Mátyás Corninus, who made a name for himself after raising the Turkish siege of Nándorfehérvár (Belgrade) in 1456. The pope at that time ordered all the church bells in Europe to celebrate the event by ringing daily at noon, which is what they still do today.

North of Széchenyi tér is the archaeological department of the **Janus Pannonius Museum**, housed in a mid-18th century building. It was named after Janus Pannonius (1434–72), a versatile and keenly observant poet. In 1459 King Mátyás made him Bishop of Pécs and royal representative at the papal court. This did not stop him from joining his uncle, the Primate of Hungary, János Vitéz, in a conspiracy against the king. Pannonius was one of the great poets in the 15th century. In one of his poems, he placed Hungarian poetry on par with other European literature: "Now Pannonia brings forth its own songs."

King Lear takes on Pécs.

A steep street leads up the hill into Káptalan utca. House No. 2, the oldest surviving house in the city, today contains the **Zsolnay Museum**. You enter the building through a Gothic gate and then pass a Gothic wall niche with a seat which was most probably used by the coachmen of wealthy citizens waiting for their masters. The stone Renaissance window frames and the wrought-iron grilles of classicism bear eloquent witness to repairs and improvements undertaken in whatever style was current at the time. Go through a baroque wrought iron gate to the upper floor, and in the rooms here you will be able to follow the history of the Zsolnay factory from a great wealth of exhibits. You probably remember the tiles from here which decorate the Pécs post office and the Secessionist style houses you will have seen on your travels.

The **Green Fountain** in Széchenyi tér, with its spout shaped like an ox

head, is also a Zsolnay product. These ceramics are not to everyone's taste, but are among the most expensive items for collectors. The ground floor of the Zsolnay Museum also shows some of the stark works of the sculptor Amerigo Tot.

In Káptalan utca, there are exhibitions by Hungarian artists. Those best known outside Hungary are Victor Vasarely and Tivadar Csontváry Kosztka. Vasarely, originator of Op Art, was born in this city in 1908 but moved to Paris in 1930. The geometric use of space in his tapestries is impressive, but many people find the 17th century Gobelins from Brussels more to their liking. They were a gift to the Bishopric of Pécs from Maria Theresa and can be viewed in the **Bishop's Palace** in Dóm tér.

Csontváry, in contrast to Vasarely, received no recognition in his lifetime (he was born in 1853, died in 1919). No one paid any attention to his ec-

centric genius, and he was wrongly pigeon-holed as naïve or surrealist. Other artists and art lovers mocked him, and he died in despair and poverty. However, in 1958, his work was awarded the Grand Prix at the World Fair in Brussels. Now no one makes fun of him, and art lovers are relieved that his paintings, of monumental proportions, were not destroyed. The inspiration for many of Csontváry's visionary, even hallucinatory, pictures, came from the birthplace of civilisation, the Middle East, and from the Mediterranean lands. Their freshness, spontaneity and colourfulness retain the power to enchant.

It is time to move on to the **cathedral**, via J. Pannonius utca, passed baroque houses, among them the 1772 **Cathedral Chapter House**. Walking across Sétatér, the popular place to meet, gossip and be seen in Pécs, and you're already in Dóm tér. Here stands the imposing four-tower "St Peter's"

Fleemarket stallholders.

of Pécs, the most beautiful of all the medieval churches in Hungary.

Work on the building began in the 11th century, not far from the foundations of a basilica dating from the 4th century. More building took place in every subsequent century. The final phase was completed in the 16th century and the building was thoroughly renovated in the 19th century. Nowadays, the cathedral has a neo-Romanesque appearance. The unearthed Roman stonework has found a home in the lapidarium of the Janus Pannonius Museum. The western towers of the cathedral date from the 11th century, the eastern towers from 100 years later. The Turks used part of the cathedral as a mosque, but made the crypt into an armoury. After the Turkish defeat, the cathedral was once again in Catholic hands and housed valuable art treasures.

The red marble Renaissance altar in the **Corpus Christi Chapel** de-serves special mention, as does the rich marble decoration in the main choir. The paintings on the ceiling are by Károly Lotz (1835–1904) and Bertalan Székely (1845–1910). You will also come across a painting by Moritz von Beckerath (1838–96), a German historical painter and a student of Moritz von Schwind.

The sloping cathedral square, equipped with flights of steps and two obelisks carved from a single stone, is remarkable for its stunning beauty, which has up until the present day remained unspoiled by any architectural blunders. Frescoes and mosaics dating from the 4th century were found in the excavated cemetery chapel, and these themselves covered other works from the year in which the chapel was built.

The early Christian tombs (you will find the entrance near the eastern obelisk) are similar to the Roman catacombs, a rarity outside Italy. Here

Wine cellar near Palkonya.

much of the former opulent painting is still preserved.

The religious centre of the Turks in Pécs was the **Pasha Hassan Jakovali Mosque**, crowned by its octagonal dome. This mosque, including the *mihrab* or prayer niche, was also stripped of all later additions and restored to its original form. The same happened to the **Minaret**, which stands on the grounds of the district hospital and has received an appropriate top to its tower. From its high gallery, protected by screens, there is a good view of Pécs. Behind the mosque's entrance, with its stalactitic ornamentation, there is an interesting "Turkish museum". The mosque is also used occasionally by Muslim students from the University of Pécs.

Starting from Pécs, you can take a number of walks through the forest of the Mecsek range. **Jakab Hill**, 5 miles (8 km) from Pécs, is a popular place for excursions. There is a forest trail marked from Egervölgy past the Illyrian fortifications – they are 10 foot (3 metres) high and impossible to miss. From the top there is a wide view of the land around. The ruins of a monastery dating from the 13th century were rescued from oblivion by archaeologists and the excavations can be visited.

Also popular for excursions is **Abaliget** with its limestone caves (some 12 miles/20 km north of Pécs). If you don't want to travel in your own car, a bus will take you in 30 minutes along the somewhat winding roads through the hills to **Orfü**, the "town of four lakes". The next two miles (3km), to the 500,000-year old limestone caves, provide a refreshing walk. Like all caves, those of Abaliget are cool. Warm clothing is advisable if you don't want to catch a cold on the 510 yards (466 metres) walk passed the bizarre limestone figurations. The caves have such special air that it is used by doctors to help people with bronchial problems. Back in Orfü,

Lake Orfü, an artificial lake, looks inviting for a swim. Unfortunately this area is no longer a secret. Tourist hotels, camp-sites, holiday homes, built right on the shore for convenience, have shot up out of the ground like mushrooms after rain.

The castle in Szigetvár: Now we must leave Pécs and its environs and drive along the Mecsek ridge on highway No. 6 to **Szigetvár**, a small town with a castle of historic importance. It dates from the 14th century and is a square brick building with angled bastions at the corners and many fortifications. It took a 100,000-strong Turkish army 33 days of siege to take this castle in 1566. The great-grandson of the castellan Count Miklós Zrínyi, a general and poet of the same name, wrote a heroic epic describing each day of siege, a broad view that at times goes into minute details. The 2,500 Hungarians and Croats (the Zrínyis were a Croat noble family) defending the **Making music.**

castle died, but the attacking Sultan Suleiman II and 25,000 Turks also failed to survive the battle. The castle was taken, but the Turks were so weakened that they gave up their plan of attacking Vienna. Instead, they rebuilt the castle and the town, recognising the importance of this fortification in the marshes of the Almás river.

Today the mosque in the castle courtyard contains a museum with an exhibition describing the history of the town and the castle. Note the splendid wrought iron gate and the screens in front of the windows. The Roman Catholic parish church in Zrínyi tér, the centre of the town, was also once a mosque. It was altered to form a single-nave baroque church. A fresco depicts the battle at the castle. Many Turkish elements – ogive arches, stalactite vault and two red marble holy water fonts (formerly wash-basins for the Turks) are evidence of the church's

Parish church in Kaposvár.

Islamic origins. The little single-storey house in Bástya utca, built of brick, was once a caravanserai.

To the south of Szigetvár is an unusual region known as **Ormánság**, where local peasant families were allowed to have only one child, thus dense population never became a problem. A museum of local history has been arranged inside a little peasant house not far from the main crossing in Vajszló. A feature of this area are the painted coffered ceilings in some of the churches, notably in **Drávaivány** and **Kovácshida**. Further east, **Harkány** is the site of a well-developed thermal spa. The weather in this part of Hungary is generally hot and dry in summer, so taking a dip at this point is one of the best antidotes to the heat and poor roads. **Siklós** also has a thermal bath, but its most prominent sight is the castle, which houses several museums, galleries and an hotel.

The church at **Máriagyüd** attracts

pilgrims in search of miraculous healing, but it is otherwise nothing more than a baroque edifice with kitschy votive trappings for venerating visitors. Far more interesting is the little church in **Nagyharsány**, with its Gothic frescoes, and the nearby Sculpture Park, where in good weather one can occasionally catch a sculptor in full creative frenzy.

As for **Villány** itself, it is known for its wines, which visitors are invited to sample. Wreaths typically hang over the doors of the private cellars offering tastings. The Wine Museum in the village of Villány provides an insight into the evolution and history of the local wine-making industry. Wine was brought to the region by the Danube-Swabians who settled in Hungary during the 18th century, and indeed German is still widely spoken in the region. The road back to Pécs leads through more wine villages, whose cellars appear as rows of quaint-fronted houses along the hillsides. **Palkonya** has, in addition, an interesting church that was once a mosque.

Back to Szigetvár: Route 67 leads northwards to **Kaposvár**, a small town surrounded by hills and greenery. The journey takes you 25 miles (40 km) straight through the **Zselic Hills** (highest point 1,171feet/357 metres), with its huge oak forests in which swineherds put their pigs out to pasture in earlier times.

Five miles (8 km) before you get to Kaposvár you reach the village of **Szenna**. Be sure to visit the **Skansen**, the open-air museum with its old farmhouses, ancient graves and old agricultural tools. But above all it is the **Reformed Church** that makes the visit worth while. It was built in 1785 in baroque style. Its interior is that of a genuine "peasant church". There are painted pews, a beautifully carved wooden altar and a coffered ceiling with 117 panels, all glowing with colourful flower patterns. Stylistically it is harmonious and not at all "kitschy".

Kaposvár was formerly a purely agricultural town (wheat, cattle, sunflowers, milling). It has become increasingly industrialised since World War II – imported cotton, wood products – but keeps its industry within bounds. Industry hasn't affected its development as a tourist centre. Kossuth Lajos tér, an extension of Majús 1 út, forms the centre. In the square there is a larger-than-life statue of Kossuth.

The **parish church** in Kossuth tér dates from the mid 18th century, but was later covered with neo-Gothic elements to such an extent that the baroque origins can hardly be recognised. Next to the church is a very beautiful baroque limestone votive pillar to the Virgin Mary. It originally belonged to the Festetics family, who were part of the upper echelons of the Hungarian nobility.

The **museum** in Jószef Rippl-Rónai tér contains an extensive ethnological collection as well as exhibitions of archaeology and civic history. In front of the building (intended as a prison when it was built in 1828) is a bust of Rippl-Rónai, who is, of course, represented by his works in the museum. The house in which he lived from 1906 until his death in 1927 is to the south of the town in park on Rómahegy (Rome Hill). His son, Ferenc Martyn, was born and raised here and went on to become one of Hungary's leading modern artists.

The town of Dombóvár, which lies some 19 miles (31 km) to the east of Kaposvár, is not the greatest of tourist attractions. It has some houses that have been well restored, a 19th -century Trinity statue, and a few remnants of an old fort. People flock here to enjoy the benefits of nearby Gunarus, whose waters are used in the treatment of gallbladder and other digestive tract ailments. The proximity to Pécs and Kaposvár makes the little spa town an ideal place to enjoy a holiday combining health and culture.

WHY THEY PICKED PÉCS

An Eastern people in the West is how the Hungarians, who have remained linguistically isolated in Europe even to this day, often describe themselves. They arrived in the Carpathian Basin following a centuries-long westward trek from east of the Urals. Their adoption of Christianity was necessary for survival and yet, even after centuries of settled life, these nomads-at-heart- have remained a special, individual people.

Their situation reflects this conflict of intellectual and spiritual connections. The Danube divides the country into two parts. To the east lies the boundless Great Plain with its reserved people living in widely separated villages. To the west is a range of gentle hills, densely populated by more open, friendly people.

There is one spot in Hungary which displays, in both culture as well as landscape, eastern, western, even southern characteristics, harmoniously united. This is Pécs in the southwest. The mild Mediterranean climate, the lush sub-tropical vegetation, the gentle hilly landscape, have harboured human settlements since prehistoric times. Orchards, vineyards, almond and fig trees were the foundation of prosperity. In modern times, the uranium and coal deposits in the neighbouring Mecsek range have added to this wealth.

The trade route from the German-speaking countries to the Middle East ran through Pécs, which boasted more than the five churches recalled in its German name, *Fünfkirchen*. Everyone who stopped here praised the land and the people and left some mark; only the Celts have disappeared without trace. The Roman emperor Hadrian made the town, known as Sopianae, the capital of Pannonia. In the 4th century, the early Christians painted frescoes in underground catacombs. Later they built their churches underground, which gave rise to the German name of the town, from Quincae Basilicae, the five Roman burial chapels founded by the Franks and later by the Moravians. The conquering Magyars also felt at home in this area. King István made it a bishopric in 1009. In 1367 the first Hungarian university was founded here by King Lajos the Great. When the Turks conquered large parts of Hungary after the battle of Mohács in 1526, it was not Buda but Pécs that became the intellectual centre of their Hungarian colony. Suleiman the

Magnificent had mosques and minarets, baths and *konaks* (palaces of the rulers) built. Unfortunately the Habsburgs destroyed nearly all the Turkish buildings, but the mosque of Pasha Hassan Jakovali survived (it now houses a museum), and in the mosque of Pasha Gazi Kassim, once built from the stones of the demolished church of St Bartholomew, Catholic services are held. Only the burial chapel of Idris Baba has retained its old appearance. Many Jews lived in Pécs. More than 3,000 of the 5,000 who lived here before the last war were murdered in German concentration camps. Now the Jewish community has some 500 members who meet in the whitewashed synagogue on Kossuth tér. The magnificent Romanesque cathedral, however, survived Turkish rule and its transformation into a mosque unharmed.

The dialogue between East and West is also visible in the work of two artists who were born here, Victor Vasarely (born 1908) and Tivadar Csontváry Kosztka (1853–1919). There is a museum devoted to each – to Vasarely, who lived in France and paints his magical geometric pictures; and to Kosztka, who followed the traces of wind, colour and light in the Mediterranean and the Middle East. ■

The Hassan Jakowali Museum.

INSIGHT GUIDES
Travel Tips

Let your message travel with Insight Guides

With 200 titles covering the world, Insight Guides can convey your advertisement to sophisticated international travellers.

HÖFER MEDIA PTE LTD

Singapore : 38, Joo Koon Road, Singapore 628990
Tel: (65)-865-1629/30 Fax: (65)-862-0694

London : PO Box 7910, London SE11 8LL, United Kingdom
Tel: (44 171)-620-0008, Fax: (44 171)-620-1074
e-mail: insight@apaguide.demon.co.uk

INSIGHT GUIDES

Getting Acquainted

The Place

Area: 93,033 sq. km (35,920 sq. miles).
Capital: Budapest.
Highest Mountain: Kékes – 1,015 metres (3,330 ft).
Longest River: Danube and Tisza.
Population: approximately 11 million.
Language: Hungarian (Magyar).
Religion: Roman Catholic.
Time Zone: Central European Time (CET), i.e. GMT plus one hour.
Currency: Forint (HUF).
Electricity: 220V.
Weights and Measures: Metric.
International Dialling Code: 00 36.

Climate

Hungary has a continental climate, although this is moderated by Atlantic troughs. Winters can be very cold and the summers are hot. The warmest region is in the south around Pécs. Hungary boasts an average of 2,015 hours of sunshine per year, more than the European average. Mean temperatures range from -2°C/28°F in January to 23°C/73°F in June, but can often be much colder and much hotter.

The best times to visit Hungary are in spring and autumn.

Geography

Hungary lies at the heart of Europe. It is bordered in the west by Austria, in the north by Slovakia and the Ukraine, in the east by Romania and in the south by Slovenia, Croatia and Serbia. The total area covers 93,033 sq. km (35,920 sq. miles), about one percent of the whole of Europe.

The country can be divided into four sections. The Small Plain (Kisalföld) lies in the northwest with Györ at the centre. The Great Plain (Alföld) lies to the east of the Danube and Tisza rivers and embraces almost half of Hun-gary. The puszta, grassless steppe now put to good use as agricultural land, is at the centre of this region. Only in the protected Hortobágy region west of Debrecen has the puszta been preserved in its original form. The Northern Highlands with no mountains higher than 1,015 metres (3,330 ft) separate the Small and Great Plain.

The River Danube cuts through the range near Esztergom. The Transdanubian Hills separate the Danube from the Dráva with the Mecsek Hill, 682 metres (2,237 ft), the highest peak. About 18 percent of this area is woodland, mostly from an altitude of about 350 metres (1,150 ft). Some six percent are pines, the rest is deciduous.

Of all the Hungarian rivers, the Tisza (579 km/359 miles on Hungarian soil) and the Danube (420 km/260 miles) are the longest. Balaton, covering an area of 492 sq. km/187 sq. miles, is the biggest lake. Lake Fertö is second-largest with 320 sq. km (122 sq. miles) on Hungarian soil.

The People

The population of Hungary is about 11 million. For each square kilometre there are on average 114 inhabitants. In rural areas this figure drops to 70 as some 60 percent of the population live in the urban areas. Women make up 52.3 percent of the population.

Hungary's major cities and populations are:

Budapest	2,115,000
Debrecen	219,000
Miskolc	208,000
Szeged	189,000
Pécs	183,000
Györ	132,000
Nyiregyháza	119,000
Székesfehérvár	114,000
Kecskemét	107,000

The majority of the population, some 95 percent, are Hungarian. Romany Gypsies form the biggest minority with 400,000 people. There are also about 220,000 German speakers. Other recognisable minorities are Romanians, Slovaks, Serbs, Croats and Jews.

About 6 million Hungarian citizens are Catholic; 2.5 million Protestant; 270,000 Greek Orthodox; and 80,000 Jewish.

Fierce patriotism has shored up the Hungarian language, the main lan-guage spoken. It belongs to the Finno-Ugric group of languages. English and German are widely spoken.

Government

Constitution

On 20 August 1989, Hungary was proclaimed a parliamentary republic. The Hungarian name is Magyar Köztársaság (Republic of Hungary). Apart from a few alterations, the constitution agreed on 20 August 1949 is still in force. The Hungarian flag consists of three horizontal stripes in red, white and green.

Parliament

The head of state is the national president who is elected by the Hungarian parliament for a period of five years. Árpád Göncz of the Alliance of Free Democrats (SZDSZ) was elected president on 2 May 1990.

The parliament consists of one chamber which is the highest legislative body. A total of 386 deputies are elected, 176 by direct mandate. The electoral system combines elements of the French and German systems. Some deputies are elected directly and some from a list. Parties with less than four percent of the total vote are excluded, but elections are repeated in the event of a low turnout and/or in the absence of an overall majority. Elections must be held every four years.

The government comprises the prime minister and ministers, some without portfolio. Elections in May 1994 returned the Socialist Workers' Party (MSZP) to power under prime minister Gyula Horn. His party won 54.15 percent of the votes. A coalition led by József Antall had ruled Hungary since the collapse of communism in 1989, but Antall, the leader of the Hungarian Democratic Forum (MDF), died at the end of 1993 and his party won only 9.59 percent of the votes. The second largest party, the Alliance of Free Democrats (SZDSZ), gained 18.13 percent of votes.

Hungary is divided into 19 smaller counties and the capital Budapest. Their regional assemblies have considerable powers.

Economy

Switching to a Western, quality market has been difficult although foreign investors have shown an interest in Hungary. Inflation has soared and unemployment has increased sharply as old, inefficient factories have closed for lack of subsidies.

Budapest is the most important economic and industrial centre in Hungary. Iron and steel, machinery, pharmaceuticals and vehicle manufacture are among the country's chief industries. Its main crops are grains, vegetables and fruits.

Planning The Trip

What To Bring

The continental climate can result in very hot summers and cold winters, so be prepared. In Budapest in summer light clothing would be suitable by day, however, in the evenings you would need a sweater or cardigan in the open air. You should expect some rain the year round, so bring along suitable protection.

Maps

Road maps and town plans to various scales can be bought from bookshops. Also useful is the practical City Atlas of Budapest, published by Cartographia, as it contains a brief guide to the capital. Simplified maps which give a general view of the towns and their sights can be obtained free in hotels and travel agencies.

Entry Regulations

Passports

To enter Hungary you will need a passport which is still valid for at least another nine months. Europeans (except citizens of Portugal, Greece and Turkey), Americans, members of the CIS, Canadians and Argentinians no longer need a visa before entering Hungary.

However, most Asians, Middle Easterners and Latin Americans require visas, as do Australians, New Zealanders and Maltese.

Animal Quarantine

Dogs and cats need an official vetinary certificate detailing their inoculations before entering the country. Dogs need an additional inoculation against rabies and distemper.
Veterinary Hospital and Clinic, Budapest XIII, Lehel ut, tel: -270-0361.

Customs

Customs are not what one might call strict. Cars are generally let through with a cursory glance and maybe a question or two as to what the passengers are carrying. However, from time to time one will be asked to open the boot and pull out a suitcase for inspection, even now.

On entering the country persons over 16 years old are allowed to import 250 cigarettes or 50 cigars or 250g tobacco, 2 litres wine and 1 litre brandy as well as items for personal use. Gifts to the value 15,000 forints may be imported free of duty once a year. Under *Currency*, below, you will find the currency regulations.

Weapons, ammunition, transmitters and the like have to be registered with the proper authorities. The best bet is to contact the Hungarian embassy or consulate in your own country.
Exporting goods: goods to the value of 10,000 forint may be exported, but licences are required for gold and silverware, works of art, antiques and objects of archaeological or historic interest. If intending to buy items in this category you are advised to call the TOURINFORM office in Budapest, tel: 117-9800, or contact the relevant authorities at the border. It is wise to keep receipts in case you are checked at the border.

Health

The standards of health treatment and hygiene in Hungary vary considerably. Rather than take a chance, it is best to have proper travel insurance cover in case of serious illness or accident. For emergencies, the ambulance number is 104, or 311-1666. For lesser problems ask your hotel to call a doctor, or simply go to a pharmacy (*gyógy-*

szertár), and explain as best you can what the problem is.

Dentistry is a Hungarian speciality, and many tourists visit the country just to benefit from lower prices. Gold fillings, however, are purchased at the market price for gold, and are hence no cheaper than elsewhere.

Articles of personal hygiene, from condoms to tampons, are readily available in supermarkets and chemists.

Public toilets in Hungary can be something of an adventure. If there is an attendant, you will be given toilet paper for a small fee ranging from 10 to 20Ft. Otherwise, as a precaution, bring your own. This applies on occasion to even the better places.

If you are intending to swim, equip yourself with an antiseptic foot powder or fluid.

Beware, too, of the food: it can be very heavy at first for the untrained stomach. Lard is used for cooking, vegetarianism is only just beginning to sink in, and off-season means few fresh items such as salad or fruit. What the Hungarian calls salad is usually pickled vegetables. A mild laxative could help to keep the digestion moving at first.

Currency

The unit of currency in Hungary is the forint: 100 fillér equal 1 forint, but the fillér is worth so little that it is falling into disuse. 10, 20 and 50 fillér coins are in circulation as are 1, 2, 5, 10 and 20, 50 and 100 forint coins. Notes are issued to the value of 100, 500, 1,000 and 5,000 forints. The exchange rate is set weekly by the Hungarian National Bank. At the time of press, the rates were £1 sterling equals about 300Ft.

Currency Restrictions/ Changing Money

There are no limits on the amounts of currency which may be imported and exported, but if large sums of money are involved, then it is recommended that these should be declared to the authorities. There is no need to be worried about taking the forints left over from the last holiday.

Most banks will change money, especially branches of the OTP, the Hungarian savings bank, but there are very few Eurocheque cash machines. Eurocheques may be cashed at most banks and bureaux de change in Budapest, but in smaller towns it may be necessary to look a little harder. The upper limit for Eurocheques is 15,000 forints. A certificate of exchange is no longer necessary. It is not advisable to change more money than is required as to change money back can lead to losses on the exchange rate.

Hotels, travel agencies, tourist offices and campsites will also change money and exchange rates are not usually any worse than at a bank, but never change money with the many "friendly" young men who approach tourists in Budapest. There is a flourishing black market in Western currencies (with rates that are noticeably more advantageous than the official ones). The temptations are great, but so are the risks. You could be cheated, or you could be caught. If arrested, you will have to pay a high fine for currency offences.

Banks are normally open on working days from 9am to 4pm, but the bureaux de change are open for longer hours and at weekends.

Most restaurants, businesses and petrol stations in Budapest and the major cities accept the main credit cards, but few outlets in country areas will be familiar with them. Cash will only be issued against credit cards at a few banks in Budapest, e.g. MKB in Türr Istvan utca 9 by the Vörösmarty tér (Mastercard and Visa). It has one of the few ATM machines to issue cash against credit cards. There is also a cash machine at the American Express offices in Déak Ferenc utca 10.

Public Holidays

1 January	New Year's day
15 March	National Holiday
	Easter Monday
1 May	Labour Day
20 August	St Stephan's Day
23 October	1956 Uprising Day
	of Remembrance
25/26 December	Christmas

If the holiday falls on a Thursday or Tuesday, the Friday or Monday will be taken off as well and added to the weekend. *See Festivals page 290.*

Getting There
By Air

Budapest is served by several European and a few non-European airlines. Malév, the Hungarian national airline, operates regular scheduled flights several times a day between the Hungarian capital and most European cities, with a non-stop service to London Heathrow and New York several times a week.

Normal scheduled air fares are subject to a variety of discounts (APEX etc.). Your travel agent will have the details, or you can contact the airlines directly. There are charter flights in the summer season.

There are two airports in Budapest: Ferihegy I and Ferihegy II. A bus service connects the two. Foreign airlines land at Ferihegy I, 20 km/12 miles from the city centre. The new airport, Ferihegy II, about 25 km/16 miles away, is reserved exclusively for the national airline Malév.

For the journey into Budapest from the airport, avoid taking a taxi. Taxi-drivers at the airport are known for demanding extortionate prices. A single journey into Budapest ought not to cost more than 2,000 forints, but often fares 10 times this amount are requested. Every half an hour buses (Volánbus) leave for the city centre bus station at Erzsébet tér. In order to overcome the problem with taxi fares, the airport management (LRI) operates a shuttle service. Minibuses will take passengers to their hotel or pension and collect them for the return flight. To find out more about the service, ask at the counter near the left luggage office. To return to the airport from the city centre, tel: 157-8555.

Malév overseas branch offices:
Britain: 10 Vigo Street, London W1X IAJ, tel: 0171-439 0577.
USA, New York: Suite 1900. Rockefeller Center, 630 Fifth Avenue, NY 10111, tel: 212-757 6480.
Malév offices in Budapest:
Malév Central Office, 1051 Budapest V, Roosevelt tér 2, tel: 226-9033.
Airport: tel: 157-2122.
Flight information (Budapest):
Central Flight Information: tel: 296-7155.
Malév (arrivals): tel: 296-8000.
Malév (departures): tel: 296-7000.

By Boat

One of the most memorable ways of arriving in Budapest is by river. A service linking Vienna and Budapest operates between April and October. There are generally two departures per day and the journey takes about four hours. Details of services and river cruises: CTC Line, 1 Regent Street, London SW1Y 4NN, tel: 0171-930 5833, 0171-839 3580.

Jetfoil: 1 April–1 October, daily, leaving at 8am, in either direction. During the main season (up until mid-September), a second boat leaves in each direction in the early afternoon from 1 May in Vienna and from 1 June in Budapest. reservations can be made at IBUSZ offices abroad and at the main MAHART office in Vienna: Karlplatz 2/8, A-1010 Vienna, tel: (0222) 505-5644.

Reservations can be made in Budapest at the central MAHART office of the Hungarian Danube Shipping Company, International Mooring Point, Budapest V, Belgrád rakpart, tel: 118-1704; fax: 118-7740.

Hovercraft: Daily (except Wednesday) from the end of April to the end of September. Three times a week throughout October, leaving Vienna Monday, Wednesday, Saturday; leaving Budapest Tuesday, Thursday, Sunday. Reservations: Erste Donau-Dampfschiffahrts-Gesellschaft (DDSG), Handelskai 265, A-1020 Vienna. Travel service, tel: 218-5919. Timetable information, tel: 218-1537.

By Rail

Many direct trains run from Germany, Austria and Switzerland to Hungary. The trains are comfortable and have all facilities. Nearly all trains arrive at Budapest's Eastern Railway station (Keleti pályaudvar).

In general, reservations are required for long-distance international trains during the high season and for sleeping cars. You can make your reservations for your return journey before leaving home, or at the customer service office of MÁV – Hungarian State Railways. MÁV Customer Services, Budapest VI, Andrássy út 35, tel: 122-8049, 122-8056. Open Monday – Friday 9am–6pm, Saturday 9am–1pm.

Railway Stations: Of the three railway stations in Budapest, two serve Western Europe:

Keleti pályaudvar (Eastern Railway Station), Budapest VIII, Baross tér, tel: 313-6835.

Deli pályaudvar (Southern Railway Station), Budapest I, Alkotás utca, tel: 175-6293.

Connections: The railway stations of Budapest have good connections to the rest of the public transport system (Metro, buses, trams). There is a direct Metro link between the Southern and Eastern railway stations.

If you prefer to travel to your hotel by taxi (which could take much longer than going by Metro), you can order a taxi at the border at Hegyeshalom by approaching an official who goes through the train. This will save you a tiresome wait on your arrival.

There are various reduced fares for young people under the age of 26, e.g. the Interail card, which are also valid in Hungary.

By Coach

There are regular long-distance coach connections between southern Germany and Austria and Budapest. Contact **Central long-distance coach station**, Budapest V, Erzsébet tér. Information and bookings, tel: 117-2966.

By Car

TRAVEL DOCUMENTS

For travellers from Western Europe, a driving licence, a nationality sticker on the car and the correct insurance documents are sufficient. A green card is not actually essential but motoring associations do recommend that you take one, and also take out an insurance policy which in the event of an emergency will guarantee the return of the damaged vehicle. Further information is available from the AA and RAC.

CROSSING THE BORDER

The shortest and easiest route into Hungary is via Vienna and the Nickelsdorf/Hegyeshalom crossing which then allows easy access to Budapest or Lake Balaton. During the summer, however, the wait for customs clearance can take several hours, so it is a good idea to choose a minor crossing point, e.g. Deutschkreuz/Sopron a few kilometres further south. This should not be confused with Klingenbach/Sopron where customs clearance also requires a long

wait. Another alternative is to cross into Hungary via Bratislava. No visas are needed for entry into Slovakia now, but the detour involves many extra miles and an additional frontier crossing. The motorway into Budapest is now complete.

To enter southern Hungary, the best crossing point is at Heiligenkreuz beyond Graz. The road to Pécs runs through pretty countryside but it is narrow and winding in places. Allow plenty of time.

DISTANCES

From Budapest to

Debrecen	266 km/164 miles
Györ	123 km/76 miles
Kecskemét	85 km/53 miles
Miskolc	179 km/111 miles
Pécs	198 km/123 miles
Sopron	210 km/130 miles
Szeged	171 km/106 miles
Eger	100 km/62 miles
Zalaegerszeg	224 km/139 miles.

TRAFFIC REGULATIONS

The Hungarian road network – especially the trunk roads – is well developed and, generally speaking, in satisfactory condition.

The highway code and the road signs follow international usage. Seat belts are obligatory.

Beware! There is a total drink-and-drive ban in Hungary. The legal limit is **0.0 milligrams**! There are strict rules and harsh penalties if you are over the limit. Up to 0.8 milligrams, there is a maximum fine of 10,000 forint; over 0.8 milligrams, prison sentences can be given (foreigners are not exempted).

MAXIMUM SPEED LIMITS

Take care – these are lower than those in Western Europe. Breaking the speed limit is not tolerated, even if the drivers are foreigners.

Built-up areas	60 km/h (37 mph)
Country roads	80 km/h (50 mph)
Trunk roads	100 km/h (62 mph)
Motorways	120 km/h (74 mph)

Drivers are required to switch their headlights on during the day as well.

FINES

Should you be stopped by the police and charged a fine for some misdemeanor, pay in forint, and request a receipt or a ticket. Police are

fairly strict, but with very few exceptions this writer has never had any troubles, nor found excessively rude officers on the job.

STOLEN CARS

Should you not find your car where you parked it, call the police headquarters at 118-0800 or 343-0848. It has either been towed or stolen. Unfortunately car theft by organised bands in Budapest is fairly frequent. Luxury vehicles are preferred, and apparently none is safe.

OTHER IMPORTANT NUMBERS

008 or 212-3952 for the Hungarian Automobile Club whose "yellow angels" travel the highways. In case of accident call the police, tel: 07, and then the Hungária Biztosító (Hungária Insurance), tel: 163-3079, 183-5359, 183-6527 in Budapest.

A word to the wise about driving in Hungary: The accident rate is very high owing to several factors. One is the abuse of alcohol, another the abuse of the speed and power of many Western cars. Hungarians are by and large not the best drivers, the main fault being recklessness, such as overtaking on blind curves, in foggy weather, or in other perfectly absurd situations.

Driving at night is especially dangerous as people, bicycle riders and horse- or ox-drawn carts tend to be on the road without any lights. Be especially careful around evening when people come in from the fields or factories.

Driving in Budapest is basically a waste of time, energy and nerves. Parking is difficult, jams are frequent especially in the inner city, and the risk of having one's car broken into is high. The best thing to do is take everything out of your vehicle, find a safe spot (parking garage or the hotel garage) and use the very efficient and cheap public transportation. Taxis are also fairly well priced: Cabbies with western automobiles may charge more. Make no deals with meterless cabbies (whereby it has been found that a number of cabbies alter their meters). There is no real way of fighting this felony, just note the name and number of the cab if you have any suspicions, say if one way cost 500Ft, and the other 800Ft.

Special Facilities

Travelling with Children

Hungarians are fond of children and there is plenty for youngsters to do (*see Activities for Children page 288*). For general information contact: **Toptour**, Budapest V, Nádor u. 26, tel: 131-6194. Toptour specialises in the care of families and children. Here you can book family-friendly private accommodation or pensions with cots. There is a baby-sitting agency avaialable. Children aged four to 12 can be cared for by the hour by trained staff.

Student

Express Youth and Student Travel Agency, Central office, Budapest VI, Szabadsag tér 16, tel: 131-7777.

Business People

The central organisation for business people to contact in Hungary is the Hungarian Chamber of Commerce: Budapest V, Kossuth Lajos tér 6-8, tel: 111-1843. Open 8am–5pm.

Useful Addresses

Tourist Information

Tourist information abroad is available from either a travel agent specialising in Eastern European travel, a branch of IBUZS, Malév, or the nearest Hungarian embassy or consulate.

GREAT BRITAIN

Hungarian National Tourist Office, 46 Eaton Place, London SW1X 8AL, tel: 0171-823 1032, 0171-823 1055.
Malév, 10 Vigo Street, London W1X 1AJ, tel: 0171-439 0577.
Danube Travel, 6 Conduit Street, London W1R 9TG, tel: 0171-493 0263.
Intra Travel, 44 Maple Street, London W1P 5GD, tel: 0171-323 3305.
Hungarian Air Tours, 87 Regent Street, London W1R 7HF, tel: 0171-437 9405.
Bridgewater Travel, 217 Monton Road, Manchester M30 9PN, tel: 0161-707 8547.
Regent Holidays, 15 John Street, Bristol BS1 2HR, tel: 0117-921 1711.
Thermalia Travel, New College Parade, London NW3 5EP, tel: 0171-483 1898.
New Millennium, 20 High Street, Solihull, W. Midlands B91 3TB, tel: 0121-711 2232; fax: 0121-711 3652.

UNITED STATES

Hungarian Tourist Board, Embassy of the Republic of Hungary, 150 East 58th Street, 33rd floor, New York, NY 10155, tel: 212-355 0240.
Malév, Suite 1900, Rockefeller Center, 630 Fifth Avenue, NY 10111, tel: 212-757 6480.

Practical Tips

Weights & Measures

The metric system is valid in Hungary. In the shops, weights are measured in kilogrammes (kg) and decagrammes (dkg). One "deka", as they say, equals 10 grammes.

Business Hours

There are no legal opening times. Most shops and department stores in the town centres open from 10am–6pm and 9am–1pm on Saturday. Many shops stay open until 8pm on Thursday. In many parts of Budapest there are food shops which stay open round the clock. Even in country regions more and more shops are staying open until late in the evening.

Listed below are the opening hours of businesses and government departments. Only to be used as a guideline.
Shops: Monday–Friday 10am–6pm; Saturday 10am–1pm; Sunday closed, with the exception of some supermarkets (8am–1pm). Thursday is "late shopping day", shops are open up until 7pm or 8pm.

The following shops in Budapest are also open on Sunday 8am–1pm: **Kispesti Centrum Áruház**, Budapest XIX, Kossuth tér 4-5. **Áruház**, Budapest Vii, Klauzál tér 11. **Sugár shopping centre**, Budapest XIV, Örs vesér tere. **ABC store**, Budapest I, Batthyány tér. **ABC store** (near Nyugati tér), Budapest XII, Szt. István körút.

A plethora of **24-hour stores** has appeared on the scene, offering basic consumer goods. They advertise either "non-stop", or "*éjjel-nappal*". After

10pm there is sometimes a small surcharge.
Department stores: Monday–Friday 9am–6pm; Saturday 9am–1pm; Sunday closed.
Food shops: Monday–Friday 7am–7/8pm; Saturday 7am–4pm; Sunday closed, with the exception of some supermarkets (8am–1pm).
Tobacconists: Monday–Friday 7am–8pm; Saturday 7am–4pm; Sunday closed.
Hairdressers: Monday–Friday 7am–9pm; Saturday 7am–4pm; Sunday closed.
Post offices: Monday–Friday 9am–6pm except the main post office in Budapest (8am–7pm) and the post offices at the Western and Eastern Railway stations (Nyugati and Keleti Pályaudvar respectively) which are open 24 hours.
Banks: Monday–Friday 9am–4pm.
Bureaux de change: Monday–Friday 8am–3/4pm; close at 7pm on Monday, and 1pm on Friday.
Petrol stations: Monday–Sunday 6am–8pm. Many stations open 24 hours.
Pharmacies: Monday–Friday 8am–6pm, with a weekend emergency cover service.
Museums: Tuesday–Friday 10am–6pm; Saturday 10am–6pm; Sunday 10am–6pm; Monday closed.
Government departments: Monday–Friday 9am–1pm.
For 24-hour tourist information including accommodation service, to go Petöfi tér 3.

Religious Services

Details of services held by the various denominations can be obtained from the notices put out by the various religious communities. Early mass is said daily in all Catholic churches.

Sunday Services

High Mass (Catholic) in Matthias Church, Budapest, with excellent musicians, every Sunday at 10am.

Religious Offices

Roman Catholic Church, Archepiscopal Office, Budapest V, Eötvös Loránd utca 7, tel: 117-4752.
Protestant Church/National Church, Office, Budapest VII, Üllöi út, tel: 117-1637.

Reformed Church, Reformed Church Episcopal Office, Budapest IX, Ráday utca, tel: 218-0753.
Jewish Community, Budapest VII, Síp utca 12, tel: 342-1355.

Newspapers & Magazines

Daily News is a bi-weekly newspaper in German and English published by the national MTI news agency.

Travel Magazin is a quarterly that is best found in the airplane. It has interesting articles on current affairs, and makes an attempt at being critical, even though it is in the business of selling the country.

Budapest Week is a fine weekly paper written by Hungarians, with critical news about the country. It's a must.

Budapest Panorama, a monthly programme magazine.

For Youth, a quarterly guide in several languages.

Foreign newspapers and magazines are also readily available at the newsstands where the foreigners tread, i.e., the train stations, in the Pest inner city and at hotels.

Radio & Television

All Eastern European radio stations broadcast on frequencies used in the West by the police and emergency services. This situation arose during the Cold War as a way of preventing the people from listening to Western radio stations. Consequently there is very little to hear on the car radio. One exception is Radio Danubius, a new private radio station with Western pop music and lightweight news summaries (100.5, 102 and 103.3MHz).

Hungarian State Radio has three main channels – Budapest I (*Kossuth*) and Budapest II (*Petöfi*) on medium wave as well as Rádió Bartók on VHF.
Radio Bridge, 102.1 Mhy, English-language news and reports.
Rádió Petöfi, Monday–Friday noon–12.05pm: News broadcast in English and German.
Rádió Bartók has excellent, almost continuous music.

Hungary has two television channels and is, relatively speaking, at an early stage of development. Every Tuesday, at 8pm, a news programme in English and German is broadcast on Channel 2. Cable and satellite TV is widely available in hotels and private homes, sometimes even in restaurants, much to the ire of those hoping for a quiet meal .

In general, post offices are open from 9am–6pm. The following post offices have longer opening hours:
Main Post Office (8am–7pm), Budapest V, Városház utca 9–11, tel: 118-5398.
Post Office 62 (24 hours), Western Railway Station, Budapest VI, Teréz körut 5, tel: 312-0436.
Post Office 72 (24 hours), Eastern Railway Station, Budapest VII, Barosstér, tel: 322-1099.
Address for poste restante: 1364 Budapest 4, Petöfi Sándor utca 13–15.

Mail boxes are emptied once or twice a day. They are red and are either fixed to the walls of buildings or free-standing on wrought-iron stands at the roadside.

Stamps can be bought at post offices or at the tobacconists.

Phone boxes use 5, 10 and 20 forint coins, but using phone cards is preferable, particularly for long-distance calls. There are a lot of card phones in Budapest now, and more and more such phones are being installed in other parts of the country. Every post office and tobacconist sells phone cards with either 50 or 120 units.

To make a call abroad, first dial 00 and then wait for a high-pitched tone or a rattling ringing sound. That sound indicates that a line out of Hungary is open. If no such sound is heard, then all lines are engaged and it will be necessary to try again later. When dialling Germany, Austria and Switzerland, dial the area code without the 0 and then the number you require.

It is cheaper to call between 10pm and 8am and also at weekends. The number for English-speaking directory enquiries is Budapest (1) 117-0170 (inland); 267-5555 (international).

Post office will accept telegrams, but a fax service is only available at larger post offices, at the East and West Stations in Budapest and at the telephone shop in Petöfi Sándor utca.

Telephone forecasts: For information tel: 135-3500 (Budapest); tel: 117-1833 (provinces).
Radio forecasts: Every hour after the news, alternately on the Kossuth and Petöfi channels, but in Hunagrian only.
TV forecasts: Following the evening news (Tuesday–Saturday about 8pm, Sunday about 8.30pm; no news on Monday).

Tourinform, Budapest V, Sütö utca 2, tel: 117-9800; fax: 117-9578. Open weedays 7am–7pm, Saturday 8am–8pm, Sunday 7am–1pm. Visitors can obtain travel information in English, plus details of accommodation, opening hours, addresses, telephone numbers, programmes and news of forthcoming events.
IBUSZ (open 24 hours), Budapest V, Petöfi tér 3, tel: 118-5707, 118-3925. State-run travel agency offering the usual services, plus organisation of sightseeing tours and tourist programmes.
Budapest Tourist, V. Roosevelt tér 5, tel: 118-1453. General information and accommodation agency for private rooms and pensions in Budapest.

Tourinform Offices Outside Budapest

Budaörs, AGIP-complex, tel: (23) 313-518.
Debrecen, Piac u. 20, tel: (52) 412-250.
Eger, Dobó tér 2, tel: (36) 321-807.
Gödöllő, Király Kastely, tel: (28) 320-331; 330-864.
Györ, Arpád u. 32, tel: (96) 317-709.
Hajdúszoboszló, Szilfákalja 2, tel: (52) 361-612.
Kaposvár, Csokonai Köz 3, tel: (82) 316-349 (responsible for the county).
Kaposvár, Fö u. 8, tel: (82) 320-404 (responsible for the town).
Kecskemét, Kossuth tér 1, tel: (76) 481-065.
Keszthely, Kossuth u. 28, tel: (83) 314-144.
Komárom, Mártírok u. 14, tel: (34) 341-790.
Mesztegnyö, Szabadság tér 6, tel: (60) 368-236.
Miskolc, Mindszent tér 1, tel: (46) 348-921.

Nyíregyháza, Hösök tere 5, tel: (42) 312-606.
Pécs, Széchenyi tér 9, tel: (72) 213-315.
Siófok, Fö u. 41, tel: (84) 310-117.
Szécsény, Ady Endre u. 12, tel: (32) 370-777.
Szeged, Victor Hugo u. 1, tel: (62) 311-711.
Székesfehérvár, Városház tér 11, tel: (22) 312-818.
Szentendre, Dumsta Jenö tér 22, tel: (26) 317-965.
Szolnok, Ságvári körut 4, tel: (56) 424-803.
Tiszafüred, Húszöles u. 21/A, tel: (59) 353-000.
Vác, Dr. Csányi körut 45, tel: (27) 316-1160.
Velence, Tópart u. 26, tel: (22) 368-037.
Zalakaros, Termál út 4, tel: (93) 340-421.

Embassies

British Embassy, 1054 Budapest V, Harmincad utca 6, tel: 266-2888.
US Embassy, 1054 Budapest V, Szabadsag tér 12, tel: 267-4700.

Emergencies

Security & Crime

Crime is sharply on the increase in Budapest, and several precautions should be taken. **Avoid certain neighbourhoods at night**: the eastern train station, the narrow streets around Rákóczi tér and Blaha Luijza tér. Your judgement here is called for as in any other major metropolis.

Do not carry purses and cameras loosely, do not count great wads of money in public, take only what you need. A good tip is to avoid carrying a purse at all. Pickpockets are very skilled in Hungary. They tend to operate in crowded places (such as shops, subway stations, Váci u.). Should you fall victim to a crime, contact the police at once.

Car robbery is the other great crime that takes place in the city. Empty your vehicle, take the radio out, lock it up, and try to find a populous place or a garage. Some hotels have car parks, but not all. Luxury cars are preferred but not exclusively.

Beware of **moneychangers** offering astronomical exchange rates. This ac-

tivity is illegal, and leaves many a Scroogey type with a handful of newspaper clippings and no legal resort. Professionals will count out ten 1000Ft bills before your very eyes and give you five.

Much of the criminal activity that takes place is mafia-style and therefore only really affects either other criminals or victims such as drug addicts, prostitutes and shop owners subjected to extortion. But the issue of prostitution must be addressed more closely: it has flourished since the communist embargo on prostitution was lifted, and is also a by-product of hard economic times. Budapest is sometimes referred to as the "Bangkok of Europe". Driving in from Austria one notices it at once, with scantily clad women hitchhiking in absurdly remote locations.

In the city, certain localities are well-known for the ladies of the night, but the business is also practised in cafés, at hotel bars, around discos, and in the countless nightclubs and striptease joints that have mushroomed. It is generally very obvious to the casual observer. The user of this ancient service should always be equipped with condoms, as AIDS and other venereal diseases are experiencing a parallel boom. Secondly, there have been stories of customers waking up with a bump on their heads and empty pockets, or not waking up at all after a night of revelry.

Emergency Numbers

These key numbers can be dialled from any telephone:
Emergency Rescue Service: 04 in Budapest; 104 in the provinces.
Ambulance, First Aid: 04 (311-1666 in Budapest); 004 in the provinces.
Fire Brigade: 05 in Budapest; 105 in the provinces.
Police: 07 in Budapest; 107 in the provinces.

Lost Property

Central Lost Property Office, Budapest V, Erzsébet tér 5, tel: 117-4961. Monday–Thursday 8am–4.30pm (Friday until 4pm).
Lost Property Office of the Budapest City Public Transport Systems, BKV, Budapest VII, Akácfa utca 18, tel: 322-6613. Monday–Friday 7.30am–3.30pm (Wednesday until 7pm).

Airport Lost Property, Ferihegy I, tel: 296-7155; Ferihegy II, tel: 296-8000.
Taxi Central Lost Property Office, Budapest VII, Akácfa utca 20, tel: 134-4787. Monday–Thursday 8am–4pm (Friday until 4pm).
Volántaxi, Budapest XIV, Jerney utca 54-56, tel: 183-5780. Daily 6am–7pm.

If you lose your passport: Contact KEOKH (Police headquarters, Aliens Department), Budapest VI, Néköztársaság utca 12, tel: 111-8667, 111-8668.

Medical Services

Medical first aid and a free ambulance are a basic right in Hungary and this also applies to tourists. Charges will be made for further treatment, so it always advisable to take out an adequate insurance policy in advance.

Accidents

Accidents have to be reported to the police immediately, and forms need to be filled even for minor collisions. Report any accident – even if it wasn't your fault – immediately to **Hungária Insurance Budapest**, Gvadányi út 69, tel: 252-6333.
Helicopter Rescue Service Aerocaritas: tel: 625-3130, 625-3950.

Doctors

First aid and doctors' visits have to be paid for, mostly in foreign currency. Make sure you obtain receipts for insurance purposes. Medical aid is available around the clock from the following clinics:
IMS Outpatient Clinic, Váci út 202, tel: 149-9349.
Trauma Inst, Lörcy Sandor 3–5, tel: 133-5593.
Children's Clinic, Üllói út 86, tel: 210-0720.

Dentists

One special feature of the medical scene in Budapest is the very cheap (by Western standards) dental treatment, which includes conservation, surgical and prosthetic treatment. The dental surgeries in the luxurious Hotel Thermál on Margaret Island and most recently in the not so luxurious Hotel Volga have been specially set up for tourists. Even including hotel costs, dental treatment in Budapest is still much cheaper than in some other Western cities.

Dental Emergency Service (day and night), Budapest VIII, Mária utca 52, tel: 133-0189.

Dentex dental practice, Városligeti (Gorki fasor) 32, tel: 351-1895.

Pharmacies

Medicines and drugs can only be obtained in pharmacies. Most are available only on prescription, only a few can be sold freely. Payments must be made in cash. Keep receipts for insurance purposes.

Opening hours: Monday–Friday 8am–6pm, Saturday 8am–2pm.

There is a regular emergency cover service for night-time and holidays. In every pharmacy there is a notice indicating the nearest pharmacy offering emergency cover.

The following remain open at night on Sundays and on public holidays:

II, Frankel Leó út 22, tel: 212-4406.
III, Szentendrei út 2/a, tel: 188-6528.
IV, Pozsonyi u. 19, tel: 189-4079.
VI, Teréz krt. 41, tel: 111-4439.
VIII, Rákóczi út 39, tel: 114-3695.
IX, Üllói út 121, tel: 215-3800.
XI, Kosztolányi Dezsö tér 11. Open 8am–8pm, tel: 166-6494.
XII, Alkotás utca 1/b, tel: 155-4691.
XIII, Gyöngyösi sétány 1, tel: 129-8401.

Getting Around

Public Transport

Public transport in Budapest is good, rapid and cheap. A closely-knit network of trams and buses, the underground railway (Metro) and the suburban railway (HÉV) provide access to all parts of the city in any direction. In the Buda Hills there are also the rack railways, the Children's Railway and the chair lift, the cable railway up Castle Hill and the minibus in the Castle Quarter. The motorboat ferries crossing the Danube also belong to the public transport system. The speed of travel is higher than in most big European cities. On aver-

age, some 1,600 million passengers are transported every year. There are ticket franking machines instead of conductors.

Tickets (best bought in bulk in advance) can be obtained from vending machines, at stations, at the tobacconists, at the Metro ticket offices and in travel agencies. Each ticket is only valid for one journey. They are not valid for transfers. Beware! If you are caught fare-dodging, you will have to pay a heavy fine. There are no exemptions for tourists.

Operating hours:
Metro, buses: 4.30am–11pm.
Trams: 4am–midnight.
24-hours and night-time routes:
Trams: 6,12, 28, 31, 49, 50.
Buses: 3, 42, 78, 11, 144, 173, 179, 182, C.

Information about the public transport system can be obtained from:
Fövinform (day and night), tel: 117-1173.

Buses & Trams

The Volánbus Company operates a comprehensive network of transportation which includes smaller towns throughout Hungary. Contact Tourinform, Budapest V, Sütö utca 2, tel: 117-9800; fax: 117-9578.

In Budapest there are about 40 tram and more than 208 bus routes. Express buses have red numbers and only stop at certain points. The 12 trolley-bus routes mostly link up with the Metro routes; route 73 is a direct link between the Western and Eastern Railway Stations. To reach the airport from the city, the Volánbus departs every half-an-hour from the central bus station at Erzsebet tér.

Metro

The Metro system is the by far the quickest way of getting around Budapest. There are three routes. The "little Metro" (1) links the city centre with Mexikói út. Route M2 runs from west–east, from the Southern Railway Station (Déli pu.) under the Danube to the other bank, passing the Eastern Railway Station (Keleti pu.) and on as far as Örs vezér tere.

The M3 runs from north–south on the Pest bank from Újpest központ to Köbánya-Kispest. The M1 is signed in yellow, the M2 in red, the M3 in blue. The three routes cross at Deák tér.

Trains

There are train connections between most of Hungary's towns. Contact MÁV Customer Services, Budapest VI, Andrássy út, tel: 322-8049, 322-8056.

Suburban Railway (HÉV)

The HÉV is a rapid link with the immediate surroundings of the capital. Within the city boundaries the yellow tickets are valid. For longer journeys tickets can be bought from the ticket offices of the individual stations. The suburban railway has four routes:

From Batthyány tér (M2 station) via Obuda (Acquincum) to Szatendre (the most interesting route for tourists). Operating hours: 3.50am–11.40pm. Journey time: 42 minutes.
From Örs vezér tere (MZ terminus) to Gödöllö. Operating hours: 4.30am–11.20pm. Journey time: 49 minutes.
From Boráros tér to Csepel Island. Operating Hours: 4.30am–11.30pm. Journey time: 15 minutes.
From Vágóhíd to Ráckeve at the southern end of Csepel Island. Operating Hours: 3.20am–12.10pm. Journey time: 72 minutes.

Taxis

For Western visitors taxi rides in Budapest are an affordable luxury. Though most taxi drivers are honest, hard-working fellows, it is always advisable to note name, number and company. Western taxis are more expensive than the Ladas, Scodas and Wartburgs. Because of the constant traffic jams, it is not advisable to take a taxi into the city centre (nor is it a good idea to take your own car).

Apart from the 4,000 taxis of the two state-owned taxi companies Fötaxi and Volántaxi – there are at least 3,000 "private" taxis. Within the city there are at least 160 taxi ranks (not for the "private" taxis); you can stop an empty taxi (the roof light will be switched on) or you can book a radio cab by phone (the trip to the pick-up point is charged).

Taxi telephone numbers:

Fötaxi	122-2222
To pre-book a taxi	118-8188
Volántaxi	166-6666
City-Taxi	211-1111
Radio-Taxi	177-7777
Buda-Taxi	129-4000
Teletaxi	155-5555

Transporting goods by taxi:
Fösped   133-0330

Water Transport

There is a ferry service which runs from both banks of the Danube in Budapest to Margaret Island. Of the 13 departure points (4 on the Buda bank, 7 on the Pest shore, 2 on Margaret Island), the ones for tourists are Buda: Batthyány tér-Gellért tér; Pest: Vigadó tér. For more information, contact: **BKV** (Budapest Public Transport Systems), Budapest XIII, Jászai Mari tér, tel: 129-5844.
MAHART also organises excursions on the Danube, tel: 118-1740.

Other Forms of Transport

Cable Railway: This runs from Clark Adam tér opposite the Chain Bridge up Castle Hill. The original wagons have recently been renovated. Every 3 minutes from 8.30am to 8pm.
Rack Railway: From Városmajor up Széchenyi HIll. 4am–12.25am, every 15 minutes. (Monthly season tickets are not valid!)
Children's Railway: From Széchenyi Hill to Hüvösvölgy (Cool Valley) and over 8 miles (12 km). Apart from the driver, the train is manned by children and young people. Fares vary according to length of journey. Tickets available at stations.
Chair Lifts: From Zugligetu út up János Hill. Terminus near the viewing tower. 8am–4pm (winter), 5pm (summer).
Microbus: Runs on Margaret Island. Tour guide (in Hungarian).
Horsedrawn Omnibus/Carriage: A horsedrawn omnibus dating from the turn of the century runs through Óbuda.
   A special tourist attraction for those who like such things is a trip through the Castle Quarter in a carriage drawn by two horses. Journey time: around 30 minutes. Fare: 3,000–4,000Ft. Carriages available outside the Matthias Church.

Private Transport

Following international trends, Hungary now also has car hire organisations which collaborate with international companies. If you have booked your car before setting out on your journey, it will be waiting for you in Budapest at the airport, station or hotel. On payment of a surcharge the car can also be delivered outside Budapest or even abroad and returned later. Hirers must be at least 21 years old.
Americana Rent-a-Car: Dósza György út 65, tel: 129-0200/120-8287.
Avis Rent-a-Car: Szervita tér 8, tel: 118-4240/118-4158.
Fox Autorent: Óbudai Hajógyári Sziget 130, tel: 457-1150.
Fötaxi: Kertész utca 24, tel: 322-1471; Aranykéz u. 4, tel: 117-7533. Airport: Ferihegy I, tel: 157-8618; Ferihegy II, tel: 157-8606.
   Fötaxi also has a chauffeur-driven limousine service available.
Europcar: Interrent, Üllöí út 60-62, tel: 113-1492, 113-0207.
   The major hotels also offer a car hire service.

Self-Drive

The Hungarian Autoclub will provide information on all matters relevant to car drivers, including a legal aid service. The Autoclub also provides forms in case of accident. These forms should be carried with you as a precaution.
Magyar Autoklub, Budapest II, Rómer Flóris utca 4-6, tel: 212-3952.

Useful Tips

The maximum speed on Hungarian motorways is 120 km/h (74 m/h), 80 km/h (50 m/h) outside built-up areas (100 km/h (62 m/h) on main highways) and 50 km/h (31 m/h) in urban areas. Maximum speeds for cars with trailers and motor-cycles are 80 km/h (50 m/h) on motorways, 70 km/h (43 m/h) outside built-up areas and 50 km/h (31 m/h) in urban areas.
   On motorways, dipped lights must be switched on even during the day.
   In Budapest, cars are not allowed into the Castle Quarter. Exceptions are made for guests of the Hilton Hotel in the Castle Quarter; the parking opportunities between the top of the hill and Matthias Church are far and few between. You can drive to the hotels on Margaret Island via the Árpád Bridge.

TRAFFIC REPORTS

Budapest, tel: 117-1173.
Provinces, tel: 122-7052, 122-7643.

Fuel

All types of fuel are available in Hungary, including lead-free petrol and diesel with anti-freeze. Most large international companies have installed their stations along the major roads and in the capital. There are very few self-service stations (attendants expect a small tip). Generally prices are just a little shy of average Western European prices.

Parking

Opportunities for parking in Budapest are limited – yet another reason to leave your car in the hotel garage when strolling around the town.
   Incidentally, if you are planning to travel in your own car, make sure that your hotel has garaging or parking space available, otherwise you could have problems!

Multi-storey Car Parks

Budapest V, Martinelli tér 8; Budapest V, Arankéz utca.
   There are also supervised car parks with varying charges (Monday–Friday 8am–6pm, Saturday 8am–2pm).
   You might have the good fortune to find a "free" parking meter which runs for two hours.
   If you park in a prohibited area the police have the right to have your car removed. In such cases, apart from the imposed fine, you will also have to pay the service fee for towing the car away. You can enquire about cars which have been towed away by ringing 307-6776.

Accidents

If you are involved in a road accident, even if no one is hurt, you must inform the police (tel: 07), who will prepare a report. You should get a statement of any damage to the car, which can be shown on leaving the country. The accident must be reported within 24 hours.
Hungária Insurance (Car damage claims), 1087 Uerepesi út 15, tel: 210-4944/210-4937.
Breakdown & Recovery Service: The "yellow angels" of the Hungarian Autoclub are on duty round the clock. Vehicle recovery service at reduced rates.
Magyar Autoclub, Breakdown Service (24 hours), tel: 252-8000; **Vehicle recovery service** (24 hours), Budapest XIV, Francia út 38B, tel: 169-1831, 169-3714; **Information service**, tel: 135-3101.

Further vehicle recovery services, (6am–11pm) Budapest XII, Petneházi utca 72, tel: 120-7119, 120-8208. **Volán** (24 hours), Budapest VI, Lenin kórút 96, tel: 112-9000; Budapest XV, Ifjú Gárda útca (24 hours), tel: 140-9326; Budapest IX, Vaskapu utca (7am–9pm), tel: 133-4783; 166-6666 (after 9pm). **AFIT**, Budapest XIII, Váci út 82-84, tel: 149-9170.

Repairs

Proper spare parts are not always easy to find in Hungary though the situation is steadily improving. The best places to find help are the following repair workshops which have specialised in Western models:
Special BMW Team, Kassák Lajos utca 75, tel: 120-9986.
Ford Petrányi-Auto Kft, Kerepsi út 105–113, tel: 260-5050.
Herceg Opel Autójavító Mühely, Miskoki utca 93, tel: 183-7849.
Peugeot-Gablini, Fogarasi út 195–197, tel: 222-1210.
Magyar Volkswagen Szerviz, Vöröskö utca 13, tel: 155-9213.
Theft Loss Insurance: Notify the appropriate police station immediately if your car is stolen.
Police Headquarters, Budapest V, Deák tér 16–18, tel: 118-0800.

To be on the safe side, it is worth enquiring at the car pound: Budapest X, Szalió utca 5, tel: 261-6441.

If you lose your **car keys**: door opening service and manufacture of replacement keys by **Sándor Simon**, Budapest VII, Kertész utca 48, tel: 142-1034. Monday–Friday 8am–6pm.

Insurance claims made against Hungarian citizens must be made through the central office of the state insurance association: **Hungária Biztosító**, V. Vadász utca 23–25, tel: 269-003.

Where To Stay

As far as accommodation is concerned, Hungary after 1945 had a great deal of catching up to do. Almost all the great hotels of Budapest had fallen victim to the war, and for 30 years this big gap was not filled. Also, because of lack of funds rather than because of complacency, the hotels that had survived were not equipped to satisfy the demands of the travelling community.

Thanks to efforts undertaken over the last few years, the Hungarian capital, in particular, once more has a series of splendid luxury and several excellent four-star hotels to offer, but most hotels are still struggling to catch up, although it must be said that many guests enjoy the "pre-war" atmosphere more than the technically better equipped but interchangeable tourist hotels of today.

Every year the Hungarian Tourist Office publishes a register of accommodation, the *Hotel, Camping* handbook which is available free in the Tourinform office, Budapest V, Sütö utca 2, tel: 117-9800; fax: 117-9578.

Don't travel on spec! As Budapest becomes more popular with visitors and for holidays, it is becoming more and more difficult to find accommodation without pre-booking, especially during the fine weather season.

Hotels

Hotel rooms in Hungary are no longer as ridiculously cheap as they once were, but measured by Western standards they are still at times modest, except in the luxury class. According to international usage, they are divided into five classes.

In the hotels of the top two classes (luxury and first class hotels), all rooms come with en suite bathrooms; for the three-star ("good quality") hotels, about 75 percent of the rooms have en suite bathrooms. Among the two-star ("plain") hotels, there are

many which are classified below their actual standard – old, traditional hotels with faded charm which more than compensates for any deficiency in modern sanitation. The one-star ("modest") establishments, however, can only be recommended to backpackers who are not interested in anything other than a roof over their heads.

The following price guidelines (dating from time of press) are per person in double rooms or suites. The rooms are with bath or shower, with a bathroom on the same floor in Class 4. Single room surcharge is about 40 percent. Breakfast is included in the room price. Prices for a double room with bath.

Class	Double (Ft)
L (5-star)	20,000–35,000
1 (4-star)	5,000–19,000
2 (3-star)	2,000–12,000
3 (2-star)	2,000–5,000
4 (1-star)	1,500–3,000

The prices above are for the main season (April–October). In the early season and out of season there are considerable price reductions, in the so-called peak season (for instance the Grand Prix weekend) there are surcharges (not in the luxury class). Reductions and surcharges are both around the 20 percent level.

Budapest

Aero, Budapest IX, Ferde utca 1-3, tel: 280-6728; fax: 127-5825. For those who prefer hotels near airports. Good restaurant. Class 2; 139 rooms.
Astoria, Budapest V, Kossuth Lajos utca 19, tel: 117-3411; fax: 118-6798. Grand hotel with old-fashioned charm, in the city centre. Class 2; 192 rooms.
Atrium-Hyatt, Budapest V, Roosevelt tér 2, tel: 266-1234; fax: 266-9101. The most recent addition to the chain of luxury hotels on the Pest bank of the Danube, with a winter garden-style courtyard. Rooms are good value, the suites expensive. Class L; 353 rooms.
Béke-Radisson, Budapest VI, Teréz krt. 43, tel: 132-3300; fax: 153-3380. Well established, recently renovated hotel in the Secessionist style, not far from the Western Railway Station. Class 1; 238 rooms.
Benczúr, Budapest VI, Benczúr utca 35, tel: 342-7970; fax: 342-1558. A guest-house hotel. Class 2; 91 rooms.

Cycling

It is *not* advisable to move about Budapest by bicycle. There are few special lanes and drivers are neither used to cyclists nor particularly friendly.

Budapest, Budapest II, Szilágy Erzsébet fasor 47, tel: 202-0044; fax: 115-0496. The hotel with the most extravagant shape – a cylindrical tower. Class 2; 280 rooms.

Corvinus Kempinski, Budapest V, Erzsébet tér 7-8, tel: 266-1000; fax: 266-2000. Very modern, excellent service, warrants its distinction.

Erzsébet, Budapest V, Károlyi Mihály utca 11, tel: 138-2111. A popular modern city centre hotel. Class 2; 123 rooms.

Gellért, Budapest XI, Gellért tér 1, tel: 185-2200; fax: 166-6631. The most famous of all the Budapest hotels – because of the gorgeous Secessionist-style baths. On the Buda bank of the Danube near Liberation Bridge. Class 1; 235 rooms.

Grand Hotel Hungária, Budapest VII, Rákóczi út 90, tel: 322-9050; fax: 268-1999. The biggest tourist hotel in Budapest, it has almost 1,000 beds. Near the Eastern Railway Station. Class 2; 582 rooms.

Grand Hotel Ramada, Budapest XIII, Margitsziget, tel: 132-1100, 111-1000; fax: 153-3029. This palace of a hotel, built in 1873 on Margaret Island, was thoroughly renovated in 1987. There is a subway to the Hotel Térmal. Class 1; 163 rooms.

Hilton, Budapest I, Hess András tér 103, tel: 175-1000; fax: 156-0285. A great architectural success – modern glass walls which reflect the ornate little towers of the Fishermen's Bastion and the Matthias Church, and into which the Gothic remains of the Dominican monastery have been integrated with the greatest care. A further attraction is the casino. Class L; 323 rooms.

Hotel Thermal, Budapest XIII, Margitsziget, tel: 311-1000; fax: 153-2753. A luxury hotel built in 1979 on Margaret Island – with its own dental clinic. Class 2; 206 rooms.

International, Budapest V, Apáczai Csere János utca 12–14, tel: 117-8088; fax: 117-9111. According to general opinion, the best-managed of the three grand hotels on the Pest bank of the Danube, classified, strangely enough, as Class 1 – though the prices certainly fall into the luxury class. 400 rooms.

Mariott, Budapest V, Apáczai Csere János utca 4, tel: 266-7000; fax: 266-5000. In the centre of the newly restored Danube promenade, next to the boat departure point. Class L; 340 rooms.

Mercure Buda, Budapest II, Krisztina körút 41-43, tel: 156-6333; fax: 155-6964. Good quality hotel right next to the Southern Railway Station. Class 1.

Nemzeti, Budapest VIII, Józsefkrt 4, tel: 269-9310; fax: 114-0019. An old-fashioned beauty, class 2; 76 rooms.

Olympia, Budapest XII, Eötvös út 40, tel/fax: 395-6447. Situated in the Buda Hills, this has a fitness centre and tennis courts and is a real El Dorado for sports fans and recreation seekers. Class 1; 168 rooms.

Park, Budapest VIII, Baross tér 10, tel: 113-1420; fax: 113-5619. Near the Eastern Railway Station. Inexpensive (however, two-thirds of the rooms have no bathrooms). Class 3; 173 rooms.

Taverna, Budapest V, Váci u. 20, tel: 138-4999; fax: 118-7188. An excellent hotel for the money (Class 2), right on the pedestrian zone. 224 rooms.

Wien, Budapest XI, Budaörsi út 88-90, tel: 310-2999. On the edge of the city near the motorway exit. Ideal for those travelling by car. Inexpensive (rooms without baths available). Class 3, 110 rooms.

OTHER SUGGESTIONS

Budai Hotel, Budapest XII, Rácz Aladár utca 45-47, tel: 249-2187. New hotel on the hillside in Buda. Fantastic view.

Buda Villa, Budapest XII, Kiss Aron utca 6, tel: 176-2679. Small but attractive pension in the Buda Hills

Liget, Budapest VI, Dózsa György út 106, tel: 269-5329. New and reasonably priced.

Lidó, Budapest III, Nánási út 7-8, tel: 188-6865. Basic hotel in Obuda.

Motel Momini Panzio, Csörsz utca, 35, tel: 175-0727. Unusual pension in a converted factory.

Balatonfüred

Blaha Lujza, 8230 Balatonfüred, Blaha Lujza serány 4, tel: (87) 343-700. Occupying the villa which was once the residence of one of Hungary's best-loved actresses, this is one of the more interesting places to stay in Balaton's most venerable resort.

Debrecen

Arany Bika, 4025 Debrecen, Piac utca 11–15, tel: (52) 416-777. Superb Secessionist style establishment dating from 1915, the largest in town and an important social centre, located on Debrecen's main street close to the city's great Reformed Church.

Civis, 4026 Debrecen, Kalvin tér 4, tel: (52) 418-522. Small modern hotel in the heart of the city.

Eger

Park Eger, 3300 Eger Szàlloda utca 1–3, tel: (36) 413-233. A combination of elegant turn of the century villa and modern 1970s extension with full range of facilities.

Senátor-haz, 3300 Eger, Dobo-István tér 11, tel: (36) 320-466. Small, charming hotel in the old town, stylishly renovated.

Korona, 3300 Eger, Tündérpart 5, tel: (36) 313-670/310/287, 422-577. Family-run impeccable small hotel with added benefit of ancient wine-cellars.

Gyor

Klastrom, 9021 Gyor, Zechmeister utca 1, tel: (96) 315-611. Stylish hotel in former monastery with correspondingly small rooms.

Kertész, 9022 Gyor, Iskola utca 11, tel: (96) 315-196. Small, pleasant pension.

Hajdúszoboszló

Béke, 4200 Hajdúszoboszló, Màtyás király sétány 10, tel: (52) 361-411. Large, traditional spa hotel.

Héviz

Thermal Aqua, 8380 Héviz, Kossuth Lajos utca 13–15, tel: (83) 341-090. Comfortable accommodation and all the facilities which characterise this spa resort.

Kecskemét

Három Gúnár, 6000 Kecskemét, Batthyány utca 1, tel: (76) 483-611. Well-restored old style hotel close to the town centre.

Marilyn, 6000 Kecskemét, Köhíd ut 13, tel: (76) 482-137. Small, well-appointed pension.

Keszthely

Abbazia Club, 8360 Keszthely, Erzsébt királyné utca 23, tel: (83) 314-426. Modern hotel with 60 rooms.

Bacchus, 8360 Keszthely, Ersébet királyné utca 18, tel: (83) 314-096. Pleasant small contemporary hotel.

Miskolc

Pannónia, 3525 Miskolc, Kossuth utca 2, tel: (46) 329-811. Standard Communist-era hotel in excellent position right in the city centre.

Palota, 3517 Miskolc-Lillafüred, Erzsébet sétány 1, tel: (46) 331-411. Huge prestige interwar hotel in the fresh air and forest surroundings of the Bükk National Park to the west of town.

Pécs

Palatinus, 7621 Pécs, Király utca 5, tel: (72) 233-022. Traditional luxury hotel in the old town, built around the turn of the century with some art nouveau features.

Siófok

Aranypart, 8600 Siófok, Beszédes Jószef sétány 82, tel: (84) 312-722. Best hotel in town.

Janus, 8600 Siófok, Fo utca 93–95, tel: (84) 312-546. An attractive alternative to the standard modern hotels lining the foreshore.

Sopron

Jégverem Fogadó, 9400 Sopron, Jégverem utca 1, tel: (99) 312-004. A comfortable contemporary pension incorporating Sopron's municipal ice-cellar in its attractive restaurant.

Szeged

Forrás, 6726 Szeged, Szent-Györgyi Albert utca 16–24, tel: (62) 430-130. Well-appointed spa hotel.

Royal, 6720 Szeged, Kölcsey utca 1–3, tel: (62) 475-275. Plain exterior, more attractive inside.

Joó, 6725 Szeged, Móra utca 10/B, tel: (62) 329-564. Small, respectable pension with only eight rooms.

Székesfehérvár

Rév, 8000 Székesfehérvár, Jószef Attila utca 42, tel: (22) 314-441. Midrange hotel with 42 rooms.

Magyar Király, 8000 Székesfehérvár, Fo utca 10, tel: (22) 311-262. Fine old-style hotel in the town centre with 57 modernised rooms.

Szentendre

Kentaur, 2000 Szentendre, Marx tér 3–5, tel: (26) 312-125. New, small, but well appointed hotel near the town centre with an excellent view of old Szentendre.

Bed & Breakfast

Another form of accommodation that has developed in the 1990s is the bed-and-breakfast (*panzió*) and the older version of the guest house. The prices range from cheap to moderate depending on the services and amenities. The key to these places is either to keep a lookout while driving around, or check in the hotel guide. Otherwise there is the tourist office at Sütö u. or on Petöfi tér 3.

Private Rooms

The hotel situation in Budapest is still precarious and rooms in private houses continue to make up an important part of the accommodation available in the Hungarian capital.

Those looking for rooms to rent can either hire direct or via a travel agency. The prices for rooms can be set by the owner, so costs vary.

Non-compulsory guidelines for double rooms or apartments of the better class: 700–3,000Ft per day. Simple beds can be had for as little as 300Ft per day. A limited number of private rooms can also be booked through travel agencies abroad. Register of private rooms available from:

Budapest Tourist, Budapest V, Roosevelt tér 5, tel: 117-3555.

IBUSZ, Budapest V, Petöfi tér 3, tel: 118-4848 (24 hours).

Campgrounds

Off-site camping is prohibited in Hungary. Space, overnight stay and parking spot prices are reckoned separately. Space hire (according to category) is between 60–550Ft and overnight stay is charged at 50–100Ft per person. Reductions are available outside the main season. A selection of campsites follows:

Csillebérci Camping, 1121 Budapest, Konkoly-Thege M. u. 21, tel: 156-3533/5772; fax: 175-9139/9327.

Hárs-hegyi Camping, 1021 Budapest, Hars-hegyi út 7, tel: 115-1482; fax: 176-1921.

Római Camping, 1031 Budapest, Szentendrei út 189, tel: 168-6260; fax: 250-0426.

Zugligeti Niche Camping, Zugligeti út 101, tel: 156-8641.

CARAVANS

In the peak holiday season of July and August the Budapest Exhibition Area offers a space of 30,000 sq. metres (36,000 sq. yards) with all the usual services for caravanners.

Youth Hostels

Youth hostels in the accepted sense do not exist in Hungary. In the holiday months (July/August) student hostels are converted into youth guest hostels. For more information, contact: **Hungarian Youth Hostel Federation**, Konkoly Thege M. u. 21, Budapest, tel: 156-3533; fax: 175-9139. It publishes a small brochure with all the necessary information.

An IYHF (International Youth Hostel Federation) pass or ISTC (International Student Tourist Conference) card is essential.

Tourist Hostels

This is where young people can find the most inexpensive accommodation with the most basic provisions (dormitories, in some places, do not have hot water).

Csúcshegyi, Category B, Budapest III, Menedéház utca 122, tel: 168-6015.

Strand, Budapest III, Pusztakúti út 3, tel: 188-7167.

Backpackers

Over the last few years free sleeping-bag space with toilets and washing facilities in the vicinity has been made available to backpackers at Budapest X, Tündérfürt utca, open mid-June–early September, from 4pm.

Eating Out

When To Eat

Breakfast (7am–10am): Hungary has joined the international trend of a buffet-style breakfast, even though it has done so reluctantly. At present only the luxury hotels conform to international standards.

A warning for coffee drinkers: in complete contrast to their usual habits (where coffee cannot be too black or too strong), Hungarians (like Italians with their *caffe latte*) love to drink an indifferent light brownish brew at breakfast time. If you want stronger coffee, you would do well to switch to mocha (*dupla*) for breakfast.

Lunch (noon–2.30pm): This is the main meal of the day and normally consists of three courses: soup, a meat dish with vegetables, dessert. After food a strong espresso is usually served.

Supper (7pm–10pm): The same as lunch. In most pubs you can find a relatively inexpensive set menu at lunchtime and in the evenings.

What To Eat

Hungarian cuisine is uncomplicated country food; heavy, substantial and anything but calorie-conscious.

Pork dominates the menu. The national spice is – without a doubt – paprika (whoever would guess that it was once imported from America?). Goulash, the Hungarian national dish, needs a little explanation. The dish known outside Hungary as goulash or *gulyás* is called *pörkölt* by the Magyars (and unusual in that it is made with beef or veal). In Hungary *gulyás* is much more of a soup. The Hungarian fish soup *halászlé* deserves its fame. Many paprika-seasoned dishes are also Hungarian specialities: apart from *pörkölt* and *gulyás* there is *Szeged* (the correct term is Székler) *gulyás*, paprika chicken and paprika potatoes. The famous stuffed paprika, like *lecsó* (sautéed paprika pods with tomatoes and onions), is a Balkan import. Preserved and stuffed cabbage come from Transylvania.

As an accompaniment to the main dish, apart from boiled potatoes, a form of pasta (*tarhonya*) is popular.

Paprika is also partly responsible for the flavour of *Liptauer*, a spread made from sheep's cheese mixed with butter, paprika, mustard, caraway and chives.

Among the desserts, the pancakes should be mentioned in first place. They are mostly made with sweet fillings (preserves, jam) but also with meat (*Hortobágy* pancakes).

Where To Eat

The generally low cost of living in Hungary is most pleasantly noticeable when visiting a restaurant. Unless you decide to eat at one of the luxury hotels or at "Gundel", which emphasises its importance with especially high prices, you can pay about half the amount you would have to put on the table in a restaurant of equal status in the West ("of equal status" here refers to the general atmosphere and service and not necessarily to the quality of the food). It is worth noting that all the major hotels in Budapest have excellent restaurants.

Budapest

Bagolyvár, Állatkerti út 2, tel: 351-6395. Honest Hungarian food provided at reasonable prices by the same ownership as the more expensive Gundel (*see below*).

Corso Etterem, Budapest V, Petőfi Sándor utca 3, tel: 267-0314. Typical Hungarian restaurant in the city centre. Pretty inner courtyard.

Fatál, Váci utca 67, tel: 266-2607. Conveniently located just off the southern stretch of Váci utca, this basement restaurant piles its wooden platters high with all kinds of traditional country dishes. Be sure to book.

Fülemüle Vendeglö, Budapest VIII, Kőfaragó u. 5, tel: 138-4048. Straightforward Hungarian restaurant, occasional jazz nights.

Gundel, Budapest XIV, Allatkerti út 2 (near the zoo), tel: 268-0446. Best restaurant in the capital, extravagantly refurbished by a Hungarian American.

Háromszív Étterem, Budapest XII, Böszörményi út 44, tel: 212-3803. Above-average Hungarian cuisine. Pleasant garden.

Kehli, Mókus utca 22, tel: 250-4241. In a pleasant position on a square of Óbuda with authentic Hungarian food and outside eating in summer.

Kistölgyfa Vendeglö, Budapest II, Budakeszi út 75, tel: 275-1337. Small restaurant in the middle of a wood. Speciality dishes cooked in wood oven.

Náncsi Néni Vendéglöje, Budapest II, Ördögárok út 80, tel: 176-5809. Small garden restaurant just out of town. Reservation essential.

Sipos Haláskert, Budapest III, Fö tér 6, tel: 188-8745. One of the city's best fish restaurants in Óbuda. Pretty courtyard.

Söröző a Szent Jupáthoz, Budapest II, Dékán u. 3, tel: 212-2928. Large portions of good food. Open 24 hours.

Sport Vendéglö, Budapest XVI, Csömöri utca 198 (N.B. There is a street with the same name in the neighbouring XV district). A little way out. Straightforward food served in large portions.

Tabáni kakas, Attila út 27, tel: 175-7156. At the foot of Castle Hill, an unpretentious eating-place with excellent plain food at a very reasonable price.

Udvárház, Hármashatárhegyi út 2, tel: 188-8780. Usually full of visitors from abroad, drawn by its Hungarian specialities and the superb views from its location high in the Buda Hills.

Vegetárium, Cukor utca 3, tel: 267-0322. A haven for herbivores, though poultry and fish are on offer too.

Badacsony

Halászkert, Park utca 5, tel: (87) 431-054. One of the most popular of the many fish restaurants along the Balaton shore.

Kisfaludy-ház, Szegedy Róza utca 87, tel: (87) 431-016. High up among the vineyards, this terrace restaurant enjoys superb views over Lake Balaton and the food is fine too.

Balatongyörök

Panorama, Balatongyörök-Szépkilátó. Pull in off the highway along Lake Balaton's north shore for good food as well as the famous panorama of the lake and the Badacsony hills.

Debrecen

Csokonai, Kossuth Lajos utca 21, tel: (52) 410-802. Long-established basement restaurant serving traditional Hungarian food.

Sörpince a Flaskához, Miklos utca 2, tel: (52) 314-582. Simple restaurant with a colourful clientele.

Eger

HBH Bajor Sörház, Bajcsy-Zsilinszky utca 19, tel: (36) 316-312. The ambience of a Bavarian beer-hall in miniature but with excellent Hungarian food.

Talizmán, Kossuth Lajos u. 19, tel: (36) 410-883. Small basement restaurant in the town centre. Easily missed. Traditional, regional specialities. Try the game dishes.

Szépasszony Fogadó, Szépasszony völgy, tel: (36) 310-777. Located in the "Valley of Beautiful Women" among Eger's famous vineyards, this large and welcoming restaurant is a good place to begin your sampling of local food and wines.

Györ

Sárkánylyuk Étterem, Arany János utca 27, tel: (96) 317-116. Straightforward restaurant with regional specialities.

Varkapu, Káptalandomb 2/4, tel: (96) 328-685. Very close to the Carmelite church on the approach ramp to the Cathedral, this is a charming restaurant with good service and fine food.

Kecskemét

Szabadság/Liberté, Szabadság tér 2, tel: (76) 480-350. The best Hungarian restaurant in the town centre.

Keszthely

Park Vendéglö, Vörösmarty utca 1a, tel: (83) 311-654. Good plain Hungarian food in a simple setting with outside service in summer.

Miskolc

Alabárdos Étterem, Kisvas-Elsösor 15, tel: (46) 353-462. Best restaurant in this industrial town and a popular meeting place.

Pécs

Aranykacsa, Teréz u. 4, tel: (72) 211-018. The "Golden Duck" is one of the best places to eat in Pécs, not least because of its careful revival of traditional regional dishes.

Bagolyvár, Felsöhavi duló 6/1, tel: (72) 211-333. The "Owl's Castle" is a fine modern building overlooking the vineyards from the slopes above the city centre and serves food and wines to match the setting.

Dóm, Kiraly utca 3. A downtown branch of the Owl Castle, the "Cathedral" features an extraordinary interior modelled on the city's basilica.

Sopron

Corvinus, Fö tér 7, tel: (99) 312-841. In a prime position on the old city's main square, this vaulted restaurant occupies part of the famous Storno House.

Szeged

Alabárdos, Oskola u. 13, tel: (62) 312-914. This is reputed to be Szeged's smoothest eating-place, with sophisticated service and dramatically flambéed dishes.

Halászcsárda, Roosevelt tér 14, tel: (62) 480-117. One of the best places in Hungary to test whether or not the country's famous fish soup is to your liking.

Öreg Körössy Haáskert, Felsö Tiszapart, tel: (62) 327-410. An alternative source of fishy specialities from the River Tisza.

Szentbékkálla

Pegazus. Popular with visitors from the various resorts on Lake Balaton, this is a large-scale establishment with a wonderful location above a pretty village in the hills to the north of the lake.

Szentendre

Görög Kancsó, Görög utca 1, tel: (26) 315-528. The "Greek Jug" has Greek dishes as well as fine Hungarian fare. During the summer months, meals are served on the terrace.

Régimodi, Fütö utca 3, tel: (26) 311-105. Attractive restaurant with a delightful terrace overlooking the rooftops of this lovely town.

Tihany

Fogas Csárda, Kossuth Lajos utca 9, tel: (87) 448-658. A deservedly popular restaurant high up on the Tihany peninsula with folksy interior and a wide terrace.

Kolostor, Kossuth Lajos utca 14, tel: (87) 448-408. The "Monastery" at the foot of the steps leading up to Tihany's abbey church is a micro-brewery as well as a busy restaurant.

Veszprém

Betyár Csárda, Nemesvámos on main road southwest of Veszprém, tel: (88) 365-087. An old inn inland from Lake Balaton's north shore which makes the most of its reputation as a one-time handg-out for outlaws and highwaymen.

Villány

Fülemüle Csárda, just north of Villány village on the main road to Pécs, tel: (72) 480-077 or (60) 361-731. Attractively renovated roadside inn offering some of the best eating in the Villány wine region.

Visegrad

Nagyvillám Vadászcsárda, Nagyvillám utca 20-25, tel: (26) 398-070. The best place to eat among the limited possibilities in Danube-side Visegrad.

Drinking Notes

Hungary has good wines. Their undisputed king is Tokay, a heavy, sweet white wine which, it must be said, is not necessarily the fashion these days. However, there are a number of excellent light white wines, especially those from around Lake Balaton.

The most famous red wine is the legendary Bull's Blood, and among the spirits the apricot brandy barack is top of the list.

Cocktails are not really that widespread in Hungary. However, at the bars of the big hotels you can still be served with the most extraordinary of drinks.

Pubs & Bars

The well-known "pub scene" actually comes alive during the day. Most of the pubs in Budapest are full of casually dressed young people. The atmosphere is loud and noisy, people gather to meet their friends and chat, without necessarily straining their wallets too much.

Beckett's, Bajcsy-Zsilinszky út 72, tel: 111-1033. This Irish import attracts locals as well as a mainly Anglophone ex-pat crowd.

Captain Cook, Bajcsy-Zsilinszky út 19A, tel: 269-3136. Antipodean atmosphere successfully created in this city centre pub where there is even famous lager from Down Under on draught.
Flashdance, Váci utca 32. Something new and vibrant in the heart of downtown.
Fregatt, Molnár utca 26, tel: 118-9997. Budapest's first English pub and proud of it.
Ipoly, Pozsonyi út 28, tel: 270-2923. Cocktail-chasing yuppies mingle with beer drinkers in this engaging pub.
Picasso Point, Hajós utca 31, tel: 269-5544. Bar upstairs and disco down below makes this a popular combination.
Talk Talk, Magyar utca 12–14, tel: 267-2878. A trendy haven for the round-the-clock crowd.

Cafés & Coffee-Houses

Even though the legendary glories of the Budapest coffee-houses may have faded, the Hungarian café trade still shows that it is something to be reckoned with.

The names of, for example, Ruszwurm and Gerbeaud, still have the same resonance as they did in the past, and the greatest care is taken to preserve the pre-war atmosphere in the furnishings and the decor. A visit to one of the great cafés of Budpest is something of a nostalgic trip into the past. Even among the clientele, you can discover relics of the "good" old days: white-haired ladies with strings of pearls, distinguished elderly gentlemen whose tailor-made suits have bravely withstood the ravages of time. Not forgetting the waitresses, members of a profession which one might have believed – especially in these parts of the world – to have long been extinct.
Café New York, Budapest VII, Erzsébet körút 9–11. The famous haunt of artists and authors around the turn of the century. Open Monday–Saturday 9am–10pm; closed Sunday.
Café Pierrot, Budapest I, Fortuna utca 14.
Gerbeaud, Budapest V, Vörösmarty tér. Open daily 9am–9pm.
Müvész, Andrássy út 29. Open 8am–8pm. Saturdays from 10am–8pm. Closed Sundays.

Ruszwurm, Budapest I, Szentháromsag utca 7. Open daily 10am–8pm.
Talu Talu Café, Budapest V, Magyar u. 12–14.

Attractions

Things To Do

Travel Agencies/Excursions

BÉKÉSCSABA

Békéstourist, Andrassy u. 10, tel/fax: (66) 323 4480. Branches in Gyula, Orosháza, Tótkomlós.
Worth seeing: Szarvas (arboretum).
Arranged visits: theatre at Gyula castle in summer; medicinal cures at thermal springs in Gyula; summer concerts in the Protestant church in Bekescsaba.

BUDAPEST

There are numerous travel agencies, of varying degrees of competence, around the city. The first listed is 50 metres from Deák tér and is perhaps the best around. It has foreign-language telephone operators (generally) which really helps.

There are also offices of travel agencies at the train stations and at the airport terminals.
Tourinform, Budapest V, Sütö utca 2, tel: 117-9800; fax: 117-9578. Open weekdays 7am–7pm, Saturday 8am–8pm and Sunday 7am–1pm. Visitors can obtain information in Hungarian, Russian, German, English and French on anything to do with tourism such as travel information, opening hours, addresses, directions, telephone numbers, programmes and forthcoming events.
Budapest Tourist, Budapest V, Roosevelt tér, tel: 117-3555. Arranges special events for your stay in Budapest, sightseeing tours, excursions of one or several days to other parts of the country. The accommodation service will book you rooms in private houses in any district of the city. The branches of Budapest Tourist offer all the usual services of a travel agency.

Cooptourist, Budapest XIII, Tátra u. 15/A, tel: 131-4318.
Dunatours, Budapest VI, Bajcsy-Zsilinszkiy út 17, tel: 131-4533.

Excursions
For details of boat trips to and from Árpád Bridge, Margaret Island, Szentendre, Visegrád, Esztergom, and to see Budapest by night, contact:
MAHART, Hungarian Shipping Company, International Shipping Office, Budapest V, Belgrád rakpart, tel: 118-1704.
Vigadó tér mooring point, tel: 118-1223, 135-4907; and other travel agencies.

Short Stays
If you only have a short time to spend seeing the city, you should try to limit yourself, first of all, to the essential sites – there will be other opportunities to increase your knowledge of Budapest at a later date.
One day: Morning: Castle Quarter, Castle Museum. Afternoon: Pest (Inner City, Parliament).
Two days: *Day 1.* Morning: Gellért Hill, Pest (Inner City), Parliament and surroundings. Afternoon: Castle Quarter, Castle Museum. *Day 2.* Morning: walk along Buda Danube bank, Rudas Baths, Király Baths, Óbuda, Aquincum, Margaret Island. Afternoon: Heroes' Square, Museum of Fine Arts, Városliget (City Park).
Three days: *Day 1.* Morning: Inner City, Parliament and surroundings. Afternoon: Castle Quarter and Castle Museum. *Day 2.* Morning: Gellért Hill, walk along the Buda Danube bank, Water City, Aquincum. Afternoon: St István körút, Basilica, Andrássy út, Liberation Square, Museum of Fine Arts, City Park, zoo. *Day 3.* Morning: National Museum, Museum of Applied and Decorative Arts. Afternoon: Margaret Island or trip to the Buda Hills; in summer, perhaps a boat trip on the Danube.
Four days: The 3-day programme plus a fourth day: whole day excursion (boat or bus) to the Danube Bend.

City Tours
Guided tours of the city, in special coaches, are organised all year round by various travel agencies. There are several tours a day in the main season. The city tours (which in summer

also take place in an open-topped bus) usually last 3–4 hours.

Detailed programmes are available from hotel receptions, travel agencies and the various organisers.

DEBRECEN

Hajdútourist, Kálvin tér 2A, tel: (52) 315 588; fax: (52) 319 616. Branches in Hajdúöbszörmény, Hajdúnánas, Hajdúszoboszló, Hortobágy.
Tourinform, Piac u. 20, tel: (52) 412 250; fax: (52) 314 139.
Worth seeing: Debrecen (Hungarian Protestant "Rome"); Hajdúszoboszló (medicinal baths); Puszta Hortobágy.
Arranged visits: riding events; medicinal cures; folk art; Hortobágy Bridge Market, 19–20 August; Debrecen Flower Show, 20 August.

EGER

Tourinform, Dobó tér 2, tel: (36) 321 807; fax: (36) 321 304.
Worth seeing: Eger (minaret, churches); Bükk national park; Gyöngyös (museum); Mátra mountains.
Arranged visits: sightseeing in Eger; village wedding; wine harvest; riding in a horse-drawn carriage; game hunting and fishing in Bukk national park.

GYÖR & SOPRON

Györ: Ciklámen Tourist, Jokai u. 12, tel: (96) 311-557; fax: (96) 316-050. Branches in Sopron, Csorna, Kapuvár, Mosonmagyaróvár, Pannonhalma.
Tourinform, Árpád u. 32, tel: (96) 317-709.
Sopron: Locomotiv Tourist, Útjutca 1, tel: (99) 311-111.
Worth seeing: Fertöd (Esterházy Palace); Pannonhalma (Benedictine abbey); Sopron (medieval town centre).
Arranged visits: sightseeing in Györ and Sopron; palaces in Fertöd and Nagycenk; Pannonhalma abbey and concerts in summer; water paradise "gravel island"; hunting parties.

KECSKEMÉT

Pusztatourist, Szabadság tér 2, tel: (76) 483-493; fax: (76) 321-215. Branches in Baja, Kalosca, Kiskunhalas, Tiszakecske.
Tourinform, Kossuth tér 1, tel: (76) 481-065.
Worth seeing: Kecskemét (town centre); Baja (museum of fishing); Bugac-Puszta; Kalocsa (cathedral); Kiskun-

félegyháza (windmills); Kiskunmajsa (stables, thermal baths).
Arranged visits: sightseeing in Kecskemét; equestrian shows in Bugac, Borbás-Puszta, Magony-Tanya, Solt; traditional folk programmes in Kalocsa and Hajós; wedding in Szeremle; farm holiday in Kiskunság.

MISKOLC

Borsod Tourist, Széchenyi u. 35, tel: (46) 350-666; fax: (46) 350-617. Branches in Jósvalö, Mezökövesd, Miskolctapolca, Sárospatak, Tokaj.
Tourinform, Mindszent tér 1, tel: (46) 348 921.
Worth seeing: Aggtelek (stalactite caverns); Mezökövesd (medicinal springs); Sárospatak (fort); Tokay (museum).
Arranged visits: excursions to the Zemplen mountains (Tokay and Sárospatak); Bükk mountains; Aggtelek; medicinal baths (Miskolctapolca, Mezökövesd).

NYÍREGYHAZA

Nyírtourist, Dózsa György u. 3, tel: (42) 311-544; fax: (42) 311-546. Branches in Kisvárda, Nyírbátor, Vásarosnamény, Mátészalka.
Tourinform, Hösök tér 5, tel: (42) 312 606.
Worth seeing: Nyíregyháza-Sóstó (medicinal salt baths); Mátészalka (regional museum); Nyírbátor (15-century churches).
Arranged visits: tours in Nyírseg, Bereg; literary tours in Szatmár; farm holidays In Tanpa.

PÉCS

Mecsek Tourist, Széchenyi tér 1 and 9, tel: (72) 213-300; fax: (72) 214-866, 214 071. Branches in Abaliget, Harkány, Mohács, Orfü, Pécsvárad, Siklós, Sikonda, Szigetvár.
Tourinform, Szechenyi ter 9, tel: (72) 213-315.
Worth seeing: Pécs (former mosque, old city); Harkány (medicinal baths); Mohács – Satorhely (site of 1526 battle); Siklós (castle museum); Szigetvár (castle museum); the Villány wine region.
Arranged visits: sightseeing in Pécs; medicinal cures in Harkány; antique and flea market in Pécs; excursions to the ethnic German areas; Satorhely memorial; Mohacs (carnival procession).

SZÉKESFEHÉRVÁR

Albatours, Városház tér 1, tel: (22) 312-494; fax. (22) 327-082.
Tourinform, Városház tér 11, tel: (22) 312 818.
Worth seeing: Székesfehérvár (the former coronation city); Gorsium (Roman excavations); Lake Velence (recreation area with nature reserves).
Arranged visits: sightseeing in Székesfehérvár; riding in Seregélyes; Beethoven concerts in Martonvásár during summer.

SZEKSZÁRD

Tolna Tourist, Széchenyi u. 38, tel: (74) 312-144; fax: (74) 315-252. Branches in Bonyhád, Dombovár, Dunaföldvár, Simontornya, Tamási.
Worth seeing: Szekszárd (former synaguogue); Décs (folk art museum); Gemene forest (narrow guage railway); Grábóc (Serbian orthodox church and monastery).
Arranged visits: Gemence nature reserve; riding in Gemence Forest; wine tasting in Szekszard; ethnic German folk evenings in Mórágy; wine harvest festival in Györköny; wedding celebration in Váralja; riding in Szekszárd.

SZOLNOK

Tiszatour, Verseghy park 8, tel: (56) 422-506; fax: (56) 341-441.
Tourinform, Ságvári körut 4, tel: (56) 424-803.
Worth seeing: Szolnok (banks of river Tisza); Jászberény (museum); Karcag (museum); Mezötur (pottery museum).
Arranged visits: concerts in the former synagogue of Szolnok; festival with gypsy orchestras; choice of boat trips on river Tisza.

SZOMBATHELY

Savaria Tourist, Mártirok tere 1, tel: (94) 312-348. Branches in Bükfürdö, Celldömölk, Ják, Körmend, Köszeg, Öriszentpéter, Sárvár, Szentgotthárd, Velem.
Worth seeing: Szombathely (town centre, museums); Bük Spa (baths); Ják (Romanesque church); Körmend (castle); Köszeg (town); Szentgottárd (baroque church and monastery).
Arranged visits: sightseeing in Szombathely; summer concerts at Sárvár fort; Savaria autumn festival; riding tours; holidays in spas and in castles for those interested in hunting, fishing, riding.

SALGÓTARJÁN

Nógrád Tourist, Erzsébet tér 5, tel: (32) 316 940; fax: (32) 316 789. Branches in Balassagyarmat, Hollókö.

Worth seeing: Balassagyarmat (Palócz museum); Karancs-Medves mountains.

Arranged visits: folk art programmes in Hollókö; Palócz wedding; Easter celebrations; "in the spinning shed", traditional dancing; spinning, woodcarving and folk dancing courses in Hollókö; holidays at the Castle Hotel, Szirák.

SIÓFOK

Siótour, Batthyány u. 2B, tel: (84) 313 111; fax: (84) 310 850. Branches in Balatonberény, Blatonfenyves, Balatonföldvár, Balatonkeresztúr, Balatonszárszó; Balatonszemes, Boglárlelle, Fonyód, Siófokfürdö, Siófok-Sóstó, Siófok-Széplak-felso, Szántód, Szántód-Puszta, Zamardi.

Tourinform, Fö u. 41, tel: (84) 315 355.

Worth seeing: Balatonszentgyörgy (star castle and landscape museum); Kaposvár (museums); Kaposszentjakab (castle ruins); Szántódpuszta (open-air museum); Igal (spa); Zala (Mihály-Zichy museum).

Arranged visits: folk dancing evenings in Balatonboglár; fishing weeks in Balatonszemes and Fonyód-Belatelep; wine harvest festivals.

SZEGED

Szeged Tourist, Dorozsmai u. 4, tel: (62) 325 800; fax: (62) 324 579. Branches in Csongrád, Hódmezövásárhely, Makó.

Tourinform, Victor Hugo u. 1, tel: (62) 311 711.

Worth seeing: Szeged town centre; Csongrád (museums, thermal springs); Hodmezövásárhely (churches); Opusztaszer (national memorial), Makó (churches).

Arranged visits: sightseeing in Szeged; open-air festival at Szeged cathedral (July and August); boat trips on the river Tisza; Piroshka programme; nostalgic train journey to the Kutasi-Puszta; portrayal of a Hungarian wedding; fruit and wine tasting.

TATA

Komtourist, Ady Endre u. 9, tel: (34) 381 805; fax: (34) 380 694. Branches in Dorog, Esztergom, Kisbér, Komáron, Tatábanya.

Worth seeing: Komárom (regional museum); Bábolna (stables); Esztergom (fort museum, Christian museum, baslica).

Arranged visits: cultural programmes including the verse chronicle of Esztergom; open-air baroque music at Fort Tata; Csatka autumn fair; gypsy folk art in Porcinkule; riding tours in Kisbér; wine tasting in Azsar; venison dinner in Majk.

VESPRÉM

Balatontourist North, Kossuth Lajos u. 21, tel: (88) 429 630; fax: (88) 427 062. Branches in Ajka, Badacsony, Balatonalmádi, Balatonfüred, Nagyvázsony, Pápa, Révfülöp, Sümeg, Tapolca, Tihany, Várpalota, Zirc.

Worth seeing: Veszprem (old town centre); Tihany peninsula; Pápa (museum of church history); Zirc (museum of natural science); Herend (museum of porcelain manufacture).

Arranged visits: wine cellars in Badacsony; peasant wedding in Nemesvámos (the old Csárda); show riding in Nagyvázsony; autumn festival and wine harvest at Lake Balaton.

ZALAEGERSZEG

Zalatour, Kovács Károly tér 1, tel: (92) 311 389; fax: (92) 311 469. Branches in Balatonyörök, Héviz, Keszthely, Lenti, Nagykanizsa, Zalakaros.

Worth seeing: Zalaegerszeg (museums, churches); Héviz (largest warm water lake in Europe); Kápolnáspuszta (buffalo reserve); Keszthely (museums, palace and grounds); Nagykanizsa (regional museum); Zalakaros (spa).

Arranged visits: guided tour of Keszthely palace; summer concerts in Festetics palace, Keszthely; botanical gardens in Budafapuszta; Helikon cultural festival in Keszthely; Göcseje village museum in Zalaegerszeg; folk art programme at Lake Balaton; wine harvest festival.

Boat Trips/Lake Balaton

Ferries run from the beginning of June until the end of August between 7am and 12.30pm, usually at 20-minute intervals. From the beginning of October to the end of April, no ferries run between 6.40pm and 7am.

Boat trips on Lake Balaton are handled by Balaton-MAHART (Siófok). In peak season, more than 50,000 passengers are transported daily by a fleet of more than 30 ships and four ferries. During the Hungarian school holidays, beginning around the end of June through August, the steamers make more than 100 regular journeys. Ferries and cruise vessels run at short intervals between the three harbours Siófok, Balatonfüred and Tihany. Nevertheless, during the peak season, refreshing drinks and a good deal of patience are vital.

MAIN SHIPPING ROUTES

The following route along the length of the northern shore is taken during the season: Balatonkenese – Balatonalmádi – Alsóörs – Csopak – Balatonfüred – Tihany-mólo (jetty) – Tihanyrév (harbour) – Kilián-telep – Balatonakali – Révfülöp – Badacsony – Szigliget – Balatongyörök – Keszthely. Travel time is 7 hours and 15 minutes.

The route from Siófok to Keszthely is charming – it passes many harbours at the southern and northern shores from Siófok – Balatonfüred – Tihanymóló (jetty) – Tihany-rév (harbour) – Balatonföldvár – Balatonszemes – Balatonlelle – Balatonboglár – Badacsony – Szigliget – Balatongyörök – Keszthely. The journey takes approximately six hours.

A 4-hour route starts from Siófok to Badacsony. The boat docks at Balatonfüred – Tihany-mólo (jetty)– Tihany-rév (harbour) – Balatonföldvár – Balatonszemes – Balatonlelle – Balatonboglár – Révfülöp – Badacsony. Between mid-June and early September there are also disco and leisure boats offering a musical programme and meals.

ROUTES ON THE EAST–WEST DIRECTION

Northern shore: Balatonkenese – Balatonalmádi – Alsóörs – Csopak – Balatonfüred – Tihany-mólo (jetty) – Tihany-rév (harbour) – Kilián-telep – Balatonakali – Révfülöp – Badacsony – Szigliget – Keszthely.

Southern shore: Siófok – Szántódi-rév (harbour) – Balatonföldvár – Balatonszemes – Balatonlelle – Balatonboglár – Fonyód – Balatonmáriafürdö.

Culture

Hungarians are known for the excellent quality of their exhibitions which emphasise both their nationality and creativity. The best way to find out what is on is to pick up a copy of *Programme*, a monthly which lists events throughout the country. Museum opening hours: Budapest 10am–6pm, country 10am–5pm, Sunday 9am/10am–1pm, closed Monday.

Museums

Baranya District

PÉCS

Csontváry Museum, Janus Pannonius utca 11. Works by the painter Csontváry.
Jakovali Hassan Museum, Rákóczi utca 2. History of the Turks in Hungary.
Janus Pannonius Museum, Kulich Gyula utca 5. Regional history until conquest.
Hungarian Modern Art Gallery, Kulich Gyula utca 4.
Victor Vasarely Museum, Káptalan utca 13. 150 works by the Op-artist.
Zsolnay Production, Exhibition of Ceramics, Káptalan utca 2.

PÉCSVARAD

Castle Museum.

SÁTORELY

Historic Memorial Park of Mohács, on the main road, No. 56.

SIKLÓS

Castle Museum, Vajda tér. History of the fort.

SZIGETVÁR

Zrinyi Miklós Museum, Vár utca 1. History of the fort.

MECSEKNADASD

Village Museum of the German ethnic minority, Munkácsy Mihály utca 45-47.

Villány Wine Museum, Bern Jószef utca 8.

Bacs-Kiskun District

BAJA

Türr István Museum, Deak Ferenc utca 1. Regional history, ethnography.

BUGACPUSZTA

Museum of the Kiskunság National Park.

KECSKEMÉT

Katona József Museum, Bethlenváros utca 75. Archaeological collection.
Museum of Naive Artists in Hungary, Gáspár A. utca 11.

KALOCSA

Paprika Museum, Marx tér 6.

Békés District

BÉKÉSCSABA

Munkácsy Mihály Museum, Szécheny utca 9. Archaeology, ethnography.

GYULA

Castle Museum, Várfürdö utca. History of the castle.
Erkel Ferenc Museum, Kossuth utca 15. Archaeology and ethnography; room of Düerr paintings.

OROSHÁZA

Szántó Kovács János Museum, Dozsa György utca 5. Ethnographic collection.

BÉKÉSCSABA

Slovak village house, Garai utca 21. Ethnographic collection of an ethnic group.

Borsod-Abauj-Zemplen District

MEZÖKÖVESD

Matyó Museum, Béke tér 20. Folk museum of the Matyó ethnic group.

MISKOLC

Castle Museum Diósgyór, Vár utca 24. History of the castle.
Hermann Otto Museum, Felsabaditok útja 28. Local and regional history.

SÁROSPATAK

Rákóczi Museum, Kadar Kata utca 21. History of the castle.

SZERENCS

Museum of the Zemplén area, Rákóczi var. History of the picture postcard – *ex libris* collection.

TOKAJ

Tokaj Museum, Bethlen Gábor utca 7. Regional history, wine industry in Tokay.

SÁROSPATAK

Museum of the Reformed Collegiate, Rákóczi utca 1. Comenius exhibition, religious art, library.
Collection of the Roman Catholic Church, Kádár Kata utca 17.

Budapest

Budapest has a wealth of museums – there are three dozen of them altogether. The most important of them are listed below. A complete list can be found in the monthly programmes.

Opening hours: 10am–6pm, Sunday 9am–1pm, closed Monday.
Agricultural Museum (Mezögazdasági Múzeum), Városliget, Budapest XIV, Széchenyi sziget.
Aquincum, Excavated site of Aquincum and museum, Budapest III, Szentendrei út 139.
Civilian Town Amphitheatre next to the excavations. Military Town Amphitheatre, Budapest III, Nagyszombat, corner of Pacsirtamezöu utca.
Ethnographical Museum, Budapest V, Kossuth Lajos tér 12. The collections concentrate on Hungarian folk history.
Ferenc Hopp East Asian Museum (Keletázsiai Múzeum), Budapest VI, Andrássy 103.
Fine Arts Museum (Szépmüvészeti Múzeum), Budapest XIV, (Hösök tere) Dósza György út 41. Considered the most important collection of paintings in Hungary.
Historical Museum/Castle Museum (Történeti Múzeum), Várpalota, Szent György tér 2. Here you can see the remains of the building and the sculptures of the medieval castle, which came to light during restoration work after 1945.
Military History Museum (Hadtörténeti Múzeum), Várpalota, Budapest I, Tóth Arpád sétány 40.
Military Town Museum (Táborvárosi Múzeum), Budapest III, Pacsirtamezö u. 64.
Mosaic floor of a Roman villa, Budapest II, Vihar utca 31.

Museum of Applied and Decorative Arts (Iparmüvészeti Múzeum), Budapest XI, Üllöi út 31-37. Built from 1893–96, it is probably the most impressive work by the great Hungarian Secessionist architect Ödön Lechner.
National Gallery (Magyar Nemzeti Galéria), Vápalota, Budapest I, Dísz tér 17. In what were once the royal reception halls of the castle of Buda (wings B, C, D). Medieval lapidarium. Gothic wooden sculpture and panel paintings of the 14th and 15th centuries, late Gothic altar panels, art of the late Renaissance and Baroque, painting and sculpture of 19th century Hungary, Hungarian art of the 20th century.
National Museum (Magyar Nemzeti Múzeum), Budapest VII, Múzeum körút 14–16. The most beautiful classical building by Mihály Pollack, built 1837–47, houses among its treasures the Hungarian coronation regalia, including St Stephen's Crown.
Remains of Roman baths, Budapest III, Flórián tér 3.

Csongrad District

HÓDMEZÖVÁSÁRHELY

Tornyai János Museum. Szantó Kovács János utca 16-18. Early historic and archaeological collection, local history, folklore.

SZEGED

Mora Ferenc Museum, Roosevelt tér 1-3. Archaeology, paintings.

HÓDMEZÖVÁSÁRHELY

Csucsi Potters House, Rákóczi utca 101.

Fejér District

SZÉKESFEHÉRVÁR

Budenz House, Arany J. utca 12. Exhibition of the town's history.
Csok Istvan Art Gallery, Bartok Béla tér 1.
István Király Museum, Gagarin tér 3. Roman excavations, town and regional history, ethnographic collection.

TÁC

Museum Gorsium. Open-air Roman excavations.

MÁRTONVÁSÁR

Beethoven Museum, former Brunswick castle.

MÓR

Castle Museum, former Lamberg castle of Jakob Fellner. Exhibitions.

Györ-Sopron District

FERTÖD

Castle Museum ("Hungarian Versailles"), Bartók Béla utca 2.

GYÖR

Xantus János Museum, Széchenyi tér 5. Prehistorical collection, Roman archaeological finds, history of guilds and ethnographic collections.

NAGYCENK

Széchenyi Istvan Memorial Museum, Széchenyi Castle. Transport museum, luxury carriages, uniforms.

PANNONHALMA

Collection of the Benedictine Abbey, Vár utca 1, Monastery Museum. History of art, coin collection, library, collection of antiques.

SOPRON

Fabricius House, Fö tér 6. Archaeological collection, Roman lapidarium.
Liszt Ferene Museum, Május 1 tér 1. Ethnographic and crafts.
Medieval Synagogue, Uj utca 11.
Museum for Town History, Fö tér 6.
House of Arcades (Lábashaz), Orsolya tér 5. Guilds; exhibitions.
Pharmacy Museum, Fö tér 2
Museum of Bakers, Bácsi út 5.
Central Museum of Mining, Templom utca 2-4 (Palais Esterházy). History of mining in Hungary.

Hajdu-Bihar District

DEBRECEN

Déri Museum, Déri tér 1. Prehistoric finds, important Egyptian, Greek, Roman and East Asian collections, collection of minerals.
Reformed Collegiate/Museum of Religious Art, Kálvin tér 16. History of the Protestant religion in Hungary, library.

HORTOBÁGY

Puszta Shepherds' Museum, Petöfi tér.

HAJDÚBÖSZÖRMENY

Hayduk Museum (Hadú székház), Kossuth utca 1.

Heves District

BÉLATPÁTFALVA

Area of Ruins, Köalja dülü, former Cistercian church.

EGER

Dobó István Castle Museum, Vár 1. Archaeology, castle and town history, ethnographic and craft collection.

KISNÁNA

Castle ruins and folk art memorial, Béke utca 22.

EGER

Museum of Astronomy, Szabadság tér 2 (housed in the Institute of Education). Observatory, library containing rare works.

PARÁDFÜRDÖ

Museum of Coaches, Cifra Istalló.

SZILVÁSVÁRAD

Museum of the History of Horse Breeding (Museum of Lippizan Horses), Szalajka völgy.

Komárom District

ESZTERGOM

Balassi Balint Museum, Bajcsy Zsilinszkyi út 28. Oldest library in Hungary with rare and beautiful works on display.
Castle Museum, Szent István tér. The Castle of the Árpád dynasty, stone masonry, fragments of frescoes, ceramics, glazed ceramic figures.
Christian Museum, Berényi utca 2. Most important art gallery in Hungary, Gothic and Renaissance paintings.
Treasury of the Basilica, Szent István tér 1.

KOMÁROM

Klapka György Museum, Imándi eröd. Roman lapidarium, local history, regional ethnography.

TATA

Kuny Domókos Museum, Öregvár. Fort, Roman finds, medieval collection, faience work.
Museum of Nationalities, Ady Endre utca 26 (Miklós mill). History of the German ethnic minority.

VÉRTESSZÖLLÖS

Exhibition of the Hungarian National Museum. Former quarry, stone age settlement, site of earliest discovery of humans in Hungary.

Lake Balaton – Northern Shore

BADACSONY

Egry-József-Museum. Permanent exhibition by the Hungarian painter.
Wine Museum. The history of wine at Lake Balaton since Roman times.

BALATONFÜRED

Balaton Gallery. Art exhibitions.
Jokaj Memorial Museum. A literary museum honouring the great Hungarian storyteller Mór Jókai (1825–1904).

BALATONRENDES

Bajcsy Zsilinszky Museum (on Pálköve hill). In memory of the writer murdered by the Gestapo in 1944.

HEREND

Museum of Porcelain. An exhibition of the most beautiful samples from the famous Herend production.

KESZTHELY

Balaton Museum. Archaeology collection, natural sciences and ethnography of the region, science and art exhibitions.
Farm Museum. Exhibition on the history of Georgikon University of Agrarian Sciences – one of the world's best agricultural institutes. Collection of old agricultural tools and machines.
Palace Museum and Helikon Library. Exhibition showing the history of the castle, the famous Helikon library with more than 50,000 books (located in the palace, which was the home of the Festetics family in the 18th–19th century. Concerts are also held here).

NAGYVÁZSONY

Kinizsi Castle Museum. Historic exhibition – archaeological finds, namely weapons and furniture from the Middle Ages.
Postal Museum. Historic exhibition with a special theme on "the post during the Turkish era", ethnographic exhibition.

SÜMEG

Castle Museum. Exhibition on the history of the castle.

Kisfaludy Sándor Memorial Museum (in the poet's birthplace). Relics, documents on the Reformation.
Stables (former stud farm). Exhibits of old saddles and harnesses are displayed in the building.

TIHANY

Museum of ethnography (Open-air). Reconstructed old farm houses, household and fishing implements, ethnic art.
History Museum. History of the northern Balaton region, stone memorials dating back to Roman times and the Middle Ages, art exhibitions.

VÁRPALOTA

Artillery museum. Located in the former Zichy castle, showing the history of war.
Hungarian Museum of Chemistry (very appropriate in the smog-filled town). History of the chemicals industry in Hungary.

VESZPRÉM

Bakony Museum. History of the Comitat from the beginning to the present, ethnographic exhibition, other exhibitions.
Bakony House. Historic farmhouse in the Bakony mountains, authentically furnished.
Castle Museum. Archaeological exhibits from Roman times, frescoes and historic buildings from the Middle Ages, exhibition on the history of the castle.
Museum of Religious Art (in the Bishop's Palace). Visitors need special permission (information from Balaton North tourist office: Münich Ferenc tér).

ZIRC

Museum of Natural Science (about the Bakony mountains). Scientific and historic exhibits from the Bakony region.
Reguly-Antal-Library. Named after the researcher into the Finno-ugric language who, in the mid-19th century, traveled to the Urals, Scandinavia and the Baltics. The library holds over 40,000 books. It is housed in the former abbey and is surrounded by valuable furniture.

Lake Balaton – Southern Shore

BALATONSZÁRSZO

Jósef Attila Memorial Museum. An exhibition about the life and work of the "proletarian" poet.

BALATONSZEMES

Postal Museum. History of telecommunications, history of the post and stamps in Hungary.

BALATONSZENTGYÖRGY

Star Castle (Csillagvár). Exhibition about life in the fortresses in the 17th century.
Talpasház (200 year old house). Folk art exhibition.

BOGLARLELLE/BALATONBOGLAR

Chapel Gallery. Art exhibitions in the Red and the Blue Chapel, sculpture exhibition in the park.

FONYÓD

Huszka Jenö Memorial Room. An exhibition in the former summer house of the most popular Hungarian operetta composer (1875–1960).

NIKLA

Brezsényi Dániel Memorial Museum. In honor of the poet (1775–1836) – with documents on his work.

SIÓFOK

Beszédes József Museum of Water. An archaeological collection, exhibition of water conservation and production.
Imre Kálmán Memorial Room. In memory of the Operatta composer who was born here in 1882 and died in 1953 in Paris.
Cultural Center. Mostly art exhibitions.

SZÁNTÓDPUSZTA

Former dairy farm. Restored buildings, in total 27 houses of a former agricultural settlement (18–19th century), a tavern, farmhands' quarters, stables, and an imposing farmhouse built in 1740, which now houses a cultural and tourist center opened by the regional travel agency Siótour.

VORS

Country House (tájház). Collection of fishing equipment from the Little Balaton region.

ZALA

Zichy Mihály Memorial Museum. Exhibition in the former residence of the painter and graphic artist (1827–1906) with books and the artist's valuable collection of old weapons, harnesses and suits of armor.

ZAMARDI

Country House (*tájház*). Local and regional folk art.

Nograd District

BALASSAGYARMAT

Palóc Museum, Palóc liget 1. Important archaeological collection, weaponry, ceramic ware.

HOLLÓKÖ

Village Museum, Kossuth utca 82. History of the Palóc ethnic group.

SALGOTARJAN

Museum of Mining, Bajcsy Zsilinszky utca.

SZÉCSÉNY

Kubinyi Ferenc Museum, Ady Endre utca 7. Castle, exhibition.

Pest District

ABONY

Abony Lajos Village Museum, Zalka M. utca 16. Local ethnography.

SZENTENDRE

Ethnographic Open Air Museum Skansen, Szabadság forrás.
Ferenczy Museum, Marx tér 6.
Margit Kovács Collection of Ceramics, Vastagh Gy. utca 1.
Serbian Orthodox Religious Art collection, Engels utca 6. Lithurgical objects, icons from 5 centuries.
Szentendre Art Gallery, Marx tér 2.
Collection of Roman Stones, Romai sánc utca 7.

VÁC

Vak Bottyán Museum, Múzeum utca 6. Archaeology, Gothic and Renaissance artifacts.

VISEGRAD

Mátyás Király Museum (King Matthias), Töutca 27-29. Gothic and Renaissance art.

Somogy District

BALATONSZENTGYÖRGY

Star castle (Csillagvár), Irtási dülö. Exhibition on history of war.

BARCS

Dráva Museum, Széchenyi utca 22.

KAPOSVÁR

Rippl Rónai Museum, Rippl Rónai tér 1. An ethnographic collection, paintings by Rippl Rónai.

SZENNA

Ethnographic Open Air Museum, Rákóczi utca 2.

SZABOLCS-SZATMAR DISTRICT

Nyírbator
Báthory-István-Museum, Károlyi utcal 15. Natural history and geography.

NYÍREGYHÁZA

Jósa András Museum, Benczúr tér 21. Archaeological collection.

MÁTÉSZALKA

Szatmár Museum, Kossuth utca 54. Regional history.

NYIREGYHÁZA

Open Air Museum (Skansen), Sosto fürdö.

Szolnok District

JÁSZBERÉNY

Jazyg Museum, Táncsics M. utca 5. Regional history of the Jasz area.

SZOLNOK

Damjanich János Museum, Kossuth tér. Archaeological exhibition, popular art, local painter.

KARCAG

Györffy István Museum, Kálvin utca 4. Chronicle of the Kuman peoples.

MEZÖTÖR

Badár Museum. Folk art, black ceramic ware by local potters.

Tolna District

SIMONTORNYA

Castle Museum, Vár tér 10. History of castle.

SKÉKSZÁRD

Béri Balog Adám Museum, Mártírok tér 26. Prehistoric and Roman archaeological finds, local history.

DUNAFÖLDVAR

Castle Museum (so-called Turkish Tower), Rátkai Köz (Fishing Museum).

SZEKSZÁRD

Gemence Hunting Museum, Szécheny utca 38.

Vas District

KÖSZEG

Jurisics Miklós Museum, Rajnis utca 9. Castle, history of town.

SÁRVÁR

Nádasdy Ferenc Museum, Vár 1. Castle, local history, hydrotherapy exhibition.

SZALAFÖ

Ethnographic Open-Air Museum, Pityeszer 12.

SZOMBATHELY

Museum of the County Vas, Árpád utca 30. I8th–19th century village.
Iseum Garden of Ruins, Rákóczi Ferenc utca 21. Roman excavations.
Savaria Museum, Kisfaludy utca 9. Roman and medieval collection.
Smidt Museum, Hollán E. utca 2. Private collection from the estate of Dr. Lajos Smidt, one of the richest and most beautiful collections of great cultural and historical value, in the former baroque institute of 1773.

Veszprém District

BAKONYBÉL

Ethnographic Open-Air Museum, Fö utca 17.

HEREND

Museum of Porcelain, Kossuth utca 140.

NAGYVÁZSONY

Kinizsi Castle Museum, Kinizsi út.

PÁPA

Museum of Geography, Fó tér 1. Várkastely Castle.
Museum of Religious Art, Fö utca 6.

SÜMEG

Castle Museum, Vár.

TIHANY

Tihany Museum, Pisky sétány 1. Roman lapidarium, history of the Lake Balaton region.
Ethnographic Museum, Batthyány utca 36. Houses of farmers and fishermen.

VESZPRÉM

Dezsö Laczkó Museum, Erzsébet sétány u. 7. Bronze Age, Roman finds, paintings, folk art.
Castle Museum, Vár utca 2; in the Bishop's Palace. Religious art.
Gizella Chapel, Vár utca 16. Third century frescoes.

VESZPRÉMFAJSZ

Baláca Puszta. Roman excavations.

ZIRC

Natural History Museum of the Bakony mountains, Rákóczi tér 1. Science library.

Zala District

KESZTHELY

Balaton Museum, Múzeum utca 2. Roman finds of Fenékpuszta.
Helikon Castle Museum, Szabadság utca 1 (Festetics Castle).

NAGYKANIZSA

Thury György Museum, Szabadsag tér 11. Archaeological collection.

ZALAEGERSZEG

Göcsej Museum, Batthyány utca 2. History of the County Zala.
Göcsej Village Museum, Falumuzeum utca 5. Popular art.

Architecture
Budapest

Basilica, see St Stephen's Church.
Castle and palace, Várpalota, Budapest I, Szent György tér. The medieval royal castle was extended in Renaissance times (King Matthias Corvinus) and completely destroyed in 1686. Not until 1749 did Empress Maria Theresa authorise the building of a new palace (completed in 1770). In 1890 the baroque building was extended to twice its size in the historicist style and given an enormous dome. The palace, completely destroyed in 1945 during the battle for Budapest, was rebuilt after 1950.

Castle Quarter. During the restoration work on Castle Hill the historic houses of the quarter were also thoroughly renovated. In the course of this work many old building elements were discovered behind the baroque facades and can now be seen.
Chain Bridge (Lánchíd). This suspension bridge, the first permanent link between Pest and Buda, was built between 1839 and 1849. The initiative came from Count István Széchenyi, the plans were drawn up by the Englishman William Tierney Clark and the building was supervised by his countryman Adam Clark. With its pillars shaped like Roman triumphal arches it has become one of the symbols of the city. It was blown up in 1945, and reopened to traffic during the centenary celebrations in 1949.
Fishermen's Bastion (Halászbástya). This construction in blinding white stone is of course not a bastion in the sense of a defensive fortification. It was built around the turn of the century in a neo-Romanesque style. Its tower-crowned viewing terraces are situated above the steep drop of Castle Hill right behind Matthias Church.
Heroes' Square (Hösök tere). This impressive square at the entrance to the City Park was laid out in 1896 for the Millennial Celebrations, the 1,000th anniversary of the Magyar conquest of Hungary. Its dominant central feature is the Millennium monument (1896–1929) and a column, 36 metres (118 ft) high, surrounded by a group of statues portraying prominent historical figures and flanked by a colonnade.
Inner City Parish Church (Belvárosi Plébánia templom), Budapest V, Március 15 tér. Situated at the Pest end of Elizabeth Bridge. Gothic choir (14th/15th century), baroque nave and double tower (18th century). A relic of Turkish times, when the church served as a mosque, is the prayer niche (*mihrab*).
Matthias Church (Mátyas templom). Little remains of the church built in the 13th century for the German population of the Castle Quarter. The present-day building, with its slender tower, is essentially the work of the architect Frigyes Schulek, who had a gift for reinterpreting a medieval church in the historicist style (1874–96).
Parliament, Budapest V, Kossuth Lajos tér 1–3. Undoubtedly the most impressive building on the Danube bank, this is a huge neo-Gothic complex dominated by its dome and, together with the Chain Bridge, it has become a symbol of the city.
St Stephen's Parish Church (Basilica), Budapest V, Szent István tér. The biggest church in Budapest, this building is the product of historicism. It was begun in 1851 in the neo-classical style by Jószef Hild. Work continued in a neo-Renaissance style under Miklós Ybl and was completed in 1905.
Synagogue, Budapest VI, Dohány utca 2-8. This mighty Byzantine-Moorish building, a three-nave hall temple with a pair of onion-domed towers (1854–59), is the work of the Viennese architect responsible for the Ringstrasse, Ludwig Förster. Newly restored.
Vajdahunyad, Budapest XIV, Városliget, Széchenyi-sziget. This building was erected in the City Park on Széchenyi Island for the Millennial Celebrations in 1896. It was designed to represent the the various building styles of Hungarian history. The dominating Gothic wing of the building is a copy of the Rákóczi castle of Vajdahunyad in Transylvania – hence the name.
Western Railway Station (Nyugati pályaudvar), Budapest VI, Nyugati tér. This wrought iron construction, built between 1874 and 1877 and restored to its original appearance in 1976, has a glass-roofed station hall which covers 25,000 sq. metres (270,000 sq. ft) and is a masterpiece of engineering. It was built by the Parisian company of Gustave Eiffel.

Art Galleries

Budapest Gallery Exhibition Hall, U. Szabadsastó u. 5, tel: 118-8097.
Exhibition Hall (Mücsarnok), Budapest XIV, (Hösök tere) Dósza György út 37, tel: 343-7401. This neo-classical Grecian temple in Heroes' Square is the biggest exhibition hall in the capital.
Studio Gallery, Budapest V, Képíró u. 6, tel: 111-9882.
Vigadó Galéria, Budapest V, Vigadó tér 1, tel: 117-6222. The Vigadó, a restored, impressive building of the Hungarian historicist period (1859–64), is the splendid setting for a variety of exhibitions. Two exhibitions can be displayed at any one time on the two floors of the building.

A complete list of the most important exhibition halls is available from: Budapest V, Dorottya utca 8, tel: 118-3899.

Music

Musicals

Budapest has risen to be one of the world centres of the musical. For years Andrew Lloyd Webber's *Cats* has been running in the old and respected Madách Theatre. Incidentally, the Budapest performance of the hit musical of the 1980s was the first to take place abroad after the London première.

These musicals, unlike in the West, are not performed in a continuous series. Repertory theatre is still valued in Budapest – this is a matter of principle, and not even the greatest financial success of a single play can change it. Take a look at the monthly programme if you want to go to a musical.

Concerts

The centre of the busy concert life of Budapest is the Music Academy, named after Franz Liszt, with its two halls. In the Ballroom (Vigadó) in Pest performances are mainly by soloists and chamber orchestras.

In fine weather, especially during the months of July and August, there are regular open-air concerts. Choral concerts, often of old music, take place every Sunday at 11am in the Castle. Concerts generally begin at 7pm, 7.30pm at the latest. For information and bookings, contact:

Filharmonia, Budapest V, Vörösmarty tér 1, tel: 117-6222.
Music Academy (Zenemüvészeti Föiskola), Budapest VI, Liszt Ferenc tér 30, tel: 342-0179.
Pest Ballroom (Pesti Vigadó), Budapest V, Vigadó tér, tel: 117-6222.
Buda Ballroom (Budai Vigadó), Budapest I, Corvin tér 8, tel: 201-5928.
Budapest Conference Centre, Budapest XII, Jagelló út. 1–3, tel: 161-2869.
MTA Congress Centre, Budapest I, Országház u. 30, tel: 175-4327.
Museum of Music History, Budapest I, Táncsis M. u. 7, tel: 175-9011.
Reformed Church, Budapest IX, Kálvin tér.
Lutheran Church, Budapest V, Deák tér 4-5.
Matthias Church, Budapest I, Szentháromság tér.

Outdoor Venues

Buda Park Theatre, Budapest XI, Kosztolányi Dezsö tér, tel: 166-9849.
Open-air stage in Városmajor Park, Budapest I, Városmajori park, tel: 175-5922.
Dominican Court in the Hilton Hotel, Budapest I, Hess András tér 1, tel: 185-3500.
Open-air stage of the Opera House on Margaret Island, Budapest XIII, Margitsziget, tel: 111-2463.
Musical Court, Budapest II, Marcibányi tér 5A, tel: 135-3786, 135-5759.
Zichy Palace, Budapest III, Fö tér 1, tel: 168-6020.

For more details on the events listed above contact:
Information, Budapest Vi, Jókai utca 24, tel: 132-1721.
Advance booking, Budapest XIII, Fürst Sándor utca 10, tel: 111-4283.

Opera & Ballet

Opera has a long and honourable tradition in Hungary. After all, Gustav Mahler, before he went to the Hofoper in Vienna, was in charge of opera in Budapest. The capital allows itself the luxury of two opera houses – the State Opera and the Erkel Theatre – which have a wide-reaching repertoire. For lighter music, there is the **Operetta Theatre**, which honours the memory of Franz Lehár and Imre Kálmán. The ballet company of the Hungarian State Opera is famous far and wide outside the country.

Ticket prices, compared to those in the West, are moderate. Performances begin at 7pm. Ticket bookings at box offices: Thursday, Friday, Saturday 3pm–5.30pm.
Central Booking Offices, Budapest VI, Andrássy út 18, tel: 112-0000.
State Opera House (Magyar Állami Operaház), Budapest VI, Andrassy út 22, tel: 131-2550.
Erkel Theatre, Budapest VIII, Köztársaság tér 30, tel: 133-0108, 333-0540.
Capital Operetta Theatre (Fövárosi Operettszinház), Budapest VI, Nagymezö utca 17-19, tel: 332-0535.

Theatre

For those who cannot speak Hungarian it is of course difficult to take part in the rich theatrical life of Budapest.

However, a visit to the theatre can have its positive side, even if you do not understand the language.
Castle Theatre, Budapest I, Színház utca 1-3, tel: 175-8649.
Katona Theatre, Budapest V, Petöfi Sándor utca 6, tel: 118-3725.
Kolibri Theatre, Jókai tér 10, tel: 153-4633.
Madách Theatre, Budapest VII, Erzsébet krt 29-33, tel: 322-2015.
Madach Chamber Theatre, Budapest VII, Madách tér 6, tel: 142-3122.
National Theatre, Budapest VII, Hevesi Sándor tér 2, tel: 122-0014.
Puppet Theatre (Bábszínház Budapest), Budapest VI, Andrássy út 69, tel: 321-5200.

Cinema

Cinema lovers from abroad have a hard time in Hungary, as foreign films here are dubbed, almost without exception.

The major hotels have their own cable television service offering (for a fee) films in other languages, including English.

Activities For Children

In general Hungarians are fond of children. There is plenty for younger guests to see and also to do, which often helps to relieve the pressure on their parents. Various organisations have their own (often free) programmes specifically for children. For general information, contact:
Toptour, Budapest V, Nádor u. 26, tel: 131-6194.

Sunday Activities

Magyar Nemzeti Múzeum, Budapest VIII, Múzeum körút 14-16, tel: 138-2122. In the National Museum on Sunday children, supervised by teachers, can work with plasticine, draw and paint.
Youth Centre, Budapest II, Marcibányi tér 5A, tel: 212-4885. In the Youth Centre in Marcibányi Square there is a children's fair every Sunday from 8am to 1pm. Young visitors take an active part.

Playgrounds

All over the city there are plenty of playgrounds for children, equipped with sand boxes, swings, and climbing

frames. Some especially attractive playgrounds are in the City Park (Városliget), in the Jubilee Park on Gellért Hill and on Margaret Island.
Children's Zoo, Budapest XIV, Állatkerti körút 6-12.
Margaret Island Zoo, Margitsziget. This is a little wildlife park where children can see native animals (deer, pheasants, peacocks) living freely.

Adventure & Amusement Parks

Children will be delighted by a trip on the Children's Railway (*Gyermekvasut*) through the Buda Hills and especially by the fact that the train is crewed entirely by children.

A further attraction of the Buda Hills for children is the Wildlife Park of Budakeszi, a compound containing native animals. Open daily from 9am to dusk.

In the amusement park in the City Park, there is a separate mini-Lunapark for children.
Vidám Park, Budapest XIV, Allatkerti körút 14-16. Open daily 10am–8pm.
Puppet Theatre, Main House, Budapest VI, Népköztársaság útca 69.
Circus, Fövárosi Nagycirkusz, Budapest XIV, Állatkerti körút 7. Local and international stars appear in the Capital Circus in City Park, which recently celebrated its 100th anniversary.

Students seem to live cheaply in Hungary because the cost of living is still low compared to the West, and also because they are entitled to all sorts of discounts and reductions.

It is important to have an International Student Card (IUS) or an international tourist card for students (ISTC). If you also happen to be a member of the Youth Hostel Association (IYHF), all the better.

The Express Youth and Student Travel Agency deals exclusively with the requirements of young people and students, ranging from cheap accommodation to cultural activities.
Express Youth and Student Travel Agency, Central Office, Budapest V, Szabadsag tér 16, tel: 131-7777.

Meeting Places

A popular meeting place, particularly for young foreigners, is the space in front of the Matthias Church and the Fishermen's Bastion on Castle Hill in Buda.

Contact with Hungarian young people and students is most easily made in the youth centres and Houses of Culture and especially in the dance halls (*táncházak* – pronounced Tahntshaasokk – *see below*), where you will immediately be invited to join in.

Dance Halls

Petöfi Csarnok (Petöfi Hall), Budapest XIV, Városliget, Zichy Mihály út. Budapest's biggest youth leisure centre in City Park. Wednesday, Friday: folk dancing (with instruction) and folk music; Saturday: disco; Friday, Saturday: foreign languages club.
Inner City House of Youth and Culture, Budapest V, Molnár utca 9. Saturday 6.30pm dance hall.
Capital House of Culture, Budapest XI, Fehérvári út 47. Tuesday 7pm dance hall.
Youth and Culture Centre, Budapest II, Marczibányi tér 5A. Saturday 6pm dance hall.

Focal points of night life in Budapest are the Castle Quarter and the Inner City of Pest. There is no shortage of nightclubs and bars; all the big hotels have them.

Nightclubs & Bars

Most places are open 10pm–4am.
Apollo, Budapest XI, Tass Vezéti utca. Monday–Saturday 10pm–4am, closed Sunday.
Fehér Györü, Budapest V, Bálint Balassi u. 27. Late-night place.
Gellért, Budapest XI, Gellért tér 1. Equally famous as the hotel to which it belongs, Monday–Saturday 10pm–4am, closed Sunday.
Halászbástya, Budapest I, Halászbástya. The elegant bar, with dancing, of the Hilton Hotel, open daily 10pm–4am.
Morrison's Music Pub, Budapest VI, Révay u. 25. Live music and CDs, snacks. A young night-crowd.
Nincs Párdon, Budapest VII, Almássy tér. The new in-crowd meets here.
Picasso Point, Budapest VI, Hajos u. 31. On two floors: upstairs for chatting, downstairs live new-age joys and other performances (also disco).
Pierrot, Budapest I, Fortuna utca 14.

Bar with live piano music in the Castle Quarter, open daily 10pm–4am.
Saigon, Budapest V, Arany János u. 13. Cellar place, exotically done-up, pin-ball machines and palm fronds.
Tilos az "A", Budapest VIII, Miksáth Kálmán tér. First excellent night joint with live bands and café theatre.

Discos

Bahnhof, Váci út 1. One of the city"s liveliest discos with action until 4am.
Fortuna, Budapest I, Hess András tér 2, tel: 155-7177. Roofed by Gothic vaults, open daily 9pm–3am.
Franklin Trocadero Café, Budapest XIII, Sg. István körút 15, tel: 111-4691. Latin and African beat.
High Life Disco 21–07, Budapest III, Kalap u. 14, tel: 250-2979.
Hully-Gully, Budapest XII, Apor Vilnes tér. Techno, etc. until 4am.
Made-Inn Music Club, Budapest VI, Andrássy út 112, tel: 111-3437. Very popular, mixed crowd.
Petöfi Csarnok. In the City Park, weekend disco, mainly young crowd.
Piaf, Budapest VI, Nagyonezö u. 25, tel: 112-3823. Upper crust, tamer music.

Cabaret

Vidám Színpad (The Merry Stage), Budapest VI, Révay utca 18, tel: 131-1311.
Mikroszkóp Színpad, Budapest VI, Nagymezö utca 11. (In the Thalla Theatre building), tel: 111-3322.

Casinos

Casino Budapest (In the Hilton Hotel, Budapest), Budapest I, Hess András tér 1-4, tel: 175-1000. Open daily from 5pm, entrance fee 5DM (can be redeemed in chips). Bets are placed in Deutschmarks – other Western currencies are accepted. You can dispose of your money – or make your fortune – playing roulette, baccarat, blackjack or the 40 "one-armed bandits". Winnings are tax free and are paid in Deutschmarks, so they can be exported without difficulty. A branch of the casino has been opened on a boat with a restaurant in front of the Hotel Fórum by the Chain Bridge. Money sources are more or less the same as in the Hilton; Hungarian nationals are not allowed to play.
Casino Budapest Gresham, Roosevelt tér 5, tel: 117-2407.

Imperial Casino, Budapest V, Szabad-sajtó út 5, tel: 118-2404.
Las Vegas Casino, Budapest V, Roosevelt tér 2, tel: 117-6022.
Orfeum Casino Hotel Béke, Radisson Teréz krt. 43, tel: 269-1799.

Festivals

February

BUDAPEST

13 February: Unofficial memorial day to mark the end of the seige of Budapest on 13 February 1945.
Mid-February: Hungarian Film festival.

DEBRECEN

Heyduck carnival.

MOHÁCS

Mardi Gras carnival to celebrate the expulsion of the Turks. Revellers in procession wear strange masks.

March

BUDAPEST

Spring Festival: Four weeks of classical music, ballet and opera.

April

HOLLÓKÖ

Traditional Easter festival with costumes in a village in the Cserhát Mountains.

MAGYARPOLÁNY

Road to Golgotha. Baroque Passion play in a village in the Bakony Mountains.

May

BALATON

Balaton festival of classical music.

BUDAPEST

1 May: Labour Day celebration in Tabán Park; bands, folk music, puppet theatre.
Late May: Trade Fair.
Last week in May: International Book Fair.

June

GYULA

Drama festival in the castle.

ZSÁMBÉK

Theatre performances in front of the Premonstratensian church.

MISKOLC-DIÓSGYÖR

Dixieland festival in the castle ruins.

July

BUDAPEST

Open-air theatre performances.

BALATONFÜRED

Operetta.

SZENTENDRE

Classical concerts, opera, folk and jazz.

SZEGED

Open-air theatre with opera, classical and rock music in the cathedral square.

NYÍRBÁTOR

Music festival. Classical music in the church.

VISEGRÁD

Plays in the palace. Renaissance festival with jousting in traditional costume.

August

BUDAPEST

Fun and games in the Castle District; open-air craft market on Tóth Árpád sétány (Castle Hill).
20 August: Festival of Guilds in honour of St Stephen. Parade in front of Parliament building; music and folk performances; evening firework display.

FERTÖD

Eszterházy festivities. Opera, ballet, puppets and plays in Eszterházy castle.

DEBRECEN

20 August: International flower carnival with grand procession through the town.

MOGYORÓD

Formula 1 Grand Prix at the Hungaroring.

HORTOBÁGY

Bridge market.
20 August: Traditional jousting and other events.

September

BUDAPEST

25 September: Béla Bartók's birthday and the start of the Budapest Festival, including concerts, theatre productions, contemporary music series, exhibitions.

SZILVÁSVÁRAD

Lippizaner festival. Horse show and other events.

October

BUDAPEST

23 October: Anniversary of the 1956 revolution.

December

Christmas is celebrated everywhere (reserve restaurant tables well in advance, many places close).

BUDAPEST

New Year's Eve: Gala evening in the Vigadó; fireworks display.

Shopping

What & Where To Buy

Arts &Crafts

In Hungary folk art has considerable status. There are thousands of craftspeople, working throughout the country, commissioned by the council which runs the craft shops in Budapest. Here you can buy hand-woven textiles, embroidery, lace, braid, ceramics, earthenware, leather goods, carpets and wood carvings based on authentic patterns.

Budapest I, Szilágyi Dezsö tér 6.
Budapest I, Országház utca 16.
Budapest II, Mártirok útja 34.
Budapest V, Kossuth Lajos utca 2.
Budapest V, Régiposta utca 12.
Budapest V, Váci utca 14 (also open Saturday and Sunday).
Budapest V, Kálvin tér 5.
Budapest VII, Erzsébet krt 5.
Budapest VII, Rákóczi út 32.
Budapest XI, Bartók Béla út 50.
Budapest XIII, Szent István körút 26.

Clothes

The tailors and cobblers of the Hungarian capital once had a legendary reputation and the "Budapest", a prototype of many men's shoe designs, has its place in fashion history.

These traditions are kept alive today, although in a more modest way. If you are patient and don't mind making a second visit to try on the items, you can have your measurements taken from head to foot for an entire new wardrobe, including shirts, and at prices that are about the same as for medium-range off-the-peg clothes. You can even bring your own material.

LADIES' WEAR

Clara Szalon, Budapest V, Váci utca 12, tel: 118-4090.
Kék Duna, Budapest V, Kristóf tér 6, tel: 117-2326.
Sikk, Budapest V, Haris köz 2, tel: 118-3313.
Ferencné Eri, Budapest V, Haris köz 3, tel: 137-4422.
Imréné Kárpáti, Budapest V, Régi posta utca 7-9, tel: 137-6385.

Shoes

The world-famous cobblers have a problem, there are not enough young people taking up the trade for the masters, all in advanced years, to pass on their skills. Consequently it takes many months before a genuine pair of "Budapests" is ready. Take care when measurements are taken: the Hungarians prefer the tightest fit possible.

László Vass, Budapest V, Haris köz 2, tel: 118-2375.
Budapest V, Kossuth Lajos utca 15, tel: 117-3571.
Budapest V, Petöfi Sándor utca 14, tel: 118-3375.

Household Goods

The range of goods on offer in the department stores does not measure up to Western standards in either quantity or quality, but the prices are low.

Corvin, Budapest VIII, Blaha Lujza tér 1–2, tel: 138-4160.
Luxus, Budapest V, Vörösmarty tér 3, tel: 118-3550.
Skála Budapest, Budapest XI, Október 23 utca, tel: 185-2222.
Skála Metro, Budapest VI, Nyugati tér.

Antiques & Books

Keep an eye out for antiques of good value. Plates, vases and embroidery can look old, but often they are not. There was once a generous supply of old books in Budapest and there are still a number of antiquarian bookshops in which to browse. Note that all pieces over 100 years old are of "national value" and may not be taken out of the country.

Markets

Every town and each district of the capital has its daily or weekly market. In Budapest you should not miss out on a visit to the recently restored **Central Market Hall**, Budapest IX, Vámház körút 1-3, near the Danube bank by Liberation Bridge. The architecture of this massive building, with its iron construction and historicist brick facade, is impressive. Inside, the quantity and quality of the produce on offer (fruit, vegetables, meat, fish and dairy produce) is overwhelming.

The fleamarket in the Budapest suburb of Kispest is worth a visit. Budapest XIX, Nagykörösi ut 156. Monday–Friday 8am–4pm, Saturday 8am–3pm.

Sports & Leisure

Participant

Fishing

Fishing is an increasingly popular leisure activity. There is a great temptation – so the regional bureaux claim – to get a catch on the dinner table for free without a permit.

Here are some tips for anglers: Each angler may catch three, or at the most five, fish per day. Pike-perch is limited by weight to three kilos in total, and other kinds of varying size, to five kilos in total. Young people under 18 can keep two (at the most three) fish of those types for which there is a minimum size. Local regulations apply. An adult is permitted to use two fishing rods in Hungary, while a youth may use only one. However, in some fishing grounds, adults are restricted to one fishing rod each.

Fishing permits are issued in all districts at short notice via the regional tourist offices, partly also by hotel receptions, camping and motel offices. For more information, contact: The Hungarian Federation of Anglers, Budapest V, Október 6 utca, tel: 132-5315.

It is important to be aware of the minimum sizes and closed season.
Eel (50 cm): 1 March–30 April.
Trout (22 cm): 15 October–30 April.
Pike (40 cm): 1–31 March.
Carp (30 cm): 2 May–15 June.
Catfish (under 50 cm): 2 May–15 June.
Pike-perch (20 cm): 1 March–30 April.

POPULAR FISHING GROUNDS

Traditionally, the most important fishing ground is Lake Balaton. Fishing is strictly prohibited between 20 April and 20 May. The best spots are on the northern shore; often a boat is necessary but (from experience) it is not always easy to hire one.

On the northern shore of Lake Balaton: carp, catfish; elsewhere: silver scaled fish; the inland lake (Belsö tó) of Tihany: the best carp and bream reserve in Hungary; the southern shore of Lake Balaton: more favorable spots than on the northern shore, but smaller catch.

Transdanubia:
Lake Velence (carp, pike-perch).
The reservoirs of Zámoly and Fehérvárcsurgo, north of Székesfehérvár.
Near Szekszárd, the former tributary of the river Fadd-Dombory (the Szálka reservoir).
Near Pécs, the reservoirs (former quarries) of Orfú and Kovácsszánája.
On the outskirts of Kaposvár: the reservoir of Deseda.

East of the Danube:
Gravel pits of Délegyháza, approximately 30 km south of Budapest.
Szélidi lake near Kalocsa.
Reservoir in the Rakaca valley north of Miskolc and the gravel pit lakes of Mályi and Nyékládháza.
Near Debrecen, the reservoir of Fanciska.
The tributary of the river Alcsisziget on the outskirts of Szolnok.
The tributary of the river Atka near Szeged.
The tributary of the river Kakafoki in Szarvas.

On the Danube:
The stretch between Kulcs and Rácalmás near Dunaújváros (carp, pike-perch, pike).
Areas around Baja and Mohács (carp, pike-perch, catfish and silver scaled fish).
Near Ráckeve south of Budapest: carp and silver scaled fish.

On the Tisza:
Near the power station Tikszalökk (mainly predatory fish).
Near the mouth of the river Körös (predatory fish, but also carp).
The huge Tisza reservoir of Kisköre.
Near Tass there are carp, pike-perch, catfish, silver scaled fish.
Connoisseurs will also appreciate the rivers Rába and Körös.

Golf

There is an 18-hole course at the northern end of the long, narrow Szentendre Island opposite Visegrád, 35 km (22 miles) from Budapest.
Hencse Golf and Country Club, Hencse, Hossuth utca 3, tel: (82) 351-209. Probably the finest golf course/country club in Hungary just 25 km (16 miles) south of Kaposvar.
Kisoroszi Golf Course. 18 holes, 36 par. Open 1 April–31 October.

Horse-Riding

Hungary has near ideal conditions in all regions for riding enthusiasts. There are numerous riding schools with overnight accommodation and leisure activities nearby.

Organised riding excursions can be arranged. Contact:
Hungarian Riding Association, National Riding School, Budapest VIII, Kerepesi út 7, tel: 113-0415.
Peneházi Riding School, Budapest II, Feketefej utca 5, tel: 116-4267.
Riding tours (day trips or longer excursions – 9, 10, 15 days) are organised by the following travel agents:
Pegazus Tours, Ferenciek tere 5, tel: 117-1644.

Hiking

For information, contact:
Hungarian Nature Lovers' Association, Budapest VI, Bajcsy-Zsilinsky út 31, tel: 153-1930.
Information Service, Budapest V, Váci utca 62-64, tel: 118-3933.

Hunting

While animal rights and environmental groups in Western countries have often protested against the destruction of the natural environment, the Hungarians have been intensifying the creation of organised hunting parties in exclusive, well-kept areas in several parts of the country.

Apart from small game, the number of trophies in Hungarian hunting grounds is – by international standards – extremely high. Red deer from Hungarian forests, fallow-deer and wild boar are particularly prized.
MAVAD, 1525 Budapest, Úri utca 39, tel: 175 9611, issues hunting permits and provides local beaters and companions. It also arranges lodgings near the hunting grounds.

Ice Skating

Cycling Track and Artificial Ice Rink, Budapest XIV, Szabó Jószef utca 3.
Outdoor Ice Skating, Budapest XIV, Népstadion út, tel: 122-8211. 5 November–8 March, open daily 10am–2pm, 4pm–8pm.

In late autumn and winter the pond of the City Park (Városliget) is turned into a skating rink.

Swimming

Budapest has more swimming pools than any other big city. Most of the pools – indoor and outdoor – are supplied from medicinal springs. Some open-air pools can be used in the winter, as they are supplied with water from hot springs. Pools are usually open from 7am–7pm. Last admission one hour before closing time.
Alfréd Hajós Indoor Sports Pool, Budapest XIII, Margitsziget.
Komjádi Sports Pool, Budapest II, Komjádi Béla utca 2-4. The roof is opened in fine weather.

SPAS WITH SWIMMING POOLS

Gellért Baths, Budapest XI, Kelenhegyi út 4, tel: 166-6166.
Lukács Baths, Budapest II, Frankel Leó út 25-29, tel: 175-4494.
Rudas Baths, Budapest I, Döbrentei tér 9, tel: 156-1322.
Szabadság-fürdö, Budapest XIII, Népfürdö utca 30, tel: 120-2203.
Széchenyi Baths, Budapest XIV, Allatkerti körút 11, tel: 121-0310.
Ujpest Baths, Budapest IV, Arpád utca 114-120, tel: 169-0344.

OUTDOOR POOLS

(Open from 1 May to 30 September)
Árpád Pool Csillaghegy, Budapest III, Pusztakúti út 3, tel: 250-1533.
Kispest Pool, Budapest XIX, Ady Endre utca 99, tel: 280-5919.
Palatinus Pool, Budapest XIII, Margitsziget, tel: 112-3069.
Pünkösd Pool, Budapest II, Királyok útja 272, tel: 188-6665.
Római fürdö (Roman Baths), Budapest III, Rozgonyi Piroska utca 2, tel: 188-9740.

HOTELS WITH INDOOR POOLS

Nearly all equipped with sauna, sunbeds and gym.
Atrium-Hyatt, Budapest V, Roosevelt tér 2, tel: 266-1234.

Mercure Buda, Budapest I, Krisztina körút 41-43, tel: 156-6333.
Flamenco, Budapest XI, Tas vezér utca 7, tel: 372-2000.
Intercontinental, Budapest V, Apáczai Csere János utca 12-14, tel: 117-8088.
Grand Hotel Ramada, Budapest XIII, Margitsziget, tel: 311-1000.
Novotel, Budapest XI, Alkotás utca 63-67, tel: 186-9588.
Olympia, Budapest XII, Eötvös út 40, tel: 395-6447.
Rege, Budapest II, Pálos út 2, tel: 200-8816.
Stadion, Budapest XIV, Ifjúság útja 1-3, tel: 251-2222.
Thermal Hotel Helia, Kárpát utca 62–64, tel: 270-3277.

LAKE BALATON

Swimming in Lake Balaton is only allowed at certain spots, despite the occasionally shallow shores. It is generally prohibited in the harbours and in the areas where boats and ferries ply. The beaches near the tourist resorts are located on danger-free stretches. There are many beaches which are open to the public free of charge.

The swimming pools (they charge a nominal entry fee) offer such facilities as restaurants, shops, sport shops, changing rooms, toilets, boat and air mattress hire, and first aid posts.

Swimmers, no matter how good they are, should not swim too far out into the lake; buoys on the beaches indicate how far out one is allowed to swim. Anyone flouting these regulations will immediately be asked by the marine police to turn back.

Storm signals are sent out through warning flares and by the hoisting of storm flags on the weather masts at the jetties. Thunderstorms at Lake Balaton tend to be brief but wild. A yellow flare draws attention to an approaching storm, a red flare announces the outbreak of a heavy storm. Anyone on the lake on lilos must return to shore as soon as the yellow flares are lit.

Tennis

Tennis Stadium, Budapest XIII, Margitsziget, tel: 131-7532.
Tennis Courts, Budapest XI, Bartók Béla út 63-65.
Club BXE, Budapest XII, Szamos utca 2c, tel: 135-0127. Open daily 8am–2pm. Tennis racquets for hire.

HOTELS WITH TENNIS COURTS

Expo, Budapest X, Albertirsai, tel: 263-7600.
Stadion, Budapest XIV, Ifjúság útja 1-3, tel: 251-2222.
Flamenco, Budapest XI, Tass vezér utca 7, tel: 372-2000.
Novotel, Budapest XII, Alokotás utca 63-67, tel: 186-9588.
Olympia, Budapest XII, Eötvös út 40, tel: 156-8011.

Water Sports

Windsurfing is popular in Hungary and is permitted, except near bathing and swimming areas.

Sailing is only possible on the larger lakes (Lake Balaton, Lake Velence) and in the large reservoirs. Sailing boats of different classes can be hired at the lakes and sailing courses are available.

The use of motor boats is restricted. On Lake Balaton and Lake Velence rowing boats and small sailing boats must not go further than one kilometre from the shore. Crossing the lake – regardless of class of boat – is prohibited. Jumping or diving into the water from boats is not allowed. The authorities are trying to minimise risks on these volatile lakes.

Spas & Health Resorts

Hungary is richly endowed with medicinal and mineral waters. Many of its 600 medicinal springs have been artificially opened up. They can be divided into springs containing carbonic acid, alkalis, sulphur or calcium, saline waters, bitter waters, and springs containing iron, iodine, bromine or radium.
Medicinal waterts containing carbonic acid: Carbonic acid, a product of post-volcanic activity, collects near Lake Balaton and in the Mátra mountains. The springs in Balatonfüred which contain carbonic acid help in the treatment of heart diseases. "The healing power of this water comes from the absorption of carbonic acid through the skin", wrote one author of a prospectus. "The blood pressure goes down, the pulse slows down, and the heart grows stronger, and the patient recuperates and can return to work."
Alkaline curative waters: These have gained their valuable salts normally as a result of the disintegration of volcanic rocks through the action of ground water containing carbonic acid. The medicinal waters rich in alkalis also contain a lot of carbonic acid and predominantly cooking salt. The finest of these springs have been opened up by deep drilling in the Great Plain and in Western Hungary, sometimes known as Transdanubia. The mineral water labelled Salvus from Bükkszék contains plenty of bicarbonate of soda.
Mineral waters containing sulphur: Sulphur springs like the curative springs in the Mátra- and Zemplén mountains are also predominantly of post-volcanic origin. In other areas (in Dunaalmás), however, the sulphur emerged as a result of the disintegration of pyrites. Drinking mineral water containing sulphur benefits the intestine and the metabolism generally. Taking a bath helps in healing and regenerating rheumatism sufferers. The two most famous sulphur spas are Héviz and Harkány.
Medicinal waters containing calcium: Most of the tepid and warm springs in Hungary, as for instance the springs in the capital, contain calcium. The curative waters in Budapest are predominantly liquids containing calcium and hydrocarbonate – the springs absorb the calcium ingredients from chalk and dolomite rock. These warm waters are also slightly radioactive.
Bitter waters: These collect in lowlands with clay soils and with no or little ground water; they are the result of the disintegration of the pyrites contained in clay. The various solutions are natural remedies for diseases of the intestine. Several of these bitter water pools enjoy a high reputation.
Medicinal waters containing cooking salt: The artesian thermal waters (65°C) in the forest near Debrecen and the springs (75°C) at Hajdúszoboszló are notable. Some of them rich in soda and chlorides may be labelled as mineral waters rich in cooking salt.
Medicinal waters rich in iodine, iron and alkalis: The medicinal waters in the spas situated mainly on the Great Plain contain dry salts with iodine. The iodine originates from decayed organisms from the ocean. These springs are particularly effective for strengthening the arteries and maintaining the blood pressure.

Parád, on the eastern edge of the Mátra mountains, is one of the Hungarian spas where the water contains iron and alum. These waters are used to treat anaemia and many other illnesses.

Budapest is a renowned health resort. The tradition of taking baths goes back to Roman times. In the 16th and 17th centuries the Turks continued the tradition, and their baths are still used today.

Every day, 40 million litres of warm water (40°–76°C) and 30 million litres of tepid water well up to the surface in the capital, giving several thousands of people the opportunity to enjoy baths and the goodness of healing.

Important: Many of the baths have alternating days for men and women, or segregated bathing facilities. It is worth mentioning that the scientific research on spas by Hungarian specialists is recognised as the most advanced in the world.
Useful Tip: the suffix "-füred" or "-fürdö" in place names means they have baths or springs (e.g. Balatonfüred, Mátrafüred, Bükfürdö, Harkányfurdö).

Budapest

Császárfürdö, Budapest II, Frankel Leó utca 31. Thermal steam baths. For treating the motor system; water drinking cures for the digestive tract, gall bladder, inflammation of joints. Tuesday, Thursday, Saturday, men only; Monday, Wednesday, Friday, women only. Monday–Saturday 6.30am–7pm, Sunday 6.30am–noon.
Gellértfürdö, Budapest XI, Gellért tér. Famous not only for its Secessionist-style swimming pool. Attached to the hotel of the same name. For treating the motor system, peripheral circulation problems, diseases of the joints and spine, chronic gynaecological complaints, asthma and bronchitis. Monday–Saturday 6am–8pm, Sunday 6am–7pm.
Királyfürdö, Budapest II, Fö utca 82–86. Built in 1565–70 by the Pasha of Buda, these baths are among the most important buildings remaining from Turkish times. For treating degenerative diseases of the digestive system and spine, inflammation of joints, neuralgia. Monday, Wednesday, Sunday, men only; Tuesday, Thursday, Saturday, women only. Thermal steam baths. Monday–Saturday 6.30am–6pm, Sunday 6.30am–noon.

Lukácsfürdö, Budapest II, Frankel Leó utca 25–29. Together with the Imperial Baths (Császár fürdö), these belong to the National Institute for Rheumatology and Physiotherapy, ORFI. For treating diseases of the joints and spine, inflammation of the digestive system, neuralgia.
Margaret Island Thermal Baths, Budapest XIII, Margitsziget. A combination of a spa and a luxury hotel, in the peaceful surroundings of Margaret Island. For treating the motor system, gynaecological problems.
Rácfürdö, Budapest I, Hadnagy utca 8-10. Situated in Tabán Park at the foot of Gellért Hill, these baths, which are under a preservation order, are perhaps the most atmospheric of all the baths of Budapest. For treating joints, damaged cartilages, bone diseases due to lack of calcium. Monday–Saturday 6.30am–7pm; closed Sunday. Tuesday, Thursday, Saturday, men only; Monday, Wednesday, Friday, women only.
Rudasfürdö, Budapest I, Döbrentei tér 9. Also situated in Tabán Park, these baths were well known as early as the 15th century. Some parts of the baths which were rebuilt in Turkish times (1566) have survived. For treating motor system; water drinking cures for digestive tract, gall bladder, respiratory system. Monday–Saturday 6am–6pm, Sunday 6am–4pm.
Széchenyifürdö, Budapest XIV, Allatkerti körút 11. These turn-of-the-century medicinal baths in the City Park have two open-air pools (open all the year round) with warm and somewhat cooler water. For treating the motor system, gynaecological problems, joints, orthopaedic degenerations as a result of injuries. Water drinking cures for stomach and gall bladder. Monday–Saturday 7am–7pm (men and women).

Last admissions are always one hour before the times listed above.

The Provinces

Many excellent spas have been built in recent years in the provinces. Here are some examples:
Balatonfüred: High blood pressure; chronic heart disease.
Balf: Wear and tear of digestive system; drinking cures for chronic stomach and intestinal complaints.
Bük: Diseases of the digestive system; rheumatism.

Csongrád: Diseases and injuries to the digestive system; aftercare of paralysis; therapy for the respiratory organs; gynaecological complaints.
Debrecen: Injuries to the joints; postoperative treatment; symptoms of paralysis; therapy for the respiratory organs.
Dombovár: Stomach, intestine and gall complaints; gynaecological complaints; dental problems; diseases of the digestive system.
Eger: Neurological complaints; anaemia, fatigue; gout.
Györ: Rheumatism; gynaecological complaints; diseases of the digestive and respiratory organs.
Gyula: Diseases of the digestive system, the heart, and the blood vessels; infections.
Hajdúszoboszló: Diseases of the digestive system; skin complaints; gynaecological problems; stomach and intestinal complaints (drinking cures); chronic diseases of the respiratory organs (inhalation).
Harkány: Diseases of the digestive system, joints and cartilages; rheumatism; poor circulation; shingles; gynaecological complaints; sterility; drinking cures for abscesses in the stomach and large intestine.
Héviz: Diseases of the digestive system; diseases of the nerves and muscles.
Kisvárda: Infections and diseases of the digestive system; aftercare for accidents.
Mezökövesd: Problems in the joints; diseases of the digestive system.
Miskolctapolca: Treatment for poor circulation, for diseases of the blood vessels and nerves.
Mosonmagyaróvár: Diseases of the nervous system; gynaecological complaints; skin diseases.
Nyíregyháza: Diseases of the nervous system; skin and gynaecological complaints.
Parád: Gynaecological complaints; stomach and intestinal complaints; anaemia; lack of calcium; exhaustion.
Szolnok: Diseases of the joints and the digestive system.
Sárvár: Gynaecological complaints; rheumatism, diseases of the digestive system.
Zalakaros: Chronic gynaecological complaints; rheumatism; diseases of the digestive system; caries.

Official Spas & Other Health Resorts

Abaliget, Agárd, Alsógöd, Alsóörs, Aszófő, Badacsonytomaj, Badacsonytördemic, Balatonakali, Balatonakarattya, Balatonmádi, Balatonberény, Balatonfenyves, Balatonföldvár, Balatonfüred, Balatongyörök, Balatonkenese, Balatonkeresztúr, Balatonmáriafürdö, Balatonöszöd, Balatonrendes, Balatonszabadi, Balatonszárszó, Balatonszemes, Balatonszepézd, Balatonudvari, Balatonvilágos, Balf, Boglárelle, Budapest, Bük, Bükkszék, Csopak, Debrecen, Dömös, Eger, Felsögöd, Fonyód, Gárdony, Gyenesdiás, Gyöngyös, Gyula, Hajdúszoboszló, Harkány, Hévíz, Igal, Keszthely, Kismaros, Köszeg, Leányfalu, Lillafüred, Lovas, Mártély, Mátrafüred, Métraháza, Miskolctapolca, Nagymaros, Nyíregyháza, Sóstó, Orfü, Orosháza, Orevényes, Parád, Pécs, Pilisszentkereszt, Révfülöp, Siófok, Sopron, Szeged, Szentendre, Szigliget, Szilvásvárad, Tahi, Tata, Tihany, Velence, Veröce, Visegrád, Vonyarcvashegy, Zalakaros, Zamárdi, Zánka, Zebegény.

Language

Even for foreign visitors who are skilled at languages, Hungarian remains a sealed book. Learning Hungarian is different from learning most other European languages. There are no similarities, no opportunities for comparison, no short cuts to understanding this language. The reason is that Hungarian has nothing whatsoever to do with the great Indo-European family of languages: it belongs to the Finno-Ugric group. Its only relatives within Europe are Finnish and Estonian, and its only other relatives are certain languages and dialects in Siberia and Central Asia.

Hungarian is an agglutinative language, i.e. grammatical forms are made by adding suffixes to the root syllable.

Stress is always on the first syllable of any word. The accent (´) does not mark the stress but indicates a long vowel (and occasionally changes its pronunciation). In all syllables the vowels are sounded clearly and fully.

In the Hungarian language the difference between "stressed" and "unstressed" syllables is slight. Diphthongs (ai, ei, eu, etc.) are always pronounced as two separate vowels.

	Pronounced	As in
a	short, deep o	on
á	long a	larder
b	short, voiced	boy
c	short, unvoiced ts	Ritz
cs	short, unvoiced ch	change
d	short, voiced	down
dz	voiced ds	Godzilla
dzs	voiced j	jungle
e	open e, higher than	pet
é	long, drawn-out	crayon
f	short, unvoiced	coffee
g	short, voiced	go
gy	voiced fricative	adieu
h	as in English	
i	long	feel
j	as English y	yes
k	unaspirated	cat
l	as in English	
ly	short voiced fricative	Goya
m	short, voiced	am
n	short, voiced	an
ng,	sounded separately,	man kind,
nk	not run together	not: tanker
ny	short, voiced fricative	vineyard
o	short, open	top
ó	long, closed	corner
p	unaspirated	stop
r	rolled r, as in Scottish	
s	short unvoiced sh	fresh
sz	short unvoiced s	sun
t	unaspirated	batter
u	short, as in Northern English	
ú	long	coop
ü	short	German münden
u	long	German Brüder
v	short, voiced	veto
z	short, voiced	doze
zs	short, voiced j	French journal

English-speaking visitors should have few difficulties being understood in Budapest, especially if they can switch to German in an emergency (these days, English is becoming more widely spoken, particularly among younger people, than German). It might, however, be a good idea to learn a few phrases, if only in order to be polite to your host nation.

Greetings

good morning	jó reggelt
hello, good day	jó napot
good evening	jó estét
good night	jó éjszakát
goodbye	viszontlátásra
enjoy your meal	jó étvágyat
pardon me	bocsánat
how are you?	hogy van?
good, well	jó, jól

Enquiries

what time is it?	hany óra van?
where is...	hol van...
when?	mikor?
where to?	hová?
how much/many	hány?/mennyi?
here	itt
there	ott
I don't understand	nem értem
how do I get to...?	merre kell menni...?
yes	igen
no	nem
please	kérem, tessék
thank you	köszönöm

Numbers

one	egy
two	kettö
three	haróm
four	négy
five	öt
six	hat
seven	hét
eight	nyolc
nine	kilenc
ten	tíz
eleven	tizenegy
twenty	húsz
twenty-one	huszonegy
thirty	harminc
forty	negyven
fifty	ötven
sixty	hatvan
seventy	hetven
eighty	nyolcvan
ninety	kilencven

one hundred .... száz	
two hundred .... kétszáz	
five hundred .... ötszáz	
one thousand .... ezer	

Time/Days Of The Week

today .... ma	
now .... most	
yesterday .... tegnap	
tomorrow .... holnap	
later .... késöbb	
Monday .... hétfö	
Tuesday .... kedd	
Wednesday .... szerda	
Thursday .... csütörtök	
Friday .... péntek	
Saturday .... szombat	
Sunday .... vasárnap	

Out Shopping

open .... nyitva	
closed .... zárva	
entrance .... bejárat	
exit .... kijárat	
how much is that? . mennyibe kerül?	
please show me.... . kerém,	
	mutassa, meg...
expensive .... drága	

In The Restaurant

menu .... étlap	
wine list .... itallap	
waiter! .... pincér!	
restaurant .... étterem	
cellar .... pince	
food .... étel	
drink .... ital	
coffee .... kávé	
wine .... bor	
beer .... sör	
red .... piros/vörös	
white .... fehér	
water .... víz	
large .... nagy	
small .... kis	

Getting Around

baths .... fürdö	
house .... ház	
hill .... hegy	
bridge .... híd	
gate .... kapu	
ring road .... körút	
park: small wood ... liget	
monument .... müemlék	
station .... pályaudvar (pu.)	
embankment .... rakpart (quay)	
island .... sziget	
theatre .... színház	
church .... templom	
square .... tér	

street/avenue .... út	
street .... útca	
(genitive form)	
street/lane .... utca (u.)	
castle .... vár	
town .... város	
inn .... vendéglö	
tram .... villamos	

Further Reading

General

Insight Guide Budapest, a comprehensive guide to the history, culture and sights. Apa Publications.

The Danube Bend, by László Cseke. Explores the beautiful Danube landscape to the north of the city. 1977, originally published in Hungarian, 1976.

Hungary: A Short History, by C.A. Macartney. Published 1962. Contains information on the capital.

Budapest 1900: A Historical Portrait of a City and its Culture, by John Lukacs. The best evocation of Budapest's glory days at the turn of the century by an American/Hungarian historian.

The Paul Street Boys, by Ferenc Molnár. Published 1907. A classic work of Hungarian literature.

Hungary: A Complete Guide, by Gyula Németh (editor). Published 1988. Translation from the Hungarian discusses the history and environs of the city.

Medieval Buda: A Study of Municipal Government and Jurisdiction in the Kingdom of Hungary, by Martyn C. Rady. Published 1985. The most authoritative work on the subject.

Hungary: A Century of Economic Development, by T.I. Berend and G. Ránki. Published 1974. Contains information on the capital.

British Travellers in Old Budapest, by Emeric W. Trencsényi (compiled). Published 1937. A collection of descriptions of the city beginning with Edward Brown in the 17th century.

Index

A
B
C
D
E
F
G

I
J
a
b
c
d
e
f
g
h

j
k
l

The Insight Approach

The book you are holding is part of the world's largest range of guidebooks. Its purpose is to help you have the most valuable travel experience possible, and we try to achieve this by providing not only information about countries, regions and cities but also genuine insight into their history, culture, institutions and people.

Since the first Insight Guide – to Bali – was published in 1970, the series has been dedicated to the proposition that, with insight into a country's people and culture, visitors can both enhance their own experience and be accepted more easily by their hosts. Now, in a world where ethnic hostilities and nationalist conflicts are all too common, such attempts to increase understanding between peoples are more important than ever.

Insight Guides:
Essentials for understanding

Because a nation's past holds the key to its present, each Insight Guide kicks off with lively history chapters. These are followed by magazine-style essays on culture and daily life. This essential background information gives readers the necessary context for using the main Places section, with its comprehensive run-down on things worth seeing and doing. Finally, a listings section contains all the information you'll need on travel, hotels, restaurants and opening times.

As far as possible, we rely on local writers and specialists to ensure that the information is authoritative. The pictures, for which Insight Guides have become so celebrated, are just as important. Our photojournalistic approach aims not only to illustrate a destination but also to communicate visually and directly to readers life as it is lived by the locals.

Compact Guides
The "great little guides"

As invaluable as such background information is, it isn't always fun to carry an Insight Guide through a crowded souk or up a church tower. Could we, readers asked, distil the key reference material into a slim volume for on-the-spot use?

Our response was to design Compact Guides as an entirely new series, with original text carefully cross-referenced to detailed maps and more than 200 photographs. In essence, they're miniature encyclopedias, concise and comprehensive, displaying reliable and up-to-date information in an accessible way.

Pocket Guides:
A local host in book form
However wide-ranging the information in a book, human beings still value the personal touch. Our editors are often asked the same questions. Where do *you* go to eat? What do *you* think is the best beach? What would you recommend if I have only three days? We invited our local correspondents to act as "substitute hosts" by revealing their preferred walks and trips, listing the restaurants they go to and structuring a visit into a series of timed itineraries.

The result is our Pocket Guides, complete with full-size fold-out maps. These 100-plus titles help readers plan a trip precisely, particularly if their time is short.

Exploring with Insight:
A valuable travel experience
In conjunction with co-publishers all over the world, we print in up to 10 languages, from German to Chinese, from Danish to Russian. But our aim remains simple: to enhance your travel experience by combining our expertise in guidebook publishing with the on-the-spot knowledge of our correspondents.